My Time
to Speak

My Time to Speak

RECLAIMING ANCESTRY
and CONFRONTING RACE

ILIA CALDERÓN

ATRIA BOOKS

New York   London   Toronto   Sydney   New Delhi

ATRIA
BOOKS

An Imprint of Simon & Schuster, Inc.
1230 Avenue of the Americas
New York, NY 10020

First Atria Books hardcover edition August 2020

ATRIA BOOKS and colophon are trademarks
of Simon & Schuster, Inc.

For information about special discounts for bulk purchases,
please contact Simon & Schuster Special Sales at 1-866-506-1949
or business@simonandschuster.com.

The Simon & Schuster Speakers Bureau can bring authors
to your live event. For more information or to book an event,
contact the Simon & Schuster Speakers Bureau at 1-866-248-3049
or visit our website at www.simonspeakers.com.

Manufactured in the United States of America

1   3   5   7   9   10   8   6   4   2

Library of Congress Cataloging-in-Publication Data

Names: Calderón, Ilia, 1972– author. | Obejas, Achy, 1956– translator.
Title: My time to speak : reclaiming ancestry and confronting race /
Ilia Calderón ; [translated from the Spanish by Achy Obejas].
Other titles: Es mi turno. English
Description: First Atria Books hardcover edition. |
New York : Atria Books, 2020.
Identifiers: LCCN 2020014940 (print) | LCCN 2020014941 (ebook)
ISBN 9781982103859 (hardcover) | ISBN 9781982103866 (ebook)
Subjects: LCSH: Calderón, Ilia, 1972– | Television journalists—United
States—Biography. | Women television journalists—Biography. | Racially
mixed people—United States—Biography.
Classification: LCC PN4874.C2184 A3 2020b (print) | LCC PN4874.C2184
(ebook) | DDC 070.92 [B]—dc23
LC record available at https://lccn.loc.gov/2020014940
LC ebook record available at https://lccn.loc.gov/2020014941

ISBN 978-1-9821-0385-9
ISBN 978-1-9821-0386-6 (ebook)

To my children.
To my daughter, Anna; my nieces, Luciana and Valeria;
my nephew, Samuel; and their right to dream.

To Gene, for his love, his patience, his critiques, and
his often silent company.

And to all of you, who at some point were afraid
to dream, I leave you my stories.
I'm no one special, just a woman who was able
to size up her obstacles.

Contents

Contents

Eyes of Hate

All my attention was focused on his face. It's what I remember most clearly more than two years after our encounter. That face that had raged red as soon as he saw me, and continued angry, indignant. His nostrils flared with his agitated breathing, which he unsuccessfully attempted to control. He responded quickly, hot, like a lit fuse, not letting anyone else talk. And then, suddenly, I heard it from his own lips, "We're going to burn you out."

We were in the middle of nowhere, in a remote area out in the countryside, and on a stranger's property. Our cell phones couldn't get a signal and the sun had begun to drop fast behind the towering trees surrounding us. Trees that seemed to remind us that it wouldn't be easy to get out of that clearing if our hosts didn't allow it. The smell of mosquito repellent on my arms fused with the whiskey and cigarettes on his breath as the conversation, at times, became more and more heated.

"Are you going to chase me out of here?" I asked, recalling the torches and the cross on the ground several feet from us.

"No, we're going to burn you out," he repeated, without hesitation, not blinking.

"You're going to burn me out? How are you going to do it?" I said, cutting him off, somewhere between irate and terrified.

"It don't matter, we killed six million Jews the last time," he shot back, his gaze defiant as he registered his displeasure with each of my features.

My nose, my lips, my cheekbones, my hair. Although there are a thousand and one bloodlines running through my veins, everything in me screams "black," and my African roots are undeniable.

There's no doubt: I, Ilia Calderón Chamat, am black. Colombian, Latina, Hispanic, Afro-Colombian, mixed, and anything else people may want to call me or I choose to call myself, but I'm always black. I may bear Castilian Jewish and Syrian Arab last names, but I'm simply black in the eyes of the world. And he—my angry interlocutor in that remote and desolate place in North Carolina—was Chris Barker, the top leader of the Order of the Loyal White Knights of the Ku Klux Klan, the Imperial Wizard of this new white supremacist branch that had proposed "to turn the United States into a white and Christian nation, founded on the word of God."

"He's not saying physically . . ." his wife said, trying to ease the tension.

"Yes, physically, we are," he quickly corrected her, then returned his gaze and sharp words toward me. "You're sitting in my property now."

Sure enough, I was on his land, surrounded by his people, and engaged in an argument that had gone well past the point of no return. The sun had vanished completely. The night engulfed the space around us. The only lights came from our cameras, aimed at the man icily pronouncing each syllable to say they were "going to burn" me.

I was afraid, I won't deny it. Afraid like I've never been before. Afraid my fate had been sealed. Afraid I wouldn't see Anna, Gene, my family again. And afraid that so many questions I'd had for so long would remain unanswered.

I should just shut up, not ask him anything else so that his fury doesn't escalate, I thought for a fraction of a second. Yes, the silence, stealth, mutism that makes us invisible . . . like we've done century after century to survive, a sure bet . . . Yes, just like I learned as a child, like we were taught at church and in school . . . to be quiet, to tiptoe . . . *Or not. Maybe I shouldn't shut up.* My head spun at a dizzying speed. *Maybe it's better if I talk back, if I tell him he's a monster, a madman, that he's sick, that he's wrong, and that no one threatens me like that. That I'm a human being like him and he has no right to talk to me in that way.*

My mind shut down from so much emotion and confusion as I sat in front of hate personified, at the mercy of the very hate I'd always wanted to look in the eye with the hope of finding answers to the many questions I'd had since I was a child. Why do they reject us? Why does skin color define us? What is the source of such pure hatred? What binds us to other human beings and what is it that keeps us so separate, to the point of such scorn? And, the most pressing question: How had I come to be here, and how was I going to get out of this—remaining quiet, as always, or facing it head-on?

Silence has a price. And, even though I'd ignored it most of my life, silence—like hatred, love, fear, and courage—also has a color.

Kerosene in Our Souls

If you hate a person, you hate something in him
that is part of yourself.
Hermann Hesse

"Look, they're marching with their faces uncovered," María Martínez told me as she pointed at the images of a street protest on the screen. "Things have changed."

That's how all of this began: with a simple observation by Univision's then vice president of News Gathering. Indeed, a lot had changed. Since the 2016 presidential election, it was undeniable that there had been a resurgence in the white supremacy movement and an increase in hate crimes in general. The headlines from the previous months served as evidence: "Hispanic beaten, told to go back where he came from" . . . "Portland man screams racial epithets before killing two" . . . "A student with white supremacist links murders a black soldier in Maryland."

Although there's always been discrimination, and racist and misogynistic insults have always been common currency, today's technology allows anyone with a cell phone to capture an image and make it go viral. Thanks to social media, we were now encountering more news stories about these discriminatory voices all over society. The images María was pointing to now weren't vintage pictures of the Ku Klux Klan or historical illustrations. These protesters were marching proudly, relaxed, wanting to be seen and identified, fearless before the law and public opinion. To ignore that would be to ignore reality, so we decided to explore the issue further and share it with our viewers.

"Let's reach out to them, to these people screaming and waving the Confederate flag," María said to Daniel Coronell, the president of our news department. "I don't know how, but we're going to interview them."

Daniel agreed and they both suggested I be a part of the reporting team.

"But only if you want to do it," María said, to clarify, because she knew it wouldn't be easy for me.

"Yes, of course." I had no doubts, not even for an instant. This was quite possibly my chance to try and understand where these emotions came from that others had expressed and directed at me: rejection, racism, unadulterated hatred.

When racism isn't expressed in words, it can be hard to explain. And for those who've never experienced it, it can be hard to understand. How can you call someone out for the way they looked you up and down, or for the smirk full of alienation and disdain that crossed their face when they saw you at a restaurant? Or when you walk down a street lined with forced smiles, or take your kids to the museum and the other parents mutter and try to keep theirs away from yours?

Even though I'd wanted to ignore these issues for a long time, especially during my adolescence, I knew deep in my heart that every time I stepped out of my environment, I'd be made to feel like a stranger, like I didn't matter anywhere else. Always living in a world where many people think you're different but no one will say it to your face. Always enveloped by a particular kind of convenient silence in which, if something isn't mentioned, it doesn't exist. A little like "Don't Ask, Don't Tell," the U.S. military policy designed to avoid having to deal with sexual orientation or gender identification in the ranks. I've spent decades of my life practicing my own "Don't Ask, Don't Tell" in terms of my skin color and facial features. From the over-the-shoulder looks at school to the thousands of products I bought to straighten my hair to try to look more like other girls. Although I never wanted to think of myself as a victim of discrimination, rejection grazed me like bullets, no matter what kind of body armor I wore to try and ignore the problem.

Now, as I reached the zenith of my journalism career, without planning or thinking about it too much, work was giving me an opportunity to go toe-to-toe with racism, to look it in the eye, and this time I wasn't going to avoid it. I wasn't going to take refuge in "Don't Ask, Don't Tell" or "let someone else take it on." Something had changed in me, and I wasn't going to say no to this assignment.

That's how the project to interview the leader of the new Ku Klux Klan came about: spontaneously, in response to what was happening and what we were sensing around us. It wasn't, like many people later suggested, a ruse by Univision to make headlines or exploit the drama in Charlottesville, Virginia, which was still weeks away. Those demonstrations by nationalists and the now unfortunately famous riots would take place almost a month after what I'm about to discuss here. Nor was the color of my skin what determined that I would lead the report. I was simply there when it was planned and I'm a journalist and I wanted to do it. Period. Univision had decided to have a sit-down with the leaders of this movement because it was an ongoing and relevant topic that affected our community and for no other reason. I got the assignment in the same way it could have been given to any one of my colleagues. It's always been important to Univision to inform and educate the Latino community in the United States about topics such as immigration, elections, the economy, security, health—in the same way it's always been very important to report the stories of Latinos who make great sacrifices and work in silence in the fields and factories so their families can get ahead, so they can pay taxes and send remittances to those anxiously waiting back home for their weekly allowance. That's why a story about the new resurgence of racism and xenophobia couldn't be left out of our coverage. It was our responsibility to reveal who was attacking us, and under what guise.

"Wait a minute—Ilia is black and she's going to meet with white supremacists?" That question came up later, as might be expected, among the members of my team. Some saw the color of my skin as an obstacle, others viewed it as a possible advantage in getting a better story. Personally, it terrified me. I was afraid the white supremacist leaders would agree to be interviewed by Univision, a network that represents minorities, but would say no to me because of the color of my skin, which is much darker than that of most Latinos. Besides fearing what might happen with me as their interviewer, I was also afraid of going deep on this subject, which was so personal to me. To prepare myself, I knew I'd have to review materials that featured black people like me beaten, harassed, killed, and that it would be like opening a Pandora's box of horrors, with those atrocities you hear about but never want to see.

I won't deny it, it hurts when you're professionally excluded because of personal circumstances. A journalist is, first and foremost, a journalist, and that's how we want to be seen—only after that can we be women, black, Latinos, or white.

"Let's not get too excited," María warned us. "These people don't even have cell phones, they're very much off the grid. All I've found is a number no one ever answers, a hotline for their announcements. I left them a message."

And they answered! Who knows why but, incredibly, they responded and accepted our invitation. María told them the reporter would be "Ilia Calderón, a Latina of color." To everyone's surprise, they didn't object. The interview would take place in a few days, on July 26, and the rendezvous would be in Yanceyville, a town of about two thousand in North Carolina, near the state line with Virginia. They'd give us the exact location once we were there.

"Get ready because they're probably going to really insult you and use the N-word," María said, in one of her now familiar reality checks while I read all I could about civil rights, the Constitution, the history of slavery, and anything else that could help me prepare for my interview.

Up until that moment, what I knew about white supremacists like the Ku Klux Klan I'd learned at a distance, through books and documentaries in my childhood and youth in Medellín, Colombia. It was through reading, especially during college in Medellín, that I discovered this aspect of American history: the ravages of slavery, the violence against African-Americans on the streets, and the great political and social battles that this had unleashed. In my elementary school in El Chocó, we didn't read much about this American chapter nor about the suffering and struggles of black communities in other places. My teachers themselves served as the texts, as well as the work of Maya Angelou and Toni Morrison that I read on my own. But to read about it was still a step removed and these stories about hooded figures, slaves in constant flight, and visionaries such as Martin Luther King Jr. echoed from far away, from Hollywood, from which we got movies like *Roots*, *Amistad,* and *The Color Purple*. I would watch the scenes with people who looked like me and experience them and live them, but they were still just movies. Undoubtedly, my life in Colombia had been different.

During the modern period in my home country, we never experienced institutionalized racism like in the United States. Slavery was abolished in 1851 and, though discrimination spread into our customs and remains latent but present, we never had laws in the twentieth century as radical as those in the United States, where segregation was legal until just a few years ago. As a result, we didn't have a civil rights movement like the kind that marked recent U.S. history and for which people are still struggling.

The Ku Klux Klan: a fear and problem as near to me as it was far away. That's why I was so intrigued as I prepared for my journey "into the lion's den." The more I researched, the more I was surprised at how the Ku Klux Klan was depicted, as if it no longer existed, as if it was a past chapter in our history, over and done with. But those beliefs were still so alive! In fact, they'd never gone away, they'd never been eradicated. They'd simply gone quiet, in that silence so complicit with survival, what everyone uses to save their own skin. A silence they were using now to make a comeback and grow in unexpected ways, almost a century later, just as immigration to the United States reached its peak.

You don't have to be an expert on the subject to understand that xenophobic and white supremacist beliefs have come back with tremendous force during the second decade of the twenty-first century, and that they operate with the same intentions although with different methods: They use the internet to recruit, they don't cover their faces or hide, and they participate in the political process, winning over the generally discontent and integrating popular movements in Germany and France and even in the current administration in Washington, DC, where you can hear their speeches from the highest levels. They also take advantage of whatever concessions other groups make to sow new fears, including the (unfounded) theory that as others gain more rights, they—white people—lose rights. That was their new weapon, their new fuel.

And this was our new reality, my new reality. I would sit face-to-face with the heir to all those crosses, all those torches, and all those ropes, as he waited to take them up again to perpetuate his hate in new generations.

On the day of this very sensitive assignment, we flew to Charlotte, North Carolina. We stayed at a hotel that night. The next morning we drove for several hours. We'd rented two vehicles to carry all our equipment: cameras, lights, batteries, and a ton of other gear. We wanted to make sure everything turned out perfectly. María was traveling in one of the SUVs with her husband, Martín Guzmán, a veteran Univision cameraman, and I was in the other, along with our excellent photojournalist, Scott Monaghan.

That morning, both eager and anxious, we ate breakfast in silence at the hotel and waited with nothing to do, looking over the generic paintings on the walls and constantly checking our phones. At three in the afternoon, María got a call and we received our instructions: we needed to go up to Yanceyville. They would wait for us at a fast food restaurant on the main street and we would follow them from there.

On the way we talked about what we'd experienced in the last year and a half, since the current president, Donald Trump, had come to power.

Verbal attacks in restaurants and shopping centers, in parks and college campuses, on neighborhood streets, had become more common. It wasn't new, we knew that. Immigrants have always been rejected, in every society, in every country. Rejected, in fact, by the children of immigrants who arrived before them: children and grandchildren of immigrants who'd completely integrated and had denied their ancestral languages in order to better assimilate to their new surroundings and camouflage themselves so they wouldn't be noticed. Now, with such a charged atmosphere because of the political moment and the complexity of our people—diverse and with many different perspectives—we found rejection both in and out of our community. Sounds strange, doesn't it?

Now, it seems some felt it their right to judge their neighbor. The hunting ban had been lifted: you could shoot at anything that moved on Twitter.

Once we got to Yanceyville, we could feel the hostility, or maybe it was just my imagination. The streets were empty, as were the local businesses, and everything seemed off. I remember construction going on in the middle of a street and, when we slowed down, I saw one of the workers in his fluorescent vest and helmet. He was a young man, tall, with dreads, skin as black as night and his eyes an intense blue. *Mixed,* I thought, ironically, as I recalled the history of these previously segregated states we'd heard so much about.

At the restaurant's parking lot, we had to wait again for almost an hour, unwilling to get out of the cars until we got a sign from our hosts. What if it was all a joke? We were plagued by doubts. What if they had just pulled one on us?

"They'll show up, believe me, they'll show up," María said to keep us calm, like always, in complete control of the situation.

And then, as if by magic, their car drove up, an old silver sedan. There were two women inside, their black shirts decorated with flags and insignias. I saw them clearly but they couldn't see me. The windows of our SUVs were tinted dark. María got out and exchanged a few words with them, then returned to her SUV and signaled for us to follow her.

The highway was straight and endless, as is always the case when you don't know where you're going. On the sides of the road, everything was green and flat, with occasional dense forests. That was the view we had of this agricultural and mining America, of the North Carolina where no great battles were fought during the Civil War, but which sent more Confederate soldiers to the front than any other state to defend the practice of slavery, that incomprehensible need to have someone submit to your will.

My heart was pounding at a thousand beats an hour, my breathing was quick, and I kept glancing at my cell while Scott tried to change the subject by talking to me about his wife, his kids, and his experiences with difficult stories such as this one.

I took one more quick look at my phone and decided to make a call to calm my nerves.

"Gene, we're losing our signal," I told my husband right off as our phones started to get spotty cell coverage.

"I'm not liking this, Ilia," he said, more worried about me than I was about myself. "I'm looking at the map and, according to what you're telling me, you're in a very isolated area. Let me know as soon as you're out of there, and don't take any risks. Remember, these guys aren't messing around."

Still, that brief call helped me relax a bit. His firm voice and words of support reminded me he's an excellent dad to Anna and that, if something did happen to me, my daughter couldn't be in better hands. So many thoughts crossed my mind! The truth is, I'd gone into this trip aware that I could be a point of contention, but my journalist heart was determined and I was too curious about finally confronting what I'd avoided all my life: racism.

Just as the very last bar of service disappeared from our cells, the silver car turned right onto a side road. All we could see was a tiny wooden house with the Confederate flag waving right at the entrance.

A skinny dog leashed to a tree welcomed us with unfriendly barking. Next to the little house there was another structure that didn't look habitable but was full of old junk and on the verge of collapsing.

It was already five in the afternoon and, though it was summer, it would be dark soon. I stayed in the car going over my notes, getting my courage up, and reminding myself why I was there. My eyes grew blurry staring at the Confederate flag, stirring in the light breeze. That worn-out piece of fabric reminded me what had brought me to this house. Even a century and a half after the Civil War, that symbol still carried an enormous power which somehow continued to divide us.

As they climbed out of the cars, María told our hosts I was getting ready and making a few calls, while Martín and Scott took photos of our surroundings. An experienced producer, María went in and out of the house, trying to measure the space. The rooms were so small, it would be impossible to get our equipment inside.

"We're leaving," said Scott as he got back in the car. "We have to follow them to a back field because we don't fit here."

As he drove down a path through the woods, Scott filled me in on what was happening.

"They treated me like a traitor because I speak a little Spanish and they tried to intimidate Martín because he's Mexican, so I told them he was my brother."

"And?" I asked, not hiding my concern.

"They left him alone but, you, you'd better get ready because they're going to insult you more than they insulted him." Scott wasn't beating around the bush; he was trying to prepare me for what was coming. "I'm not even going to repeat what they said to Martín."

As we crossed those six acres in silence, I was grateful for his honesty. I've never liked when people hide things or soften the truth. No need to sugarcoat it; I prefer bluntness, even when I may be walking straight into the lion's den. And that's where we appeared to be headed, following our hosts deep into the woods.

When we reached a small clearing, the cars stopped and everyone got out, except me. While María decided where to place the chairs and lights and Scott and Martín carried cables and cameras, I sat back and carefully observed them. There was Christopher Barker, the main leader and the one who would sit down with me for the interview, with another of his fellow Klansmen. Amanda, his wife, was chatting with Wendy, the other woman who'd gone with her to get us at the restaurant. They were basically two couples roughly the same age and of similar appearance: two men and two women between forty and fifty years old, white, three of them somewhat overweight, dressed modestly in jeans and the black shirts that appeared to be the group's uniform. Nearby, two skinny and disheveled youngsters wandered around in their own world; I imagined they were the Barkers' sons. Even though they were at somewhat of a distance, I could see the adults' faces, which betrayed their unhealthy habits. In fact, soon there were cigarettes, one after the other, and then whiskey.

Out of nowhere, somebody knocked on the car window and nearly scared me to death. For a second, I felt a cold wave run up and down my body, immediately followed by a kind of tingling, like when your nerve endings are trying to alert you to danger. I lowered the window so as not to seem rude.

"Hi, how are you? Do you need anything?" It was Wendy, the other woman, greeting me with genuine friendliness, without a trace of surprise or rejection when she laid eyes on me.

"No, I'm good, thank you, thank you very much," I responded, looking into her eyes, observing her sweet yet afflicted face and her messy hair.

Her very appearance told me she hadn't had an easy life, that she was likely where she was because she believed it was all she could aspire to, and because of that need we all have to belong to something, even a group like the KKK. Often, amid the most sordid poverty, being part of a group, regardless of its purpose, is the only thing that can save us from our misery. I've seen it with gangs, when kids just want to be a part of something, be someone, and matter to somebody, even if it's to a killer or tyrant.

Or, who knows, maybe Wendy was there simply out of love, to please the man she shared her life with. Without a doubt, the sweet woman who peered curiously over my car window was not an ideologue or a fanatic, nor did she feel the slightest need to insult me when she saw me.

"My name is Ilia Calderón. Nice to meet you, and thank you for having us." I wanted to respond with the same courtesy.

"Ilia, that's a pretty name. Do you want some water?" She was intrigued and wanted to keep the conversation going.

"No, thank you." It was clear I wasn't going to drink anything under these circumstances, even the glass of water sincerely offered to the enemy.

Finally, María gave me a signal and I knew it was time to start. It was time to confront hate. I sprayed my arms with bug repellent because, on a late afternoon in that type of setting, mosquitoes abound. I opened the car door and slowly strolled toward the circle of light generated by our equipment in the center of the clearing. It was approximately six in the evening and the sun was quickly dropping behind the highest trees. The crickets were the only sound—hundreds, thousands of invisible crickets—as everyone stood quietly, staring at me. I suddenly realized what had happened: the others had no idea I was black, even though María had told them on the phone!

"Hi, my name is Ilia Calderón," I said, introducing myself as I sat in the empty chair facing Christopher and Amanda.

This is how I came to be in this situation. And I had to come out of it successfully, no matter what. That's also when I saw his face for the first time. A face that's hard to forget because no one in my more than forty years of life had ever looked at me like that. At first, it wasn't the hatred I'd imagined. The look on his face was more cold indifference, the way you might look at someone beneath you, a being so insignificant they don't inspire anything more than slight repugnance. That attitude struck me and made me shiver. In his eyes, I wasn't even a human being deserving of hatred; I was a "thing," a soulless vessel, a creature who didn't even merit disdain. A more passionate and real hatred would come later when I, "the thing," the soulless vessel, began to talk and make him uncomfortable with my questions. For certain people, inferior beings should be quiet and live in silence. So, when I began to talk, he was not happy. Christopher Barker, the Imperial Wizard of the White Knights, sitting next to his wife, Amanda, on his home turf, wasn't going to allow a black person to contradict him or question his beliefs in front of a camera.

"You never told me you were bringing a black person on my property." That was the first thing with which he reproached María.

"Yes, I did, I told you she was 'a Latina of color.'" María tried to calm him and remind him about the phone conversation they'd had.

"Yes, yes, she did tell us," said Amanda, proving to be a little less hostile, and seemingly enjoying the attention she was receiving, as well as the increasing tension.

"I thought you meant colored, like all of you," he insisted, indignant, referring to María's dark hair and more or less light skin, which fits the image most people who aren't aware of our diversity have of Latinos.

After overcoming the initial shock of my blackness, and with a very pronounced Southern accent, Chris Barker agreed to start the interview and respond to my questions. The cameras were already rolling when he told us the property we were on, which was surrounded by mining towns, belonged to the KKK and that he'd moved there because he'd been the victim of constant robberies in the city and of the instability brought by immigrants and other races. Amanda emphatically denied they were a hate group or violent and Chris immediately mentioned the Bible to justify his practices and beliefs.

I was astonished with how they cited biblical passages by memory, interpreting them in a way that gave them license to reject or discriminate against anyone who wasn't a white-skinned Aryan. When I mentioned the U.S. Constitution, which grants the same rights to everyone under the law, he answered again with the Bible, his supreme text, and said in the Bible God asks us to love and respect our neighbors but not if they're of another race or from somewhere else. He said Jesus was white and that there was irrefutable proof in the Library of Congress. He said Jesus wasn't a Jew and that he hated Jews and even beat them up. That they raised their left arm in salute, not the right like the Nazis. That they hated Jews because they killed Christ. That most racial crimes are committed by blacks against whites. That Trump is a coward, a millionaire thanks to his father, and that, just like Bill Clinton, he wasn't going to do anything he promised. That it was black drug addicts who voted and elected Obama. That the famous Pharaohs were white and that it was white people who built the pyramids in the desert and all other great works of humanity. That the Bible warns: "They will sit at your table, they will look with lust upon your woman, and burn your cities," and he said that's why they don't break bread with black people. That the KKK had never hung a single person of color, that that was pure myth, and that the Bible told them they, the white people of Israel, Hebrews but not Jews, are the real chosen people mentioned in the Old Testament. And, to finish off, that immigrants come to take white people's jobs and that they will run them out of the country.

"Are you going to chase me out of here?" After listening to such an avalanche of crazy theories, I wanted to try and understand his logic.

And so, at this point, the fuse was lit and the scene I described at the very beginning of this story unfolded. Unfortunately, it would go on to make headlines all over the world.

"No, we're going to burn you out," he said staring me right in the eye, without the slightest doubt about what he had just said.

"You're going to burn me out? How are you going to do it?" My heart was in my throat, I held my breath because everything in me had been shaken. But I kept asking questions, pretending his threat hadn't scared me. "And how are you going to do that with eleven million immigrants?"

"Don't matter. Hey, we killed six million Jews the last time, eleven million is nothing."

And there it was! That pure, direct hatred in his eyes. And I had decided to keep talking, to keep asking questions without backing down. To be silent or use my voice? I had chosen to let my voice flow, even if that bothered him. There was no longer any distance between us; I was no longer that being who wasn't quite human and, as a result, I'd now turned into a threat against him.

You can only really hate a member of the same species, someone who can defend themselves and show you when you're wrong. As hard as he had tried not to, Barker had allowed me to become human and thus given rein to the rage he'd carried for decades, maybe generations, toward me and those like me. That's the hatred in its purest form that I'd always wanted to see up close, that I'd always wanted to investigate. That hatred without excuses, without social hypocrisies or political correctness or glances or tact. That hatred which I knew existed and intuited since I was a little girl, but which I had never seen like this, so brutally up front, so undisguised.

"He's not saying physically," his wife said to soften the most horrible words anyone had ever directed at me.

"Yes, physically we are," he countered, quickly correcting her and returning his eyes to mine. "You're sitting in my property now . . ."

"Yes, it's your property, and I understand I'm probably the first black person on your property," I said, continuing in my reporter role so the situation wouldn't get out of control, keeping to my promise to not let my fears silence me.

"To me you're a nigger, that's it." Barker hit bottom and hurled the forbidden word at me.

Nigger! María's eyes widened and her hand covered her mouth, as if she was thinking: *How could he?* Scott and Martín were outraged, and so was I, but I kept my composure: serious and collected. My eyes never strayed from his. I had an intense impulse to let go with the mouthy, rebellious Ilia of my youth, but I wasn't going to be the one to lose control in this situation. His wife asked him to watch what he said but Barker didn't pull back. Instead, he lost his temper again and twice threatened to cut the interview, getting up in a rage, taking a few puffs of his cigarette, then returning to the chair facing the camera, even more disturbed, only to continue shouting more and more insults at me at every opportunity. Soon I was a dummy, a dope, and retarded. The KKK's new top leader was no longer hiding his purest racist feelings.

"Look at your eyes, and look at mine." He challenged me as he got angrier and angrier. "I'm way more superior than you'll ever be."

"I can feel your anger," I said, trying to bore deeper into that hatred. "When you look at me, what do you see?"

"I see you, and I see your kind all the time, and what bothers me is that this property was given to me by the Klan and I've been here twenty years and we'd never had a black person, or whatever you want to call yourself, on it. To me, you're a mongrel."

Mongrel! That was the most heinous insult used during slavery to refer to mestizos, to mixed people like me, to whomever they considered physically inferior, an abomination, against the laws of God. Mutts. That's what he saw when he looked at me: an aberration. What could I expect after this? There were six of them, counting the Barkers' two teenage sons, and we were four. We were on their property, with no cell signal or neighbors who could come to the rescue. If they were carrying weapons and one of them got carried away, there would be nothing we could do. This little clearing in the woods somewhere in North Carolina would be the last thing my eyes would see. The shivers and tingling on my skin confirmed the danger. *I would be the first to fall,* I thought, remembering they'd brought several kerosene tanks for the ceremony they'd be carrying out afterward in the dark. *Would they actually be capable of hurting me?* I asked myself, with a lump in my throat. My body language and the firmness in my voice were the only weapons I had to defend myself.

I looked at the sky and saw it was already dark. I knew Scott and Martín would defend me if Barker pounced on me, or if any of the others tried anything, but it was María's convincing power, like a lioness protecting her cub, which gave me confidence. María guided me with her eyes: *You're doing fine, everything's fine, don't be afraid.* I clung to that thought so I wouldn't fall apart. It was the power of the word and presence of this incredible woman and colleague that gave me the courage I needed in that moment.

Without tempting fate too much, yet steadfast to my decision of no longer being silent, I went from question to question, the target of more and more insults until, finally, when my eyes met María's, I sensed we'd reached the end. It was better to end the interview. It wasn't worth adding more fuel to the fire, although this sounds quite macabre in this context.

The mosquitoes, huge and persistent, buzzed loudly in our ears, the smell of cigarettes and bug repellent made me nauseous, but the party hadn't ended yet. I still couldn't get in the car, declare victory, and feel safe. Barker and his acolytes had agreed to let us film the disturbing and mysterious ritual of the burning cross that has distinguished the KKK since its founding in 1865.

Still looking at me sideways as Amanda kept on talking—still excited from so much attention in front of the cameras—Barker put on his purple Imperial Wizard robe and his cone-shaped hood. James Spears, Wendy's husband, would be the officiant, dressed in red, according to the Klan's hierarchy. The two teenagers and the two women also dressed and hooded. They wore white.

First, they sprayed the wooden rope-wrapped cross with kerosene from one of the plastic containers they'd brought. Then they picked it up, now drenched in fuel, and drove it into the ground. It was a huge cross, which could well bear the weight of a person.

"We don't actually 'burn' the cross," explained James, the ritual leader, in a very pragmatic and conciliatory tone. "We light it, we light it to ward off darkness and honor God." The look Barker gave me through the two holes in his hood did not let up.

They then lit their torches and formed a circle, reciting their liturgy by repeating, "For God, for the race, for the nation, for the Ku Klux Klan."

I stayed to the side, trying to decipher what they were doing. I only wanted to see it in order to tell it. The image recalled all the frightening KKK rituals I'd read about. The flames, the bonfires . . . and here was a black woman witnessing a moment that exalted all the atrocities committed against her people. I wanted so much to cry. Even though I was there doing my job, that night everything was so intense and so overwhelming that it was tough not to give in to the personal and to take Barker's threat seriously: *We're going to burn you out.* Staring at that fiery cross in the middle of the woods, I inevitably thought about all those human beings, people of other races and colors, orientations and religions, who had lost their lives in this cruel fashion.

For an instant in the middle of the ceremony, the kerosene, the mosquitoes, the poverty, and the forest transported me: They made me travel, crossing a sea of memories, to a very different land thousands of miles away, in which I wasn't a foreigner or hated. A land green like this, but in which poverty wasn't so sad, the smell of kerosene meant home, sweet home, and my skin was neither strange nor despised.

It's where I needed to go if I wanted to find the answers to the questions this profound encounter on a hot night in Yanceyville had awakened in me. Questions I had carried with me always, deep in my heart, but now, with what was happening around us, politically and socially, and in the moment of my life in which I found myself, they were questions I had to face, not silence.

Although it bothers me, because I don't like and I'm not interested in being a victim, it was time to go back and review, step by step, experience by experience, when and how the silence had turned off our internal music and turned black.

2.

This Is How We Dance in El Chocó

I want to paint too,
to paint a black saint.

"Tío Guachupecito," Afro-Colombian folk song

"*Hija*, turn on the light, you're going to go blind." My mother would come into that huge kitchen in that huge wooden house where everything creaked and screeched with every step and help me pour the kerosene to light the lamp.

Surrounded by that blue and orange light, I'd finish the last of my homework and go to bed in one of the eight rooms on the second floor.

That's how simple life was in Istmina, my hometown. It had no residential electricity or public lighting, wide roads or highways, or any of the basic amenities the rest of the planet already enjoyed in the seventies. Back then the smell of kerosene wouldn't arouse fears and suspicion in me; it was the fuel that nurtured reading, imagination, and my dreams of becoming somebody. While others thought coal was black and dirty, to me it meant clean clothes, like my school uniform's shirt, which was pressed to perfection with our coal iron. When others crossed rivers via modern bridges that were true engineering feats, I crossed mine, the San Juan River, on a boat or canoe to get to school every morning and returned with the hot afternoon sun.

Istmina is a colloquial contraction of "isthmus of mines." It's a tiny town located in Colombia on the border with Panamá. It's a region of mines and jungle, where we're always in spring or summer, and thousands of wet days have helped denote our state, El Chocó, as "The Land of Constant Rain." In fact, we have one of the highest rainfall rates in the world. One of our other little towns, Tutunendo, has been deemed one of the rainiest places on the planet. The capital, Quibdó, is approximately forty-five miles away. We were so isolated from the rest of the world and so hard to get to that, for decades, neither good nor bad had any effect on us. Perhaps that's why, three centuries ago, when some African slaves achieved freedom in Cartagena de Indias, they decided to head toward the Pacific coast and settle in this area, remote and left behind by the hand of God and the white man; a land of lush landscape that reminded them of their Motherland. A jungle so thick, only a strong body could survive the illnesses native to its soil. Once slavery was abolished throughout the national territory, they established their own communities, at their own pace and in their own way, under the curious gaze of the indigenous tribes who only left the deepest forests to trade seafood and meat with them. Afterward, these tribes vanished again into the tropical rain forest.

This is how my native land, El Chocó, and so many other coastal areas became the "best kept secret in Colombia." There are black people in Colombia? I think that question—with an exclamation mark—will haunt me until the day I die, just as it hounds our Peruvian, Ecuadorian, Honduran, and Mexican neighbors. We are many varied communities on the Pacific and Atlantic coasts descended from those men and women dragged against their will to this new continent. Colombia has one of the largest Afro-descendant populations in the Americas, together with Brazil and Venezuela. African blood runs through the streets and customs of many of the country's most important cities, such as Cartagena, Cali, Barranquilla, and Medellín. But in our settlements, we live our Africanness with passion. It's impossible not to hear our drums and percussion, to see our joyful and rapturous dances with hip movements and steps we learn as kids, and our braids, which have always been present and are gaining on all that hair straightened with chemicals.

We're more than five million Afro-Colombians and make up more than 10 percent of the total population, but nobody reads these statistics or seems to pay attention. That data doesn't matter much to us in Istmina either, where, in our little world, being black wasn't "out of this world."

Everything around me was familiar, and everything made sense: from the smell of kerosene at night—which meant our family was together, doing homework, and getting ready for bed—to the strong scent of the blue-paste soap with which we laundered our clothes in the river when the aqueduct that served the whole town went dry. Around the San Pablo River, a community of five thousand led the same kinds of lives, whether we were rich or poor. Neither constant flooding nor terrible droughts cared much for social status. This was my personal Macondo, where the streets were paved with cement because tar melted like chocolate ice cream in the summer, and where our closest contacts with civilization were via Medellín and Cali, which we could only get to by flying over the jungle in a double-helix plane, because the highway was, and remains, a chasm. And yet it's a road used by thousands who don't have enough money for airfare. Not surprisingly, the great Gabriel García Márquez called that ill-paved road "pure cartographic speculation," and a "road more theoretical than real."

The great García Márquez also dedicated a few words to the small planes that defied the storms, the mountains, and the jungle, calling them the "airlift savior, whose crew members have the same intrepid spirit as the first settlers." On those old machines, which would eventually bring my family great misfortune, there were only about twenty terrified passengers, and we made the whole trip in silence, thinking that what kept us suspended in the air were prayers and not the engines and fuel.

In that isolated world where everything was "normal," I spent my days wandering around with friends, feeling precisely normal and trouble free. From dawn until dusk, my life happened on those narrow streets, where an occasional old Jeep or ladder bus, which we called *líneas*, would pass, completely open on one side. The passing by of the *línea* buses was the only thing that interrupted our favorite game, *la golosa* or "the sweet tooth." We played it with bottle caps in the middle of the street. Between games, I also liked talking to the town's crazy people and visiting the families who lived on the other side of the ravine, in the San Agustín neighborhood, which we called El Alambique because they distilled the local moonshine. The houses were made of wood with zinc roofs and clay floors. The voices of women in that same neighborhood would rise and reach me during funerals, singing *alabaos* to those who died as adults and *gualíes* to those who left this world as children.

Looking out at this landscape of need, I realized not all of us were so equal, and that some were less deprived than others. On my walks to the ravine, I tried to bring canned food, bags of beans, and clothes I snuck out of the house for the families in Alambique. Many of those girls went to my school and came to class with their shoes full of holes or dragging their soles. At recess, we all played together and, when the droughts came, we swam together in the river that separated our neighborhoods.

Over time, electricity came to some of the houses, and it was quite an event. Doña Blanquita, a neighbor who was better off than the rest of the families on my street, bought a gigantic generator and, two or three times a week, she'd run a line to our house. Now we could read later and even watch TV! The other nights, we went back to our kerosene lamps or simply to sleep as soon as it got dark. If we couldn't sleep, we'd gather in a room and tell stories.

As I recall, the only neighbor who couldn't afford electricity even three days a week was Miguel Antonio. Don Miguel was widowed young and left with five girls and a boy under his care. His wife died giving birth to his fifth daughter. To feed so many mouths, Don Miguel sold newspapers on the streets and worked at whatever he could find. But it was barely enough for candles, and his house was always dark. My mother and the other neighbors took turns sharing a pot of hot food every day with the six kids. Whenever the neighbors passed by, they'd let him know they were coming, *"Ya voy, Toño,"* they'd shout. "I'm coming, Toño!" The nickname stuck: he became Don Ya-Voy-Toño.

"Girl, I'm going to tell your grandfather!" Don Miguel would scold me from the steps of his front porch whenever he saw I was up to some mischief.

Since we often repeated the same pranks, we'd all run down to the river to avoid getting punished. The only ones who saw us out there were the sly *mazamorrera* women panning for gold in the water. Dressed in their colorful clothes and headscarves, a thousand lines drawn on their faces, they'd spend long hours hunched over, their feet in the water, a filterless cigarette in their mouths that they moved skillfully with their lips. They smoked incessantly, without using their hands, always busy wiggling the pan in a special way to separate the sand from any piece of gold or platinum the waters of the San Juan River might have dragged south. This eternal shaking of the round wooden pan was called *mazamorreo*, and it was always accompanied by songs I can still remember about enslaved ancestors: "Although my master might kill me / I won't go to the mine / I don't want to die in a sinkhole." At dusk, everyone headed to weigh what the waters had brought them, which was always scarce. The old and rusty scales they used didn't measure in grams, but in grains of corn. So many nuggets of gold equaled so many grains. An inaccurate and very improvised method, but that's how imprecise and spontaneous our lives were. With what history left us and what Mother Nature gave us, we worked wonders.

I think it was one day at the river while watching the *mazamorreras* that I realized there was another infallible science. A science much more accurate than corn grains: the harder the jobs, the darker the skin of those who performed them. In Istmina, it was okay to be black or white, it was okay to be mixed or indigenous, and that is how I felt: okay. But it was also typical for color to determine our guilds and labor.

As a case in point, the Emberá, with their reddish skin and straight black hair, were in charge of bringing us meat and fish from deep in the forests. They came once or twice a week, in groups, and without too many words, they'd trade fish and armadillo for medicine, sugar, or anything else they needed from town. The men used only the typical loincloth that barely covered their parts, and the women wore simple wraparound skirts, leaving their breasts exposed, covered in some cases by their long hair or seed necklaces. The Emberá have been Chocoanos since the beginning of time. It's estimated only 42,000 are alive in all of Colombia, according to the Ministry of Culture. Some decided to leave the jungle and they were given jobs according to their skills. For example, Emberá women were hired in the kitchens of black, white, and mixed-race homes, and they immediately went on to clean floors next to black peasants. The indigenous were the forgotten among the forgotten. I've always felt those of us from El Chocó are indebted to them, that we need to include them and make them more visible.

But whether white or black, mixed or indigenous, we all looked forward to the most celebrated time of the year: the festivities in honor of the Virgin of Mercy, patron saint of Istmina, held between the sixteenth and twenty-fourth of September. For eight days, the entire town explodes in music and color. Back then, we started before dawn, praying to the Virgin in a small procession that went down the streets.

"Get up, lazy bones," my mother would say as she woke us before the first ray of light. "If you don't get up, I won't let you party tonight."

Still sleepy, we went to a different neighborhood each morning to deliver the flag and the image of the Virgin of Mercy, welcomed by the breathless murmur of the devotees reciting the rosary nonstop.

The fun began at noon, when the first troupe of costumed children went dancing and singing out in the streets, followed by hornpipes. Accompanied by a clarinet, a drum, a cymbal, and a snare, my feet delighted in the typical rhythms of the land of my birth. At four in the afternoon, the first adult group joined in and the great parade began. The float was built on a simple dump truck and the whole town followed, dancing. The beat of the African drums boomed in my chest until nightfall, when the parade ended and the neighborhood festival began. With power provided by a neighbor, they connected a pair of speakers and a couple of lights. There was always someone who volunteered their turntable for when the musicians were on break. We'd play the day's hits, mostly salsa, and took over the streets as everyone danced together, chanting the lyrics to Héctor Lavoe, La Sonora Ponceña, El Gran Combo, and other radio hits that came to us from Puerto Rico.

Dance, dance, dance: some danced in pairs, others in groups, and plenty of people danced alone, in a corner, dreaming of a lost love or a love to come. Dance was our way of expressing ourselves, our true language. During those nighttime jamborees we'd inadvertently reveal everything that had happened to us that year. Some couples danced apart, a hand or two from each other, because their marriage wasn't going so well. Others danced pulled up close to each other, trying to be forgiven for something they'd done. Still others danced with babies in their arms, grateful for the new family member. That was our true language in El Chocó: dance. We said it all as we danced. And this body language became so ingrained in me that, even now, if I don't dance, I feel gagged, mute, and misunderstood.

While we were dancing at those festivities deep in the valleys and mountains, we were all truly equal, because we danced each step with our souls, with every ounce of life. When we danced, the way we danced in El Chocó, the poor were no longer so poor, nor were black people so black, or white people so white.

After working so hard in the mines, battling mosquitoes and heat, dealing with streets full of potholes, and roads that were impassable, our poverty was not tinged with hatred like in other parts of the world. It simply became more bearable.

How could I imagine that, away from these mountains and valleys, there was a world in which people couldn't connect even when dancing! A world in which music couldn't move us because silence overwhelmed it.

The only thing we lacked in our noisy and musical El Chocó, a place that seemed almost perfect in my eyes, were opportunities. In spite of its shortfalls, it was a real paradise for a girl like me. True, once childhood was behind us, there wasn't much to dream about or fight for. You could be a teacher, or open a small business in your home and sell what you could, or work in a forgotten government office. If your parents broke their backs working, and you didn't have many siblings with whom you had to share, and if they asked for credit from the local loan sharks, you might be lucky enough to have the opportunity to go study in the big city.

Opportunity, the magic word in all this time travel, throughout my life and my experiences. To find opportunities, I'd have to go very far, in one of those small planes that Chocoanos were so uneasy about, to go where our music couldn't be heard except in the distance. But before I left for good, El Chocó had a few more lessons to teach me, the kind that stay with you for the rest of your life.

3

Coffee, Roots, and Blood

More than a place in the world,
Macondo is a state of mind.

Gabriel García Márquez, *The Fragrance of Guava* (1982)

They say a home is only as good as the people who live there, and as strong as its foundation. The house where I grew up was not supported just by the giant guaiacum trunks that lifted it above the river. Our two strongest pillars were, without question, my mother and grandfather: Doña Ana Beatriz Chamat García and Don Carlos Alberto Chamat Figueroa.

In Istmina, all the stores were on Commerce Street, so that was where my grandfather had his small book and stationery shop. There was a grocery in the back which overlooked the river, and a little room where he slept. On the second floor, which hung over the waters of the San Pablo ravine, there was a kitchen and eight rooms that rocked with the rhythm of the swaying floors and walls, all built of wood.

Every time the river—fueled by incessant rains—unleashed its fury, we had to quickly take everything from the first floor to the second: books, merchandise, chairs, tables, lamps, clothes, and my grandfather's bed. The floodwaters of the San Juan River would reach my waist and, when the waters receded, we had to clean the mud and mold, and start again, as if nothing had happened. Because so long as our two pillars were present, not even the worst of tragedies could shake us.

Besides my grandfather and my mother, my two older sisters, Lizbeth and Beatriz, lived with us. My cousin Flor also stayed with us so she could go to school. Flor had been raised by my grandmother since she was a baby, and then my mother took over when my grandmother passed. That's how Flor became my older sister. As for my father, his presence was always distant and, after the divorce, he disappeared from our lives. Over time, we kept adding to our blood relatives all the girls who came from the countryside to stay with us so they could study in Istmina. Some came, others went, but my mother provided them all with food and shelter in the huge house on the river as long as they stayed in school. All those students from peasant families stay in touch with my family to this day, but there were two who never left our lives: Rubiela, a university graduate, and William, her brother and the only boy, who got a degree in accounting and still lives in Istmina with my mother, in his role as "the son who stays." If you ask me how many brothers and sisters I have, I always hesitate: two, three . . . no, four, five! Because to be family, the least important thing is blood. Although Chamat blood has a long and storied history, and many characters to introduce.

First, I'll start with my mother, who summarizes her long lineage of first and last names in two syllables: Betty. She doesn't need any other introduction because she has plenty of personality and character. Betty is very disciplined and, as a mother, she was always present in our lives. She still is, even though we live in different countries. When we were little, she never allowed the rough periods she experienced with my father to rob us of a moment of her time, or her love, or her attention. Although she was going through a bad patch in her marriage, she helped us with our homework and took us to friends' birthday parties. She didn't miss a meeting with our teachers and personally checked our clothes and made our meals every day.

Her reprimands haven't waned with the passing years. Betty had to be the authority, especially in the absence of our father, and that, coupled with her strong character, was explosive. During my adolescence, we clashed a lot. It was as if we were mirror images: both equally stubborn, firm, and armed with arguments to vanquish the other. If I didn't shut up explaining the reasons for this or that mischief, she got all the

Perrot Memorial Library

www.perrotlibrary.org

203-637-1066

09/30/2022

TITLE: **A place in the world : finding**
BARCODE: **32021004354773**
DUE DATE: **10-21-22**

TITLE: **My time to speak : reclaiming**
BARCODE: **32021004487458**
DUE DATE: **10-21-22**

---

more imperial. Betty had studied pedagogy and had been a teacher for several decades in Istmina. However, the years had bestowed another degree on her: a doctorate in survival, and she could give us all life lessons.

Doña Betty did a lot with very little, taking down the most horrific family dramas to zero. She never let anyone offend her or us. She was and is a woman so practical and strong that if we don't celebrate her birthday with candles and gifts she doesn't mind, or if Christmas isn't perfect and we don't even put up a tree, she doesn't care. I got that from her too! We don't get caught up in the thick of things.

If you want to win over Doña Betty, you have to study hard, work ethically, and show how much you love her through your deeds, not with Hallmark cards. The pride and self-esteem I have is due to her; she taught me, between reprimands and punishments, to love myself as I am, without sentimentality or great emotional drama.

In addition to these teachings, Doña Betty gave me another possibly much more valuable lesson, the one that would help me most in the life on which I was about to embark, and the career I would later choose. My mother taught me, from a very young age, to never feel like a victim, even when those around you want to see you as such. To this day, I dislike that word, in whatever context it's used.

With three daughters of her own and so many girls who came to live in our house, there was no time to raise "victims of anything," or weak women. There was also no time to fool around. If my mother saw us hanging out on the huge balcony overlooking the street and the stationery shop, she always repeated this phrase, "A woman has to be like a violet: the more discreet, the more appreciated and desired."

Doña Betty wanted to make sure none of us went astray, nor ended up believing the silly things depicted in soap operas, where falling in love with the dreamboat was everything and none of the protagonists ever think of getting an education.

If my mother's role was that of bad cop and forger of character, then my grandfather was the good cop. My magical moments with

Don Carlos began very early, when the sun was barely rising. Just before five o'clock, he'd heat up some water for his coffee. Later, my grandfather left punctually for the market to buy freshly ground meat and fish that would later be prepared for lunch and dinner. If it was Saturday, he'd pick up bananas, potatoes, cassavas, and rice to stock up for the week.

Upon his return, the smell of coffee continued to permeate the corners of the house, and we were all up by then, running down the halls, getting ready for the day. Breakfast was almost always the same, and we always devoured it with the same enthusiasm: an oatmeal smoothie with bread, or with thin fried plantains, fried cheese, and coffee, even for the kids. If I were asked when I took my first sip of coffee, I couldn't say. I only know it was with my grandfather in that huge kitchen, listening to him give advice or plucking out his gray hairs, for which he'd pay us a few cents.

Don Carlos knew that once we were off to school, to play, or to work, he wouldn't see us again until evening, so he gave us his lessons early in the day, around the always full table. While we all helped serve the food, he'd talk passionately about various topics. He was a great teacher.

Some mornings were dedicated to having savings and how important it was; other times, he'd talk about work and how it validates us in the world. Some days during those cool early hours, still illuminated by the kerosene lamps, he'd talk about men, boyfriends, and relationships, and how we needed to value ourselves as women. Along with the oatmeal, fried cheese, and rice, my grandfather fed us three other ingredients at those delicious breakfasts which I remember to this day: honesty, responsibility, and respect.

The rest of the day, Don Carlos Chamat was rather quiet. Always polite and kind to everyone, but reserved. He never complained about my father's attitude toward him, which left much to be desired. He simply waited patiently until he left our lives so he could support his eldest daughter and granddaughters. Once his son-in-law disappeared,

Don Carlos continued like always, patient and loving, helping us finish our homework while dealing with customers at the stationery shop.

"Look, Don Carlos, it's just that the boy needs these two books but I can't afford them right now . . ." a neighbor would say in a low voice so no one would know about their troubles.

"Don't worry, just take them, we'll figure it out later," he'd say, just as discreetly, and then record the debt in a notebook under the counter.

When there weren't customers around, he'd teach us to wrap gifts and label merchandise, to order notebooks for the shelves and unpack school supplies. Over time, he also taught us that half those red numbers he ceremoniously wrote down in the secret notebook would never change. He simply crossed them off and turned the page. If they paid him, great, and if not, that was fine too. His heart was like a giant eraser that deleted debts for anyone who had to choose between food and school supplies.

Although he was always surrounded by many people, my grandfather was very solitary. Since he'd been widowed, he had dedicated himself to us and his business. After the workday, he'd retire to his little room to rest. My grandmother, Ilia, had passed away a few months before I was born. She died alongside her daughter, Jenny Petrona, in an accident aboard one of those small planes that terrified us so much but, along with the dangerous road, were our only contact with the outside world.

After the tragedy, my mother was the only one who stayed with him in that house he'd built with our grandmother and in which they'd raised all their children. He ended up calling the stationery shop Jenny, in honor of my late aunt, and I was baptized with the name of his beloved wife, Ilia. They tell me that, after this great tragedy, Don Carlos was never the same. Maybe that's why he was a man of brief words and long silences. Pain haunted every memory.

"*Mija*, you're just like your grandmother," he'd tell me, thoughtfully, when he saw me talking to customers. "You have her determination and confidence when you do things, and you have her presence too."

I remember those wonderful breakfasts when he'd leave his sorrows aside and talk with ease, when he told us countless stories about his six children, and how, after widowing, and with my mother's help (because she was the eldest), he helped pave the way for everyone to get ahead. My uncle Óscar became a doctor after studying at the National University in Bogotá; my aunt Aleyda, a pharmaceutical chemist at University of Antioquia in Medellín; Alberto graduated with a degree in languages from University of Quindío in Armenia; and Alexis became a civil engineer, graduating from the National University in Medellín. None of them ever returned, with the exception of Óscar, who worked for a few years in Istmina while he was getting his career off the ground and then settled in Ibagué. In the end, everyone decided to make their lives away from El Chocó, wherever they fell in love and started their families instead.

Don Carlos never hesitated to talk about his children's feats and achievements, or about his late and beloved wife, but there was a subject he never included in his early morning lessons. He hardly ever talked to us about his parents, his grandparents, or his childhood. I know very little about the old Chamats. All I know is that his father, Alberto Chamat, left my great-grandmother, Celsa, with her two sons, my grandfather and his brother, Óscar.

Over the years, relatives were able to draw a family tree, more or less, which is why I know my grandfather was the son of a Syrian father and an Afro-Colombian mother. My grandmother Ilia had a black father and a mestizo mother, and her complexion was darker than my grandfather's, which revealed an undeniable Arab ancestry.

Given this information, it's not surprising that, in our family, it's pretty hard to predict what a baby will look like. Between cousins and aunts and uncles, between brothers and sisters, features are so varied it makes no sense to compare. And, in fact, we never do. Those who come from multiracial families know what I mean: we're so proud to belong to so many different inheritances that there isn't one we can single out. Like other people of Arab descent, my grandfather was called "The Turk," and I liked that, just like I liked to hear stories about my grandmother Ilia and her imposing blackness. Everyone could hear her heels clicking as soon as she entered church; without turning around, everyone became aware Doña Ilia had arrived.

Some of my uncles are white or almost white, and others have very African features. I have first cousins who seem right out of the Jordanian desert, like my cousin Marien, but my sister Beatriz is so light-skinned people don't always believe she's Afro-Colombian. The most curious thing is that we never realized we were different because the elders treated us all the same. I never heard of colors and hierarchies at parties and family gatherings. I never heard any of that "Ah, look, your cousin came out whiter," or, "your cousin looks more mixed."

Although, I have to confess that the Chamats, like the rest of the planet, had one obsession, a great racial weakness: our hair. That could be a matter of war!

"I want you to look flawless," my mother would say to me every morning as she pulled to straighten my hair, using dozens of products to force my rebellious African curls to look perfect in an impossible ponytail.

"Look at your cousin, how well combed her hair is, and your sister with that braid." The haranguing went on and on, and not just in my house, but in every home in Istmina, in all of El Chocó.

The most popular hairdo, with which all the mothers tortured us, featured a straight center part that split our manes in two, then two pigtails tied with two rubber bands so tight we couldn't even blink. To finish these off, they'd top off our braids with more rubber bands at the ends, so there wasn't one free hair. Not one!

Fortunately, all that drama around hair only affected me in my early adolescence, and then I left El Chocó to face an army of girls with straight, long, silky hair in white Medellín. But I overcame this trauma pretty quickly and, ever since I was a young girl, I've left it curly whenever I feel like it, to the outrage of my mother and my aunt. When it suits me, I straighten it. To date, I comb my hair however I find it more comfortable, without drama. For me, it's easier now to wear it straight for work, because it takes me less time to straighten it than to comb the curls, so that's how I wear it, without complexes. I understand my blackness doesn't depend on the color I dye it, nor the cut I choose, nor the curls I keep.

Other than the hair nightmare, racial issues never kept any of the Chamats up at night. We were simply used to being Chamats, related to the Jenny Stationery Shop on Commerce Street, the children and grandchildren of Don Carlos. And that was enough for us.

During my childhood, my grandfather, the patriarch, fell in love again. This time it was with a woman a little younger than he who had a troublesome adult son. One morning, emboldened by drugs, the young man wanted to kill Don Carlos, jealous because his mother wouldn't give him money for his addiction. My grandfather raised his arm and blocked the machete aimed straight at his neck. But the metal edge sliced his flesh and broke the bones in his forearm. The woman's son fled, terrified, shouting all over town, "I killed Carlos Chamat!" while my grandfather was rushed to Istmina's only hospital.

The news spread like wildfire: "Don Carlos Chamat was almost killed, and he's bleeding out." One by one, the neighbors—though no one had called them—began arriving at the door of the medical center to offer him their gift of life. There were so many blood donors, it was impossible to remember all their names and thank them. White, black, mixed, indigenous, and even Arab blood from some of the Lebanese families who are also part of the history of Istmina, they all joined in to help. Once they managed to stop the bleeding and stabilize him, he was flown by air ambulance to Medellín, where they saved his arm and his life after a long operation.

That wasn't his time; it wouldn't be until years later that Don Carlos said goodbye to this world. My grandfather suffered from athero-sclerosis, smoked, and didn't care about what he ate, so the implacable disease began to squeeze his enormous and noble heart until it stopped beating. I managed to see him just as he was taken by ambulance in what would be his last trip to the hospital. There, next to the stretcher, I heard him say, "Tell Ilia to leave, tell her to leave." We soon realized he meant my grandmother, not me. In his dreams, his beloved wife had returned to look for him, and he, at seventy-seven, didn't want to leave yet, clinging to what little he had left of life and to the idea of seeing us graduate and get on with our lives. Once they put him on the stretcher to get him in the ambulance, I hugged his legs and he clumsily caressed my head. His last words were, "I'll be fine, *mijita*."

On May 21, 1989, with the death of Don Carlos Chamat, the world collapsed for all of us. Until today, it's the biggest loss I've ever had in my life and the deepest emptiness I've felt in my heart. As a teenager about to finish high school, it was impossible to imagine life without him.

Almost thirty years have passed since his death, and every time I go home to Istmina, someone will tell me the story of the machete again; every version ends the same way: "And then, that same day, I donated blood." The blood of all Istmina in one, as a sealed covenant to remind us we're all, without exceptions, mixed, one way or another, because we are all Chocoanos.

For us, mixed doesn't mean mestizo, mulatto, or simply black and white. Mixed is something much bigger, richer, and more complex, which we carry with great pride. With as much pride and honor as Don Carlos felt when he came back from the hospital, with a little of each neighbor's blood running through his body.

When my grandfather died, the Jenny Stationery Shop passed to my mother. More recently, William, one of our soul brothers, bought it and moved it to another locale. He also changed the name to Doña Betty. So, one way or another, our saga and our mix continue in our town, where my family tree keeps taking root like the guaiacum trees that hold up the old wooden house, fixed in the waters of the river.

Unfortunately, those roots and that mix weren't enough to anchor me, no matter how rich they were or how deep they grew.

"Mamá, I'm going to Medellín," I told Doña Betty when I turned ten, just as I'd finished elementary school. "I want to continue my studies in the city."

I knew that great opportunities had to be sought out, and neither the rich smell of coffee in the mornings nor that enormous wooden house where everything made so much sense was going to hold me back. I knew I'd always carry those things with me, but it was time to take flight.

Of course, I probably wasn't as prepared as I thought to face the outside world, where coffee is sold in little instant packets, brick replaces wood, and nobody cares who your grandfather is, nor the blood that runs through your veins.

4.

Black Horse

Now you understand
Just why my head's not bowed.
  Maya Angelou, "Phenomenal Woman"

The hollow feeling in my stomach even stopped me from swallowing, and it wasn't exactly because of the way we were being tossed about on the plane, now caught in a fit of turbulence. That unpleasant sensation had begun in the morning, on the snaking, uneven road to the airport in neighboring Condoto, toward the flight that would take me to my new life.

"I don't want to study pedagogy and be a teacher, and I don't want to go to vocational school to be a secretary or a dressmaker," I implored my mother. These were some of the options in Istmina, and none of them caught my attention. My curious heart dreamed of other adventures and my family had no choice but to give in and enroll me in a school in Medellín. In El Chocó, which is practically abandoned by the state, there are very few resources, and most of these end up swallowed by corruption. The quality of education was deeply affected. But in Medellín, I could be part of a regular high school and have a better chance at college later. I still didn't know what I wanted, career-wise, or what I would do when I grew up, but I sensed it would be something different. I was sure my calling would not be satisfied by any of the careers offered in my beloved hometown.

In Medellín, I'd live with my aunt Aleyda, my mother's sister. She was my closest aunt, the one I trusted the most. But not even the thought of them—my aunt, my four cousins, and her husband—waiting for me with open arms could calm that feeling I'd never felt before. From the plane window, I looked out at the forests and rivers that covered my beloved El Chocó. I wanted the plane to turn one hundred and eighty degrees back to my little village, like in the movies, and go back to the Mandinga airport, from where we'd taken off. My mother was quiet by my side. Her eldest daughter was leaving and she was still a child! Yet Doña Betty respected my decision, no matter how much it hurt. We were both equally firm and stubborn. In the end, like in many families with few resources, everything's invested in the eldest child, and that was me.

Upon reaching our destination, the unease doubled. How was I going to wake up every day away from my grandfather? Suddenly, I really needed that wooden house, its smells and noises. From kerosene to coffee to the freedom of playing outside without fear of being hit by a car. In my new city, I would even miss my mother's scolding. And the music and the parties! In Medellín, I would soon discover the only parties were birthday parties, and the soundtrack was eighties rock sung in English while I was dying to dance a little salsa.

I've only felt that emptiness in my soul two other times in my life, and one would be, as I already mentioned, many years later, when we lost my grandfather forever. The third great feeling of emptiness came when I had to say goodbye to Colombia to move to a new country.

Luckily, on that first big trip to Medellín, my mother stayed with me a few days to buy my school uniform, textbooks, and all the supplies I needed for my new school. The morning before she went home, she left me a little money in an envelope and came to an agreement with my aunt to send a monthly remittance to cover my expenses.

As I watched her leave, the emptiness turned to anguish. Why did I think I could be so brave! I had been so happy swimming in the San Juan River and running up and down the streets! That anguish grew to a deep sense of desolation when I first stepped on the Colegio de la Presentación campus, a Catholic school with a very good reputation ruled by very strict nuns, where I'd be the only black or mixed student. I think there had been one other the previous year, but she had graduated and left. In the meantime, lost among so many new faces, my little girl eyes only noticed the difference in the hair all around me: all my classmates had long, smooth locks that fluttered in the breeze, while I had to keep on with my little ribbons, braids, and ponytails, which I had to learn to do every morning. In my new school, there were very high expectations about our personal appearance, and they didn't accept scruffy heads.

With a dark blue jumper dress uniform, white shirt, and dark blue stockings, I showed up for my first day and didn't go unnoticed. My skin color, my height—I was much taller than average, with acne beginning to blossom on my face—didn't help at all. The new girl was not only new, but black, big, and pimply. What I would have given to go back to that house on the river and listen to my mother's constant scolding! Not even the worst of times in my dear Istmina could be compared to those first days of sixth grade in the big city, among so many girls who saw me and were reminded of their employees back home. I was already quiet and half-reserved by nature, although no one would believe it now, but during that first year in Medellín, I became doubly introverted. I never knew if they didn't talk to me in class because I was new, because they saw me as different, or because I took refuge in my own timid silence. It was a new kind of silence for me. By instinct, I think we all learn that mutism, in a way, protects us in environments in which we don't feel safe, like stealthy gazelles in the jungle trying not to fall into the claws of a lion. How interesting! We humans unwittingly resort to this same kind of silence to save our skins but, in the long run, it actually does us a great deal of harm. Wearing my school uniform, I adopted a gazelle-like stride and quietly observed while trying to figure out who my allies would be.

But not even the silence that made me almost invisible could save me from the odd look, the whispers, or the strange contempt I tried to ignore.

As my mother had taught me, I wasn't going to be a victim, no matter how much others insisted. I wasn't going to give up because, while I might have been the only black or mixed girl at that expensive school, beyond the walls of the school, in the busy streets of Medellín, I wasn't the only one struggling to find opportunities. Those blessed opportunities I'd come from so far to catch.

Every morning on the way to school, I got in the chauffeured van that picked up six or seven other girls and took us punctually to class. I'd focus on the city: the middle-class neighborhood where we lived, with wide streets and orange brick buildings with apartments above and shops below; huge avenues lined with giant houses, luxurious cars, and security guards at some doors. In both neighborhoods, I saw well-dressed white ladies and service women, nannies and housekeepers who were like me: black, mixed, mestizo, and a few whites who came from the countryside, where they also lacked opportunities.

At each stop, I tried to examine the faces of all those women out early in their well-ironed uniforms, dragging heavy shopping baskets, or pushing baby carriages. I played a game to try to guess where they came from: she's from El Chocó, she's from north of Antioquia, she's from the Atlantic coast. I imagine that to my classmates, still sleepy in the van as we headed to school, they all looked the same. For me, each was special and different, and I wondered if they missed their wooden houses as much as I missed mine, the smell of coffee, the festivals in their villages, and the commotion of street musicians.

Luckily, I soon made a couple of friends in class who helped me feel a little more at home. Daisy and Giomar were twins, very studious, straightforward, and predisposed to avoiding those typical little cliques that sprout in schools. The two sisters were as strong willed as me, but calm and serene. The three of us organized a small study group in which they studied more than me. Later we were joined by new girls with more rebellious personalities, like mine: sisters Mónica and Olga Marcela, and the always fun Ángela. Four of us remain lifelong friends.

In my group, I was simply Ilia, but to many other girls at school, even though they didn't say it, I could read in their eyes that I'd never be more than "the black girl" or, at best, "the peasant girl."

Well, actually, there was one student who told me what she thought, loudly and to my face, and I've never forgotten it. It was the first time anyone had insulted me for being who and how I am. I think, like all first times, we never forget no matter how much we may want to minimize or downplay it. It's like the first time you find out Santa Claus doesn't exist, or the first time you have a tooth pulled, or the first time a boyfriend leaves you. It hurts, and something fragile is forever broken inside you. In my case, what was shattered was the innocence of believing that, even if they thought about it, they were never going to express it to me in words, as Chris Barker would many years later at his Ku Klux Klan base. As Maya Angelou wrote: "People will forget what you said, people will forget what you did, but people will never forget how you made them feel." And what this girl made me feel would leave an indelible mark on my memory.

That day, I remember we were in the civic events line, on the steps of the school's playground where there was a huge almond tree that provided shade. I walked by to get to my place and I heard her clearly.

"Ugh, not even my horse is black!"

The student who said it accompanied her comment with a jolt backward, as if I had been close to touching her and giving her a fatal disease.

I felt bad, very bad, and for a second, I didn't know whether to keep walking or turn to look at her. Quickly, I recovered and continued, completely ignoring what I'd just heard. *That poor girl . . .* was the only thing that came to mind, and I decided not to say anything. The girl who'd made the dire comment was seventeen years old, and much taller than me. Considering I was a mere eleven and a newcomer, I had much more to lose!

With my head up, and pretending I hadn't heard a thing, I got in line with the girls in my class and didn't tell anyone.

The next morning, in that van again, stopping to pick up the other students on the way to school, I once more gazed at the domestic workers busy with their comings and goings from the stores and mansions. *She must have heard what she said to me at home*, I thought, unable to forget the big girl's words. There was something in those conservative homes that let me know many people in that city saw us differently, and that made me feel very lonely. *I can't tell my mom about this; she's so far away, and she's only going to worry*, I told myself, ready to turn the page and not give up. *Besides, what could she do? She's sacrificing enough already so I can study here.* This is how I came to realize I needed to carry this burden by myself, in private.

I should say that in the five years I spent at the Colegio de la Presentación, nothing like that ever happened again. I began to blossom and trust that my group of good friends had my back. Plus, I wasn't going to tolerate anyone ever saying anything like that to me ever again. I used my way of walking and my general attitude to communicate a very clear message: "Be careful, don't mess with me. I might seem quiet, but I'm not dumb." However, with or without my new attitude, a subtle rejection was always present; it's hard to explain. "Don't let them get to you . . . you're so pretty and so smart," Mónica, Olga Marcela, Ángela, and the twins chorused to encourage me.

As time passed, I put aside what happened that morning in line. I made it seem as inconsequential as I could in my mind, just like my mother had taught me to do with all the drama in our lives. I put it in a drawer, a drawer that kept only silence, and downplayed it. For many years, I lied to myself. I would talk about discrimination as if it had never directly affected me. I always thought that whomever experienced discrimination had a problem, and it took me a long time to understand a problem exists when you're discriminated against and don't respond.

In my defense, I would argue that, back then, there was nowhere to complain about this kind of thing. To the nuns? To the other girls' moms? It's different today. If you feel harassed, you have somewhere to go, you have someone to listen to you and support you, your voice has an echo. Besides, in those days I thought Medellín was almost a different country and my home was far away. As if I were a foreigner in my own country. Anyone who's emigrated or moved from a town to the big city knows what I'm talking about. But because of the ironies of life, Medellín would be where I would later get my first great opportunity, the place that would accept me as I am in all those homes that were so inhospitable those first years.

But until the world changed, and during that first year of high school in Medellín at the beginning of the eighties, I thought it'd be better to focus on being a "good girl": don't complain, don't listen to them, don't talk back, don't confront them. You bury it so deep that you grow to believe it never happened. Then, in the future, as my career took off, I'd be asked, "Have you ever experienced discrimination?" My answer would always be, "No, no, never, nothing serious, just anecdotal things." Today, as an adult woman, I can face and weigh the consequences a bad word or a mean look can cause in our hearts and in society. Today, that drawer of silence has already been opened for me, and later in this story, I'll explain how and why.

To be honest, that silence and the subtle art of ignoring and minimizing what hurts is only useful until your cup overflows and you can't take it anymore, or until you're a mother and you explode, which is what happened to me.

Before, I'll say it again, I evaded, I dodged. Today, I can say it without fear: I face the hate monster, I look for it to go face-to-face with it, as I sought out Barker and looked him in the eyes during the interview with which I began my story.

With the exception of this incident with the poisonous girl, and one more or less unpleasant moment, my life as a student in Medellín wasn't so bad. At my aunt's house, they took care of me and made me feel very loved. I never lacked for anything and, when I went back to Istmina during the holidays, I became "the interesting girl." I showed up with my city clothes to be admired by my neighbors, and with my cassettes full of Menudo's new songs. With my boots, bomber shirts, Menudo jeans, Menudo lipstick, and Menudo bag, we sang all the group's big hits and even learned their choreography. Once more, dance brought us together in a great conversation in which we all understood each other wonderfully between potholed streets, skinny dogs, and half-collapsed houses.

Inevitably, when the holidays were over, a great emptiness returned to my chest because it was time to say goodbye to my little sisters, my grandfather, and my mother. Unintentionally, on that plane I never liked and that still scares me, my mind would bring back those detestable words: "Ugh, not even my horse is black!" I closed my eyes and imagined those jet-colored horses that ran free through the valleys of El Chocó, which I could see from the plane window. Black steeds, wild and bright like the night.

Wild is exactly how I would soon return to Istmina, much to my mother's dismay. I was on the verge of getting an ultimatum from the nuns after already unleashing my rebelliousness. About to turn fifteen, I was entering the most disobedient stage of my life.

5.

Rebel

If they give you ruled paper, write the other way.
    Juan Ramón Jiménez

"Mamá." I called Istmina without the slightest remorse. "I'm coming back to El Chocó. The nuns say I can't come back here next year."

I was holding the letter they'd sent to my aunt's house: due to my misconduct, they wouldn't let me register for the following year, much to my aunt Aleyda's consternation, since she'd recommended me in the first place.

"Ilia, it's October, you have one month left until your tenth-grade graduation. Just finish and we'll see what we can do later," said Doña Betty, trying uselessly to inject some common sense into my rattled brain.

"No, if they don't want to see me anymore at their school, then I won't go back; I'm leaving for Istmina tomorrow," I responded, flatly refusing her efforts.

The game was over. I'd had months of pure rebellion, poisoning the lives of my aunt and the nuns. I'd hit adolescence like a bomb. I'd never liked to be told what to do and now, with my hormones surging, much less.

There were mornings I'd wake up and declare, "I'm not going to school," and I wouldn't go. It wasn't due to laziness or because I didn't like studying—I actually loved studying. It was because I just felt like it, because I felt different and, ironically, indifferent. I couldn't identify with anything around me; most of the students seemed so perfect and obedient. So many rules overwhelmed me, and my hormones gave me no respite. At the time, I didn't understand what was happening in me. I was aware being in that school was a privilege many would have liked to have, but no matter how good it was, it just didn't go with my personality. It didn't satisfy the questions I had about God, sin, or punishment, and I didn't like that I had to confess to priests and apologize to another human being who made mistakes like everyone else.

Everything started to bother me: My skirt had to extend four fingers below the knee, my socks had to reach the bottom of the knee, my shoes could only be blue or black, and my white shirtsleeves had to hit the elbow. Hair accessories and bags couldn't be bright colored.

With so many rules, my rebelliousness went through the roof. Between classes, I'd skip school with a friend. "Oh, look, we have to go and buy supplies for our science project," we lied to the sweet doorkeeper, Mrs. María, who almost always believed us, and so we were loose on the streets. We ran free, to the mall where we walked happily, without a care, convinced we weren't doing anything wrong. Dazed, we stared at displays of expensive bags, fancy shoes, and jewelry we could never dream of buying. We didn't carry cash, and we were none the worse for it. Looking and imagining was enough.

In class, I left my tests blank. At the end of the day, Sister Javier would wait for us with her sermon, livid, impotent before this pair of "shameless" girls, as she called us. When the doorkeeper refused to be fooled and there was no way around her, we stayed at our desks, brainstorming the mischief of the day: using red masking tape on our nails to pretend we'd painted them with enamel, which was totally forbidden. Or taping up our skirts to make them shorter.

And that wild streak wasn't reserved for school. I acted out at my aunt Aleyda's house as well. I remember the party they threw to celebrate my quinceañera, totally against my will. My mother flew in expressly to help plan it, and I simply disappeared as soon as they took the official photos with the cake, right at the start of the festivities. I vanished, just like that, with my friend Germán, and left them stranded with the balloons, food, music, and guests. That was my revenge for throwing me a party I didn't want. I've never liked to be celebrated, although I am the first to say yes when it comes to celebrating others.

Challenging authority was my new modus operandi, for no apparent reason, although I'm sure there was one somewhere. There always is, even if it's hard for us to see it.

Around that time, my parents were getting divorced, and the news affected me, although Doña Betty tried to protect us and minimize the impact on our lives. Once more, silence descended on our home and surroundings to avoid deeper wounds. Like her, I pretended the inevitable lesion that follows all separations didn't affect me. To this day, it's hard for me to admit that our family situation, coupled with my experience as a "foreigner" in Medellín, plus the always unpredictable effect of hormones, made me lose my way. Perhaps all these things influenced me more than I could ever admit.

Back in El Chocó, and in spite of my arrogance and stubbornness and the feeling of utter defeat with which I got off the plane, everything tasted like glory: my streets, my people, my music, the traditions to which we all danced to the same beat. I saw and felt the essence of my little Macondo blacker than ever. I'd never thought about it before, since children don't often think about those things! Now, with new and more adult eyes, Istmina looked black and stunning. I saw it and felt it black, like my skin and my hair, and I delighted in every party and every walk through its streets and ravines. Neither the inhuman heat we felt under the zinc roof during the tedious afternoon shift at my new school, nor Professor Bonilla, director of discipline, who watched us tirelessly, managed to embitter my homecoming.

During my childhood, I'd never stopped to think about what color my life was because, as I said, in my family, we were so mixed, there was no talk of race. And out on the streets and in the neighborhoods, even the few whites felt black. Being black in El Chocó was less a matter of skin and more a matter of a history of scarcity and shared abandonment. And on my happy return, I decided to reconnect with my African roots.

My mom was happy to have me back, despite my frequent insolence and defiance. I wanted to come and go as I pleased; I didn't want anyone imposing schedules or responsibilities on me.

Like that first night, when I decided to escape to the club El Propio. According to the rules of the house, at fifteen I was too young to go to a disco. So I had no choice but to sneak out. I left without warning.

When I got to the club, everyone knew me, mostly because they were neighbors and childhood friends. One of them left early and ran into my mom down the street. He shared my whereabouts at that hour, and she decided to head over to the noisy and shady club. The news that Doña Betty was on the hunt for her daughter in the club spread like wildfire. The waiters tried to warn me, "Your mother's here, your mother's here." But I didn't have time to hide. When I got up to go, she was right there, huge and powerful, furious and offended.

"Who gave you permission to be here?" was all she said.

Those seven words and her fiery gaze were all it took for me, my face expressionless as I swallowed my anger, to head straight for the door and not stop until we got home.

The punishments came quickly: weeks grounded, floors to sweep, and entire evenings without TV or visits to friends. My mother never resorted to blows, but even if she had, I wouldn't have given up. That mother-daughter battle wasn't going to be resolved even with a United Nations intervention. Only time and maturity would bring the peace and love we both enjoy today as adults.

In those days of family warfare, the only one who seemed to understand my rebelliousness was my grandfather, and I truly enjoyed my time with him. I'm sure he didn't approve of my antics, but his hugs and words had a great effect on me. "Calm down, *mija,* I understand you, but you also have to understand your mother," he'd explain to me with infinite patience. "It's been very hard for her and she wants to raise good and independent women."

In the midst of all this teenage drama, Don Carlos was mine again, all mine, during those afternoons at the stationery shop after school, and during those magical breakfast conversations. Although Don Carlos had to play a father-like role even before my mother divorced, he preferred to be a grandfather, and as a grandfather, he listened to us, understood us, and played his role as a reconciling arbitrator perfectly in our house of women.

Those two beautiful, unruly years passed quickly and the beginning of the real end of my days in Istmina came. In a short time I would leave for college, back in Medellín and in the outside world. Only this time there would be no coming back. We were all growing up, starting to fly the nest, and my grandfather would enter the final stretch of his life.

This time, Medellín was waiting for me but singing a very different song. The same city where I'd been singled out as black was now opening doors, precisely because of my blackness.

6.

The Perfect Tone

For me, the challenge isn't to be different
but to be consistent.
　　Joan Jett

"Social work," I'd answer whenever I was asked about my major in college.

It was easy for me to lean that way career-wise. It fit perfectly with all my concerns and rebelliousness, and with what I'd learned at home: to fight for the needy.

I still wasn't sure about my true calling but at least I was clear it would be something to do with helping the less unfortunate. I'd never stopped questioning social inequality, from the Emberá to the *mazamorreras* to the mestizas and black women who worked as domestic servants and walked the streets of Medellín.

I always noticed that division in the world, in some places more pronounced than in others. Differences that piqued my curiosity and my doubts. It was the late eighties and early nineties and that was the life in any Colombian city. Those who had nothing walked right next to those who had everything in excess, on the same sidewalks and avenues. The question was inevitable: Why do these people have food, education, and health, and these others don't?

I understand and respect the fact that those who have things have worked very hard for them, have prepared themselves or taken risks. This is what they also taught me at home: those who have things earned them. I blindly believe success belongs to those who work for it, and that nothing should be given away. But all that effort and dedication will never bear fruit if we aren't given an opportunity first. The key is in the opportunities not everyone gets. I saw whole families, working hard and thinking positively, who still couldn't aspire to something as basic as access to school or a doctor.

During that decade, Colombia was, and continues to be in the twenty-first century, a society as classist as it is racist. It's a phenomenon repeated throughout the world: skin seems to lighten up with money. How sad! Class and race are entangled in a vicious circle: If you're of color, you're more likely to be born poor, therefore you'll have fewer opportunities at your disposal to make money, and so you'll stay poor. Your children will be born poor and they'll have it just as hard, and so on. Like the chicken and the egg: Which came first, poverty or race? This strange dance of class and opportunity disturbed me, even more when I was in further advanced courses in college. What separates us? What makes us so different?

Those questions were becoming increasingly urgent for me, just from looking at my surroundings and remembering where I'd come from, from that land where race and poverty merged into a single dance.

Likewise, I questioned other things, such as the rules my family imposed on me concerning my comings and goings from home, or what society dictated for me to be considered a good girl. Like having to go to social gatherings, marrying after college—before turning twenty-five and to a white guy—and having children. My strong character called into question those and other comfortably established standards. I felt each person should choose what to do in their life and when, because we're all different, we have different dreams and different expectations. I didn't understand why they insisted on applying the same rules to everyone, without any tolerance for dissent.

Now, during this new stage in Medellín, and as I grappled with so much doubt and dilemma, it was up to my mother's younger brother to host me. Poor Uncle Alexis and his wife, Dollys! They were already so frustrated with their firstborn, my cousin Tatiana, who was still a baby, to deal with me and my tribulations.

Luckily, I was almost eighteen and didn't need to be watched and taken care of like a naive teenager. Finally, I understood that if I wanted to pretend to be indomitable and independent, I had to be equally responsible. So I continued doing what I wanted but, this time, I didn't fail in school. I was already very aware of how expensive my tuition was and all of my mother's efforts to pay for it. Doña Betty had even taken out a loan so I could graduate one day.

My sisters in Istmina were never jealous because I was allowed to study in another city while they remained at the local schools. I've always thanked them for not complaining and supporting me in all my adventures. Our mother had sacrificed before and did it again to pay for my degree at the Pontifical Bolivarian University. It was time for me to put all my rebellion to work so Doña Betty could breathe a little easier—and my little sisters too. On a whim, I decided to look for a job so I could finish paying the debt my mother had incurred.

My first jobs involved clothing and fashion. Medellín is known worldwide for its textile industry and, with a classmate's help, I bought baby clothes direct from a factory and sent them to my mother in El Chocó to sell for me. This was my first job as a great businesswoman! I soon realized all these factories produced countless catalogs and runway shows, and ad agencies abounded.

"Ilia, why don't you send them a photo?" Lilián, another friend from college, suggested. "Look, my dancer friend was chosen to model for a billboard. They need a black family and you could play the mom."

I immediately sent a picture and the agency handling the project called me. That's how I met Gloria, the owner, who offered me more gigs right away. Times were changing. Medellín was increasingly multicultural and needed faces like mine. Who would have imagined it? In Istmina, naturally, no one.

"You're modeling?" my mom asked, surprised. "But, *mija*, if they tell you to smile, you're just going to do the opposite and cry. If they tell you, walk over here, you'll walk over there."

"No, Mamá, I like it, they pay me well and it leaves me time to study. They already called me for a few runway shows, not just for billboards." I was trying to calm her down.

"I don't like it. I work hard for you to go to college and become a real professional." She didn't sound convinced.

As a woman whose mother had taught her that just stepping out on the balcony to be seen was an act of total frivolity, it was practically impossible for her to approve of modeling, although the companies I worked for were all well-known brands in the textile world, such as Fabricato, Coltejer, and other local designers. With or without Doña Betty's blessing, these companies kept calling me for small ad projects and I accepted.

Fortunately, at that time in Colombia, size zero was not in style, so I fit the norm. Plus, the agencies saw my look as exotic, and liked it. *Exotic?* I wondered, confused. There was nothing exotic about me. The streets were jammed with young women like me: walking, taking the bus, cleaning houses, cooking, babysitting. We had always been part of society but, now, as if by magic, we were suddenly visible.

It was so ironic! I'd never been invisible, especially among my people in El Chocó. Ever since I was ten years old, I'd felt people's eyes on me wherever I went. "Mamá, why are they looking at me so much?" I'd ask Doña Betty, who'd answer with her usual earnestness, "There's something called magnetism, and you have it. When you grow up, you'll understand." And she'd change the subject, insisting that the key was for me to become a good person and a strong woman, because that's what others should see in me. She didn't want to praise our physical appearance nor encourage the cult of beauty at home. I think that's why I never asked myself if I was pretty, never felt special, although my height and color didn't allow me to go unnoticed. Maybe they stared at me, as my grandfather used to say, because of the bearing and determination I inherited from my grandmother Ilia. But I never cared about any of that. And back in my modeling days, I simply took advantage of my natural height and weight to be a mannequin and strut on the occasional catwalk.

After I quit modeling, which I only worked at for a couple of years, I got a job at my college's hospital. I needed to complete a minimum of practice hours to graduate on time. I spent a year evaluating families enrolling in the UPB hospital health programs and making weekly visits to community groups. I liked it. I felt useful sharing and explaining information that could help improve lives, until one day my cousin Mónica called.

"Ilia, one of my professors, Lucas, is the editor in chief for a local newscast. He's looking for someone to replace a black girl going on a sabbatical for a few months. He told me they're going to have auditions."

"What do I have to do?" I asked, without much hope. I'd never studied communications!

"Memorize some texts and perform them well." Mónica was studying journalism and encouraged me; she even offered to help me practice. At home, we recorded my voice on a cassette reading the news over and over until we were satisfied with what we heard.

"Okay, I see the job is only for a month and a half, but I could finish paying for college with that." I gathered courage and decided to go to the audition, without suspecting my life was about to change forever.

When I got to Quanta Televisión, I was invited to wait in a patio which only had a glass table with metal legs, typical of garden furniture, and a small light and camera. Soon, Lays Vargas, the news director, arrived and looked me over.

"Can you do this?" she asked defiantly.

"Of course," I replied, without hesitation.

All I need is for someone to suggest I can't do something for me to try and do it better than expected. And, apparently, the late Lays Vargas liked people who "defied the challenge."

"That's what I wanted to hear. Read this," she said, handing me a few pages.

I must have done all right because two days later, Lucas called and gave me the news: "We loved your audition; you start tomor—"

"I'm ready," I said, not even letting him finish.

A week later, all of Medellín saw my face on television, on *Noticiero día y noche*, which would later be called *Hora 13*, because it started at one in the afternoon. I took over Magali Caicedo's anchor spot. She's Afro-Colombian, also from a family from El Chocó, which she'd represented in the Miss Colombia pageant. Magali had taken a few weeks off to work on another project and the station wanted to keep white and black anchors on the air because, to date, it had worked well. Medellín—the entire country—was changing. Thousands were arriving in the cities from rural areas, displaced by a war in which guerrillas and paramilitaries sowed uncertainty. All those new faces in search of a place to live and work in peace were transforming the TV audience and their needs.

In the midst of that changing Medellín, I sat down to lead a news program with Silvia María Hoyos, an experienced Colombian journalist with whom there was such an immediate connection that we're still great friends, consultants, and counselors, although now at a distance.

In those days, I had long, straight hair with bangs and they thought that was fine. What they changed was my clothes, to make me look older, more serious, because otherwise it was easy to see I was only twenty-two years old. I'd get nervous and my entire body would burst into sweat, soaking through my blouse by the end of the day. Talking and reading live in front of those huge cameras and blinding lights wasn't as easy as it seemed. It was a demanding, intriguing, and appealing job. It was perfect for my stubborn, challenging, and rebellious spirit, although at times I wish I hadn't accepted. I was, and still am, shy, although no one believes me. But my eagerness to meet challenges always surpasses that shyness I've never been able to shed.

Besides, this new world I'd just discovered almost by chance intrigued me. Curiously, during my foray into modeling, I'd felt no sense of calling, with all due respect to that very complicated and competitive profession. But after reading the news for the first time, something lured me like a magnet. The possibility of transforming lives through information made me feel useful. I'd always wanted to help the community and this new profession was opening my eyes and giving me a chance to do just that.

"My beautiful black girl, you can do this and so much more. Go for it, *mija*, onward and forward." This is how my new partner, Silvia María, dragging her *S* with her El Chocó accent during those first days of apprenticeship, would encourage me.

Silvia María became my best teacher. I was already familiar with her work and admired her reports. I remember watching her, pregnant, reporting day and night for a national network on Pablo Escobar's capture and escape, along with the rest of the journalists encamped in front of the famous jail La Catedral. I wanted to take advantage of having her by my side to absorb her wisdom and advice and to listen to her unorthodox views and concerns, which so closely resembled mine. I never hesitated to ask her opinion about everything I was learning. With her professionalism, but especially with her great generosity, she never neglected to share her experience and counsel with me. Silvia María, Professor Lucas, and my many other newsroom partners taught me the basic language of journalism, and the rest I learned from my mistakes, which is how we learn best, and with the strength I always get from facing difficulty and knowing I'm going to get through it.

But not everyone had faith in the new girl, who was hired "because she's black." The sports anchor was a stuck-up and arrogant man. He'd been in that job for a long time and was a well-known figure in the local sports community. Unfortunately, however professional he was on his job, he was utterly lacking in humanity.

"I give this black girl forty-five days until they kick her off the air; I don't see a future for her," he predicted, but he had such bad luck that he was fired before me.

I was never told why he was let go a few months after I started. I only know he was replaced by Jorge Eliecer Campuzano, one of the best in the trade, and someone who would soon become another of my teachers and a great friend.

To top everything off, Magali, the anchor I was subbing for, never came back. She'd done a nude scene for the telenovela she was filming, the reason she'd taken leave from this position. However, management and the news director considered that a conflict with her job as a reporter, and that's the reason they gave me when they offered me a contract to stay. They'd liked what I'd been doing during those first weeks and wouldn't be holding any more auditions to find a permanent replacement.

This is a capricious and tough job: some come, others go, and some—the lucky few—stay until you, the public, decide, or until it's time to turn off the lights.

Obviously, my skin color gave me that first chance we all need and an even bigger opportunity: to make my race and my community visible, to tell Medellín we were there and always had been.

In life there are different factors that open and close doors, but your true value is what you contribute as a professional and as a human being; that's what will empower you down the line. That's why they say it's harder to stay than to get there!

Paradoxically, in my case the color of my skin—for which I'd received my share of side glances—turned out to be the attribute that allowed me into the game. The city that made me feel foreign and strange when I was a child became the city that opened the doors to my future, my calling, and my dreams of having a real career. Medellín and its viewers gave me what my people are almost always denied: opportunity. Later, my future in my new career would be determined by my effort and dedication, coupled with the help of great teachers who would guide me and continue to provide new opportunities in the face of changing times.

As I've said, Medellín had an ever-increasing Afro-descendant population that came in search of work from all over Colombia. Many arrived from the banana growing areas around Antioquia, a region of Afro-descendants where several great soccer players and sports figures were born. However, representation in other fields, such as journalism and politics, was lacking. There was also a lack of recognition among those Afro-Colombians who dedicated themselves to the arts and literature.

Apparently, my city, the second most populous in all of Colombia, was prepared to accept black anchors. Would the capital, Bogotá, and the rest of the country be ready to do the same one day?

At the moment, I never even considered it. The world of news fascinated and attracted me and I wanted to learn everything. I soon realized the power of information. I'd always known it was valuable, but now I experienced it on another level. Information gives power to those who own it, and distributing it meant empowering our audience. This feeling of being useful to my community calmed my restlessness and made everything more meaningful. I just wanted to be better at what I did, to continue learning, while I finished my studies and graduated as a social worker. I don't like leaving loose ends, although I'd already realized my service and work with the community was going to be in front of a camera, not behind a desk.

TV anchor: the choice surprised many of my friends, who didn't expect Ilia, who never missed a party and hated formalities, who was kind of shy and didn't like rules, to now appear on-screen so well-coiffed, so stiff, and so pleasant. Although those who knew me best understood I'd finally found how to channel my curious and restive spirit, which had caused me so much trouble.

There would be more surprises waiting for me along the way because, interestingly, the very thing that made my first great opportunity possible almost denied me entrance to the next stage of my life. On this occasion, my perfect skin tone would not be so perfect and almost knocked me out of the game. I say "almost" because fate doesn't understand color, and no one can take away what's yours—even if you don't get invited to the party, and even if you choose to stay quiet.

7.

This Audition Is Not for You

Luck is what happens when preparation
meets opportunity.
    Seneca

True romance, that's what I had. I fell in love little by little as the days went by, and I soon knew this would be a love that would last a lifetime. The rebel girl who'd never been satisfied with anything, suddenly woke up happy, wanting to dash to the newsroom where, with each report, each story, and each interview, I fell more and more in love . . . with my trade.

I've had three great loves in my life, and this was decades before the other two came along. I was prepared for this first love, for journalism, and ready to give myself to it 100 percent. A job becomes a calling the day you are as happy at work as at home, and that happened to me.

I was twenty-two years old and my life had changed dramatically. I still loved going to parties, dancing, and going out with friends. But a new passion had been born in me: listening to reporters discuss the topic of the day at editorial meetings, reading, researching, participating, and reviewing everything I could. I was dead serious about each and every word I said on the air; I still am. I like that responsibility and it doesn't scare me. I enjoy the complicated work involved in informing and empowering viewers.

In those first years on Teleantioquia anchoring *Hora 13*, I also fell in love with the investigative process. It was fascinating to see how a call or a comment would blossom into a story our audience could relate to. Skepticism is something I carry in my blood, just ask my dear mother. Now I'd found a profession in which inquiry was applauded instead of punished, and my boldness wasn't an obstacle but expected and approved. I could now put a spotlight on all the questions I'd had as a child whenever I watched the news. I was playing them out live, in front of the cameras, and thousands of viewers were waiting for answers with the same urgency as me.

The Colombian public is a passionate audience, involved, with a thirst for information like few others. Colombia is a land of good journalism. Because of our history, and what has been experienced in recent decades, a school of excellent journalists emerged, along with an equally demanding audience who care about what is said and how it's said. And they let you know if they like it or not.

Letters and calls from our viewers flooded the newsroom, and not all of them applauded my performance. But I used the comments to enrich, correct, refine, learn, and prepare myself better.

These were three wonderful years, watching and listening to great teachers. Besides helping me grow professionally and personally, journalism was giving me a measure of economic freedom. I had a biweekly check! With what I earned, I finished paying for college and bought my first car, a secondhand white Mazda 323 Coupe. I was the first in my family to have a car; my parents had never owned one. I even had to learn to drive. I felt like the queen of the world, going everywhere in my Coupe! But what gave me the most pride, what filled me with the most satisfaction, was that I could send money to Istmina. Now it was Lizbeth and Beatriz's turn. My younger sisters could finish their studies and my mother was no longer the only one working to get us off the ground.

What we were going through in Medellín in those days, however, wasn't easy. I started on Teleantioquia in June 1994, six months after Pablo Escobar's much publicized death. Drug trafficking obviously didn't end with his demise. It was tense and the questions everyone asked were: What would happen to his business, who would step in, who would take over? On buses, taxis, on the streets, and in coffee shops, people wondered: What will happen to all the hitmen left without a boss? Will this increase crime in our neighborhoods? There was widespread fear. The same fear we feel when the snake's head is cut off and then the twitching begins.

Medellín had been the center of a war with three fronts: Escobar, his enemies (called "Los Pepes"), and the government. Voices from the shadows offered one million pesos for every dead police officer. It was confusing and, for many, keeping silent was the golden rule. Again, the silence behind which we hide when we sense danger was near. Although the media reported the massacres and complaints and did not let up, my interests went further. I wanted to understand and explain to our audience why our children had become hitmen, why our shortcomings were leading us to this endless violence. I wanted to dig deep to empower my people in that world, which was a far cry from the glamour and fantasy now portrayed in dozens of series and telenovelas. Living in Medellín in the nineties, I learned firsthand there was nothing fascinating about any of this. It was our daily bread but a hard and bitter one. Over the years, the scene in Colombia gradually changed and, although the problem never disappeared completely, there were other additional realities, such as the corruption that continues to eat at the fiber of our society and takes lives as well, but in other ways. Children die of hunger and thirst while officials steal food subsidies allocated for their care and education. Like the so-called Hemophilia Cartel, a criminal alliance that bled the poorest patients, seizing money allotted for their healthcare.

Those were turbulent times and we Colombians lived with our daily personal struggles: working to make a living and to support and protect our families. Toward the end of the summer of 1997, after three years and a few months at Teleantioquia, my dear Pilar Vélez, an anchor on another news show on the same local station, came to me concerned. A woman of great nobility and strong ideals, she's not afraid to say what she thinks. At that time we weren't great friends yet, but she made a most generous gesture toward me. In a public meeting, she said something very simple that did right by me and changed my life.

It happened at an offsite business meeting, to which I hadn't been invited. "There's someone missing here," people told me she said in protest, and fearlessly.

Like all the other young women who already worked in journalism in Medellín, or who wanted to, Pilar had been expressly invited by an important television expert to attend a decisive casting call. *CM&*, the national news show with the most audience, was looking for a new anchor. The managers had decided Medellín would be one of the sites where they would conduct the search because the city had been a center for excellent journalists and anchors, such as María Cristina "Tata" Uribe, Félix de Bedout, and Paula Jaramillo.

By the way, Paula and I go back to our college years. It was Paula and her boyfriend who stopped to help me when I had a car accident on the road from Medellín to the airport. They were just behind the vehicle I was in with a friend and her boyfriend when we were hit by another driver at full speed. An accident I'll remember forever because of the scar on my forehead. The upside to that terrible accident is that Paula, my good Samaritan, ended up being my ex officio colleague over the years.

Now, for the casting in question . . . friends from several production companies had been invited by this so-called expert *CM&* had hired to organize the on-camera auditions.

"There's someone missing here," Pilar said with her usual sincerity. "Ilia Calderón is missing."

The casting director knew about my existence and the work I did every day with *Hora 13*. But he still didn't include me. I was the only one from the new generation of anchors, to be more precise, who had not been invited. Needless to say, and curiously, I was also the only black anchor. I didn't even have time to be offended, though, because I didn't find out I'd been excluded until someone had already fixed the problem.

Pilar Vélez's words had an immediate effect. The very next day, I received a call from Gloria Vecino, personal assistant to Mr. Yamid Amat, a famous and admired journalist, and the *CM&* news director.

"Miss Calderón, please forgive the misunderstanding and that you couldn't make the audition in Medellín. Don Yamid is wondering if you could come to Bogotá next week. The other finalists—those they chose yesterday—will also be here."

"Of course," I replied, excited about the new challenge.

When I hung up after this thirty-second call, I couldn't believe it. What audition was she talking about? Why hadn't they called me? But nothing could diminish the feeling of knowing one of the most respected journalists in the country was considering me for a job. My nerves mixed with hope, and my stomach knotted up.

On the plane on the way to the final and decisive test, I had the opportunity to thank Pilar Vélez for her generous gesture; she had also been chosen among the three finalists. I'd be the fourth, and the four of us were encouraging each other. Meeting Yamid in person was a great event. Yamid is a legend in the world of journalism and his presence alone demanded respect. Many journalism greats had learned at his knee and his reputation as a serious, demanding, and committed boss preceded him. To add to the excitement, we were taken to the *CM&* studios to meet the journalists we admired and saw every day on the national news.

Once we landed, Don Carlitos, the station's driver, picked us up and took us directly to the set. On arrival at *CM&* headquarters, we were surprised. We wouldn't be doing the audition with Néstor Morales, the coanchor. He'd been promoted to news deputy director and in his place was Claudia Gurisatti, a young, relatively new reporter, who hadn't been on the air for too many years but was ready to take a leadership role. The candidates had come to take over the vacant and coveted chair previously belonging to María Elvira Arango, who'd decided to move out of the country with her husband after decades of a successful career on Colombian TV.

As in almost all other countries, in Colombia the man-woman format was common on news shows, although a new format with two women had recently been tried out. Apparently, Mr. Amat liked taking risks as much as I did. He was like a little kid and got excited in the face of a challenge. I could offer the public something new. Claudia had already been chosen. Now they had to decide who'd be the other anchor filling the enormous shoes left behind by María Elvira with her departure. María Elvira is a critical and highly respected journalist. With her soft but determined tone, she is always firm. She's elegant, beautiful, with green eyes, a light complexion, and blond hair, like Claudia.

I'm screwed, there's nothing for me here, I thought for a moment, overwhelmed by a wave of doubts. No black anchor had ever sat in that chair and I wasn't sure if I could pull off being the first! But why not?

One by one, my colleagues from Medellín sat with Claudia to see how they looked together, to check their chemistry and how they read and improvised. This is how news auditions go. The content matters but television is obviously a visual medium and how you look next to your partner, if there's a certain affinity, is always a decisive factor. The human eye is demanding and knows if something doesn't fit right away. I wasn't sure if I fit in this major league club, in which everyone around me was white and harmonized perfectly with each other. I was the girl from El Chocó, who'd just crashed the middle of the dance, without an invitation.

When my turn came, I took a seat next to Claudia, who greeted me with a sincere smile I returned with the same sincerity. Her marked Valluno accent made me feel confident. The Valle del Cauca and El Chocó belong to the Colombian Pacific coast and, although we're physically very different, we have many things in common—things only the jungle, the rains, and the hidden and forgotten Macondos can teach you.

Apparently, those two smiles from distant provinces gelled and the chemistry between the two of us pierced the screen because we immediately heard voices from the control room and behind the cameras.

"Oh, that's it!"

Yamid, who had been watching from a somewhat quiet corner, approached me.

"What news story would you like to talk about?" he asked very kindly.

"The Gianni Versace murder," I said without giving it a second thought.

The story was fresh in my head. During the last two months, the assassination and subsequent hunt for the fashion king's killer had monopolized the international scene. I thought it would be a relatively easy topic; it was a test and I was nervous. What I had to do was let Yamid see me in action and how Claudia and I interacted.

I knew I had it hard, if not impossible, every time I remembered I was the only Afro-Colombian on the whole set. But as they say, thoughts beget results. So, even with all my doubts, I just kept repeating in my head, *Hey, why not?* What if they choose me? Pushed by the hope that wonderful things happen every day, I improvised with gusto and then read from the teleprompter, that little machine that guides anchors. I was motivated by the challenge, by the way this whole thing stirred my senses, and this gave me even more strength. I always like it better when things aren't easy; it makes me want it even more.

I think I wanted it so much even Pilar sensed it.

"The job is yours. I saw everybody's faces and I can tell you, Ilia, they're going to offer it to you," she said when we had a moment alone.

Pilar surprised me again with her honesty; her self-confidence didn't allow for jealousy. I wanted to stay real, though, to be grounded in the world where I had to live.

"I'm not getting my hopes up, Pilar. I'd rather wait for them to tell us their choice," I replied as we stood by for the flight back to Medellín.

I like to dream but with one foot on the ground. That's why, though I felt fairly sure they were going to give me the job, I also wanted to be prudent. As I mentioned, Colombia had never had a black anchor, locally or nationally. That was a fact, and I like to rely on references, statistics, and precedents. There was an Afro-Colombian anchor on the sports segment on another station, Aura Serna, whose family also came from El Chocó, and a few journalists who reported from the Pacific and Caribbean regions, but news anchor, not one.

We were a few years from closing the twentieth century and Colombia, a country that boasted about being among the most developed in Latin America, whose universities, art, literature, and industry resonated throughout the world, had never had an Afro-descendant anchor.

Consider this: Colombia, one of the world's leading exporters of soap operas (second only to Mexico) had never had a dark-skinned protagonist either. My country had dedicated itself to selling the image of the Colombian blonde in the eighties and now, on our way to the twenty-first century, the ruling stereotype was of a woman with white skin and jet-black hair, with huge and perfectly arched eyebrows. We were a country blind to real color. It was a Colombia that wanted to be European, perhaps with soft and romantic Arab tones, but not African. On TV, the only black people we saw were service characters, slaves, or thugs. No one wrote stories for us, or roles in which the millions of Afro-Colombians could be the protagonists. We were there, and had always been there, but remained invisible, our stories untold.

Every Colombian has read *María* by Jorge Isaacs, a novel that highlights an intense love story. But little is made of the background story, in which the tribal struggles in Africa and the painful sale and purchase of men and women is told. On TV, I only remember *Azúcar*, a soap opera in which we first witnessed a romance between a white person and a black person. Interestingly, that show came to us from Hollywood and the protagonists of color were members of the family, not servants. I thought, *Why don't I see black families like that on Colombian TV, with a nice house, a glamorous mom who ascends professionally, and with a decent car in the garage?* The lack of opportunities was even reflected on-screen, and always as a determining factor.

This time, opportunity came in a phone call.

"So, do you want to come to Bogotá and work with us?" It was the manager of *CM&*, excited to give me the news. "We choose you and we can offer you this salary and these benefits. Think about it and let us know."

"Yes," I managed to say amid my joy. "When do they need me?"

"As soon as you can get here. Let's say next week."

"I'm ready. Let me say goodbye to my people here in Medellín, and you can count on me," I promised and hung up, still in shock.

Without even putting the receiver down, I dialed my mom and sisters in Istmina.

"I can't believe it, Ilia, I can't believe it." It was the only thing Doña Betty said, repeatedly, filled with excitement. "You're going to work with Yamid Amat and you're going to be the first black anchor on the national news. The first!"

I don't remember if I cried, or if I just cried inside and didn't shed a tear. On the one hand, my mind was stuck on thinking it was a great honor to be the first. I didn't want to sound ungrateful before such an important opportunity. But I also thought, *It's almost the year 2000, did we have to wait until the end of the century for this to happen? How many mixed, black, mestizo girls, or whatever they want to call themselves, dreamed of this before me, prepared but weren't given the opportunity to audition?*

I was very proud to be the first and life would give me two other opportunities to be a pioneer again. But I questioned this achievement, even while celebrating it, even alongside my endless gratitude.

Once the initial euphoria passed and I finished talking with my sisters and cousins, two other feelings washed over me: first, sadness, because my dear grandfather wasn't here to celebrate this important family event. The other was a sense of responsibility. Although I'd always been attracted to challenges and trying the most difficult tricks, like trapeze artists in the circus, this time the weight was enormous. Many people would be waiting to see me on the first day on that set with Claudia Gurisatti, and some would be hoping I wasn't up to it, so they could go and tell Yamid, "See? You were wrong."

There's a horrible saying in Colombia that's often repeated on the streets and in social media: "The black person who doesn't screw it up at the beginning will do so in the end." The first time I heard it was in Medellín, when I'd moved to study with the nuns ten years before. It's a concept thousands of Colombians believed (and still believe).

Now, I—Istmina's rebellious girl, the one who'd never stood up to the big girl who'd treated me like a leper at school; the one whom the nuns expelled for being incorrigible; the one who questioned her own shadow—could not fuck it up! Neither at the beginning nor at the end because all of Colombia would be watching.

That's what it's like to be first, which isn't as much fun as they make it seem.

As it turned out, I never crossed paths with the TV expert Yamid and *CM&* had hired to oversee the Medellín auditions. I guess he adhered to so-called marketing rules and the artificial sciences that study what sells and what doesn't. I'm well aware that those in key positions in any industry or organization can make a difference, and they know it. They just need to arm themselves with a little courage, think differently, and not be so afraid of being pioneers. Because not everyone is going to have a Pilar Vélez to stick up for them and raise their voice, forcing changes that lead to fairer decisions.

Luckily, Yamid Amat dared to let me participate in a simple audition. The opportunity we all deserve. The rest you earn, showing the world what you can do. In a few days, I'd be going through a trial by fire: with the viewers.

8.

The First Time, the First One

In the middle of difficulty lies opportunity.
Albert Einstein

"We're not going to make any kind of announcement about the new hire because this shouldn't be a big deal," Yamid Amat said as the head of *CM&* news.

At that time in my life, my new boss's decision not to shout to the four corners of the earth that they'd contracted their first national Afro-descendant anchor seemed very respectable and proper. It was still an achievement because it was important that diversity on our TV screens become a norm and not an exception. But this fell in line with what I'd always practiced: not to make too much noise about this sort of thing. I wanted to stay above the fray and let my work speak for itself, to be valued for that and nothing else. A dignified silence, which many black people deployed in those years in Colombia if we wanted to get ahead in a profession. Only a handful of brave souls dared raise their voices when they were denied. In the nineties, there was still no open debate about racial inclusion in my country, and only with the passing of the years, and then the arrival of social media, did the notion of a "dignified silence" begin to break. With Twitter and Facebook, those voices of protest that already existed at academic and street levels finally reached mass media and provoked a real debate about race and discrimination. But this was 1997 and neither Yamid nor I were sure Colombia was ready for that discussion.

Within this context, the relaunching of the newscast with our new faces was mostly kept secret, while I began to quietly attend the editorial meetings at *CM&*, as one more journalist, trying to connect with my new colleagues and learn the dynamics of my new job.

CM& was a programming and production company that, like all the others, bought time on government channels. Private TV was about to take off in Colombia and the labor landscape would soon be transformed. Many changes would come and Yamid, always ahead of the pack, wanted to start with a double play: two women, one of them Afro-Colombian, a formula without a doubt innovative for its time. I wanted to have an organic, natural debut. The legendary Amat was a man who didn't like to make a fuss. He knew how to earn viewers' loyalty naturally, a practice I've always defended and adopted.

I remember my first night as if it were yesterday, although it's been more than twenty years. It was November 1997 and I arrived wrapped up in scarves and a jacket I'd just bought. From my beloved and steamy El Chocó, I'd moved to Medellín's spring, and now to cold Bogotá. My body didn't know how to contend with real winters. The capital was dark, sad, and icy. The Urapanes, the hotel where I stayed until I found an apartment, was gray and that morning, trying to brighten my new space a little, I'd decided to wear yellow—a bright yellow jacket I kept for a long time and that I ended up giving away later. I couldn't have chosen a less discreet color! The sun had to be brought to Bogotá.

Once again, I wanted to face the challenge head-on, without camouflaging myself or going unnoticed. I didn't want to copy anyone or look like anyone or pretend to be who I wasn't. I was Ilia Calderón, Doña Betty's daughter, Liz and Beatriz's sister, granddaughter of Don Carlos, the owner of the Istmina stationery shop. I was the girl from El Chocó, where we like color. Having donned my banner, and with a firm step, I arrived in the newsroom to prepare what would be my first script for my first newscast with Claudia. When the moment of truth arrived, Yamid called me.

"I'm betting everything on you, *mijita*. I'm not telling you this to make you nervous, because I know you're very capable. I wouldn't have hired you if I wasn't sure of your talent." The big boss—a man who'd faced thousands of challenges in the aggressive world of news—sounded a bit emotional. "I wanted to tell you I'm not going to be here tonight. I'm going to watch the news from my house for once. I wish you luck. I'm counting on you."

He gave me a fatherly hug and left. The world swirled around me! Yamid Amat Ruiz, one of the most honored journalists in Colombia, creator and director of many a radio program, former editor of national newspapers, and cofounder of *CM&*, was nervous!

It was then I realized it wasn't just my career at stake and I began to worry less about what anyone thought of me or if I was going to be liked. Deep down, I've never cared what anyone says. I wasn't feeling less than anyone nor stressing more than usual thinking I might be rejected because of who I am. That night my doubts focused on the ratings, the blessed audience numbers, and the advertisers because, hand in hand, those figures would more or less reflect the number of people who wanted to watch me and wouldn't change the channel. I wasn't worried about what my colleagues in the print media would say the next day, relentless critics who rarely give us, their television colleagues, any kind of break. My head revolved around the business, Yamid's reputation, the ratings, and all the work my new colleagues were putting in.

For us, news is a vocation and an obsession but it's still a way to make a living. There's a whole sales machinery that supports and provides us with the fuel to keep going. And that fuel is advertising money—I didn't want my debut to bankrupt us.

Yamid would have already arrived home when I sat next to Claudia at that perfectly lit desk surrounded by cameras. My partner encouraged me and gave me a calm and confident look, the way people who believe in you do. Just like at Teleantioquia with Silvia, here I had another copilot who didn't hesitate to guide me, step by step. That night, Colombia would have its first black anchor. "So what? Let them get used to it," said Claudia. Yamid liked being a pioneer and he was going to be one again, whether from home or the office. There was no going back.

Two minutes before going live, I fixed my hair—I wore it very short at the time—adjusted my yellow jacket, and, with Yamid, my family, my mother, and my people in El Chocó very present in my thoughts, I gathered my courage. The image of my grandfather and how much he would have enjoyed this moment was the last thing I remembered before greeting the whole country and starting to read.

As always, when you're really focused, time flies and half an hour turned into ten minutes. When I looked up, we were already saying goodbye with our official sign-off: "The news from *CM&*." I was so nervous, I said it with my most Chocoano accent, almost singing it and dragging the last vowel, which later became my personal seal.

As we stood up, our crew began to applaud. The entire editorial staff was clapping. Even before we knew what the outside world thought of this new adventure, I felt it was a battle won, thanks to everyone present. The victory wasn't just Claudia's and mine. It belonged to all of them, and to Yamid, who must have been home biting his nails.

"Mamá." She was the first person I called, because I wanted to hear the harshest and most honest criticism first. "Mamá . . . are you crying?"

"No, well, yes, yes, a little." Doña Betty, a strong woman who'd never liked sentimentality, was melting with pride and joy.

No, I hadn't set foot on the moon. I hadn't won a Pulitzer and I wasn't Rosa Parks. I hadn't changed the world or triggered a whole wave of civil rights. I wasn't Oprah or Nelson Mandela. But in Istmina, and in many parts of El Chocó, the feeling was as if Jesse Owens had won the gold medal again at the 1936 Olympics. Only this win was shown on TV and the winner was one of theirs, someone who spoke like them and looked like them: "Our anchor . . . our girl . . . our Ilia." There's a particular pleasure in the word "our" that we all feel when we say it, wherever we're from.

The next morning, I woke up in a hotel that no longer seemed so gray. My room was filled with huge bouquets of flowers of all colors and the phone wouldn't stop ringing. I was inundated with invitations to radio shows and interviews with magazines wanting to know more about me. Who was I? Where did I come from? What was my story? I didn't understand the phenomenon very well. I was clear I was the first black woman national news anchor in Colombia but, in the end, it was just journalism. And, like my mother, I didn't like that kind of attention.

Fortunately for me, when I arrived in the newsroom the next morning, my boss reacted as if nothing had happened.

"Well, *mijita*, everything went well," he said.

He never said we'd made history, never praised my work more than Claudia's, and didn't waste time responding to the noise and comments coming from outside. Yamid made us feel like things were completely normal, and I appreciated that. His message was straightforward: "Okay, let's go, we passed the first test, let's go for more."

In the next few days, my news director focused on letting me develop a love for my work; he made tough demands to get the best out of me. The veteran journalist knew it was time to give this new girl a chance, but the girl had to be up to the job. What I didn't know for sure was if Colombia was really prepared for a different face in prime time, or if what happened the night before was just because of the novelty. We would find out soon enough, when the sales department gave its reports.

As it turned out, Colombia was ready to watch a woman of color talking about politics, the economy, health, and other vital issues to its citizens. Colombia had said yes to the girl from El Chocó leading the news with her partner, Claudia. The sponsors were happy with the ratings and the popular response. The challenge now was to focus our efforts on showing that our talent and professionalism, as two women, had lasting power.

They say that on TV, as in many other trades, you're as good as your last interview or your last presentation. But nobody remembers what you did yesterday. It's an ephemeral, accelerated medium; so much that it may seem cold. Today you're up and everyone applauds you, and tomorrow you're down, you're fired, and in two months nobody remembers your name. It's not that the audience is ungrateful; it's simply the pace at which we live. The viewers have their own problems, their own struggles, and whether the news is read by Jane Doe or Joe Blow doesn't make anyone lose sleep, which is as it should be. It's important to not give weight to what's basically weightless. Which is why, in this profession I chose, I soon realized today's success and applause are tomorrow's great challenge. I'd stood out as the first woman with dark skin and African features in this kind of job. And I was sincerely grateful. Nevertheless, the fight would continue tomorrow because winning a battle doesn't mean you've won the war, nor that the world has become more just.

That night, after my second newscast with *CM&*, my goal was to be better than the day before, and to be even more invested. The door of opportunity was already open and now we couldn't let it close, because doors that open can just as easily be closed with the slightest breeze. The winds sometimes blow favorably, and sometimes not so much. Just as there would be more achievements to celebrate in my career, there would be more auditions that would exclude me.

It already seemed completely normal not to invite the Chocoana to the dance. And to think I like to dance so much!

9

Not This Audition Either

The first time it's a whim, the second time it's a rule.
Chinese proverb

"Pass me the phone book," my friend Erika said, very determined. "I'll call and see if we can visit the station."

"Yeah, c'mon," Carolina, our second travel companion, echoed. "Call and see if they'll let us tour their studio."

We'd just celebrated both the end of the year and the end of the century and two of my best friends had decided to commemorate it by getting away from Bogotá. We chose Miami for our minivacation, hoping to do some shopping as well. At the hotel, I turned on the TV and clicked to Telemundo. Because my friends were studying communications, we liked the idea of visiting a Hispanic station on American soil, although we didn't know if they'd allow the merely curious on their sets. In Colombia we watched Telemundo and some Univision and admired their production quality and the diversity of stories they told; it was different from what we did on newscasts in our country. Just as we were about to call to request a tour, we were told our taxi was waiting to take us to dinner and we took off. One of those capricious twists of fate. When we got back that night, we'd completely forgotten about the visit to the station and returned to Colombia, where life resumed its usual pace: writing, interviewing, recording special segments, and hard daily work to weather the political storms we were experiencing.

The new millennium came in with a fury: kidnappings, followed by attacks, and, later, failed negotiations between the government of

Andrés Pastrana and the FARC guerrillas while the ELN—the second guerrilla front—continued with its criminal enterprises.

I'd finished my third year at *CM&*. Claudia Gurisatti had gone on to RCN and wasn't my partner anymore. Now I shared anchoring duties with my dear Pilar Vélez, the woman who'd spoken up because they hadn't invited me to the audition for the job! When Claudia decided to go with one of the new private channels, naturally I suggested my bosses should bring in Pilar. The universe works like this: when you do something good, it comes back to you. And when *CM&* chose her, I knew this was her reward for her generosity, and undoubtedly, for the quality of her journalistic work.

Pili (as I call Pilar) and I were solid on the nightly news, supported by an incredible team of producers and reporters.

This was also around the time I was consolidating my work as a presenter. My stories appeared on *Agenda CM&*, our weekly magazine, and had opened the door for me to travel and interview our viewers, Colombians like me from different regions who were contributing to the growth of our country. I was fascinated, listening and learning from their stories and sharing them with the rest of the country.

Slowly, we began to see reporters from different races, and this filled me with pride. But when it came to high visibility on-screen positions, not much had changed.

How long am I going to be the only black person in an anchor chair? I wondered with a certain frustration. When would Colombia wake up to the reality we refused to see? Being the first shouldn't mean being the only one. They're two different concepts that need not coexist for any length of time because the first to achieve something in this world would like to celebrate the arrival of the second and the third. It's natural. It'd be like amassing a great fortune and having no heirs to whom to leave your achievements, your wealth. An unbequeathed legacy: I'd experience this feeling repeatedly throughout my career. All this would come back to haunt me again years later, during another very significant chapter of my life that I'll also recount here.

In Colombia there was talent in all social strata and of all races and colors because more and more doors were opening to education and there was a growing number of professionals of color in more fields and industries. However, the country was still governed by the same powerful middle managers unable to make decisions that went beyond precedent, and the great opportunities that make a difference remained available only to certain people: those who enjoyed the possibility of reaching their goals were the ones who had access to better schools, better jobs, and "wonderful" contacts with politicians and other powerful people. Those valuable opportunities didn't reach remote communities, for whom it was far more difficult to get ahead.

How was it possible we'd never had a black president in the modern era? In the past, Colombia had a mulatto president, and for more than a century and a half, leaders, historians, and teachers hid him, buried him in oblivion, far from our textbooks. In 1861, Juan José Nieto, a mestizo man with African features, began governing the Grenadian Confederation, what is modern-day Colombia. The "whitening" of our history reached such heights that, after he died, his portrait was sent to Paris so professional artists could erase the African features from his face. That painting ended up hidden in the basement of a historic building in Cartagena, wrapped in a cloak of shame, until recently, when Juan Manuel Santos, in his last days as president of the republic, ordered that it be hung in the presidential gallery at Casa Nariño, along with the portraits of all our other presidents. After 157 years in oblivion, we finally claimed the painting and its origin as a part of the black history of Colombia.

Juan José Nieto Gil was the first and, so far, the only one. I'm not comparing myself to that great self-taught military man and novelist, but I didn't want to be alone on this journey, like he was. Fortunately, and although it would take a while, opportunities were slowly coming along for other colleagues and journalists of color. And I rejoice each and every time they come. Each time I see a new Afro-Colombian face on camera in my native country, I feel it's a big little win.

And speaking of opportunities, I was about to be denied again, for reasons that would never be officially explained to me.

"Ilia, did you see this article in the paper three days ago?" A friend handed me the crumpled and folded newspaper, pointing to a small article in the TV section. "Didn't they let you know?"

The story said Telemundo executives had come to Bogotá in search of new anchors and presenters and were auditioning the country's leading professionals. This was pretty familiar: nobody had invited me.

"No, no one said anything," I answered.

As always, I opted to minimize the drama and not let myself be seen as a victim. However, even though I didn't want to accept it, I was still the only black woman in the major leagues and, coincidentally, the only one left out. My short but solid career, my ratings, my performance, and my popularity among viewers made me at the very least a candidate for an audition, and the colleague Telemundo had hired to organize this new casting call knew this all too well. Once more, what sells, marketing, and the desire to give what they think the public wants were messing with me, weren't they?

I was happy at *CM&*. I wasn't even thinking about looking for another job. I felt my time of service to the Colombian people wasn't over yet. As a professional, I was living one of my best moments, but the rebel in me always looked forward to more obstacles to overcome. At the time, the challenge of working in news in the United States was beyond my reach. It made me sad and annoyed me that they hadn't called, but I also liked the idea of staying where I was, doing my job in my country and for my people.

A few months later, fate decided to reopen this chapter that I thought was over and done. It happened in the simplest way. I returned to Miami for vacation, this time with a friend who knew Maggie Van de Water, Telemundo's vice president of talent.

"Oh no! This time I'm taking the studio tour," I told my friend. "Last year Erika, Carolina, and I couldn't make it." So she called and made the arrangements.

I went to Telemundo without any hope of grabbing that lost opportunity in Bogotá. I was convinced they'd already hired for the position many months before and that my visit would be merely anecdotal. Even so, I wanted to see how the world of news worked in the United States, how they managed behind the scenes in a country that has been and continues to be the standard for big news stations. My first surprise came when Maggie Van de Water herself was waiting for me at the door.

"Do you currently have a job?" Those were her first words after greeting me.

"Yes, I'm anchoring the nightly news on Channel 1 in Colombia," I said, trying to make it clear I'd only come as a tourist.

"Oh, they just held auditions in Colombia. Didn't they call you?"

"No, I didn't find out until later. Those things happen," I said, trying to downplay the situation.

I didn't want to talk about the reason I thought they hadn't included me. After all, nobody had offered an official explanation and I didn't want to speculate. I'd just stepped into Telemundo and the last thing I wanted was to talk about personal things, or let them think I saw myself as a victim. My plan was just to learn a little about journalism in the United States, a world so similar and so different from mine.

"Excuse me one second," Maggie said, her smile gone as she set out to make a call. "Hi, Joe, I'm here with the person I think we're looking for . . . No, no, now . . . yes . . . I know you're busy but don't say I didn't tell you . . . you're going to miss it."

I didn't know who she was talking to or about what because my English was very limited at the time but, in less than five minutes, Joe Peyronnin, Telemundo's vice president of News, had come down to Maggie's office, where she'd invited me to chat.

"What am I going to miss?" he asked, not realizing I was there, in a corner, silent, not sure what was happening.

Maggie gestured toward me and gave me a wink. "Her. Let me introduce her. Her name is Ilia Calderón."

"Don't you work in news in Colombia?" Joe asked. "If you want to come to the editorial meeting, follow me."

This is how everything moves in the world of journalism, at a thousand beats per minute and straight to the point. There's no time to mess around because there's always a deadline ahead. The clock is always ticking. I rushed after Joe to the meeting, where they were discussing the day's agenda. Joe asked my opinion on a couple of stories and Diana Maldonado, one of the main producers, translated.

"Are you interested in doing an audition?" Joe asked when we finished. I understood this without any help.

"Of course," I responded, driven by my passion for risks and the opportunities life presents.

Joe Peyronnin is a veteran journalist who began his career as a producer for the local CBS station, then was assigned to the White House. He served as president of Fox News and then vice president of NBC. Because of his experience, and although he didn't speak much Spanish, Joe understood the needs of the immigrant community very well. Studious and observant, he could anticipate the new direction Latino journalism would take in the United States. I think I was part of that plan because, smiling at my answer, he accompanied me to the set to prep me for my on-camera audition.

In makeup, they did me up in a way I wasn't used to, with dark shadows and a lot of blush on my cheeks. It's something that happens frequently when someone doesn't know your face, your style, or what you like. I didn't want to be rude or complacent, so I asked for the restroom and washed my face clean. I put on a little blush and, without even checking my hair, I sat down in front of the camera. If this was going to be a play for a new job, I preferred to be more natural, plus I wanted to feel more "me." As great life experts have said, "Less is more." This time I was wearing a black sweater, quite the opposite of that cheerful yellow with which I first appeared to all of Colombia.

About to start the unexpected and spontaneous test, I have to confess I felt lost. I wasn't sure what I was doing. I loved my life in Bogotá, I felt fulfilled and happy at *CM&* and working in my country, but my competitive instinct told me: "Read, read with vigor, take advantage of the opportunity you were denied and that is denied daily to your people; they always lack opportunities and today life is giving this to you. You can't let it get away!" The girl from El Chocó I always have inside asked me to try, to forget about the times when I hadn't been taken into account. Many consider working in the U.S. market a dream or, at the very least— even if it wasn't a dream—it represents an opportunity, and a big one!

When I heard "on cue!," I started reading. I read with urgency and, although I was sweating from nerves, like that first time at Tele-antioquia in Medellín, I did the best I could. As soon as I finished, they thanked me and sent me to see Berta Castañer and Anjanette Delgado, two executives who reviewed the recording right away and gave their approval.

In less than an hour I was sitting in front of Jim McNamara, president of Telemundo. Jim, a very nice and polite Panamanian, made the unexpected offer.

"Look, would you be interested in going to New York? We need an anchor for the local news there."

"Yes," I said, accepting instantly, like I always did when it came to professional opportunities—even if I hadn't been looking for or expecting them in any way.

"Are you sure? It's cold there, you'll be far from your family . . ." He tried to warn me.

"Yes, I'm sure, I'm going to New York," I said, now determined, and remembering that if I'd survived the cold in the Colombian capital all these years, I could easily survive New York, although this time I'd have to buy a store's worth of coats.

Besides, how could I reject what Bogotá had denied me? I hadn't been told about the audition and, here I was, being offered the job anyway.

"Okay, we'll send you a written offer," Jim promised as we said goodbye.

The next day, I returned to Colombia sure they'd call me and that it was a done deal. At this point I was convinced that, in this life, nobody can deny you what's destined for you, not even an audition you're not invited to. So when I received the fax with Telemundo's proposal, I was ready for it. My astonishment came when I read the details. The offer wasn't what McNamara had talked to me about. I wasn't going to New York to anchor the local news. The formal and definitive proposal was to anchor the national weekend news, from hot and colorful Miami. It wasn't going to be easy to work on the weekends. I had already done it for a few months in Medellín and it felt like living opposite everyone else's schedules. But I understood it was a new beginning and that in all battles fought and won, there are sacrifices we have to make. Dues that have to be paid, which ultimately represent the foundation of all learning.

"And, really, who cares if it's weekends?" I told my mom when I called to tell her the news. "This is a national newscast, and from Miami! In Florida, I'll be closer to Colombia than if I was in New York, so I can come see you, and many people in Miami speak Spanish."

Obviously, Doña Betty was happy, but she couldn't hide a hint of sadness every matriarch feels when her chicks fly farther and farther from the nest.

After the excitement of telling my mom and my sisters, and imagining my new life in another city and another country, I forgot another sad fact: I would also have to say goodbye to Pili and my news team, both of whom I adored.

"Okay, let's talk money," the *CM&* manager said when I told him I was leaving. "How much of a raise do you want?"

"No, I've already made my decision," I explained.

I think he thought I was joking, or that I was strategizing to get more money. But at that point in my career, it wasn't about money. It was about taking on the challenges life offered me. Although, as I said, I felt useful and accomplished informing my people in Colombia, I also knew it was time to look for new and bigger frontiers.

I started packing two bags and with every shoe and every dress I folded, I remembered my first day of school in Medellín, among the blond girls who didn't need to tie up their locks and tame them in impossible braids. I remembered my afternoons modeling and entire nights studying at the university. My memory traveled through my first newscast in Medellín and my first day at *CM&*, that night when Yamid Amat went home so he wouldn't have a nervous breakdown in the newsroom, waiting, waiting for reactions from all over Colombia after they'd seen me on their screens. I'd had quite a journey!

Once I finished packing and said goodbye to friends and family, I got on the same flight I'd taken before to go on vacation. But this time I had no return date.

It's good nobody ever told me I was going to be the first Afro-descendant to anchor national newscasts in Spanish media wherever I went! That way I didn't feel so much pressure. I thought, in the land of Oprah Winfrey, Whitney Houston, and Michael Jordan, black people had already been fronting TV news for years, whether they were immigrants or not, and whether they worked in English or Spanish. I thought that in cities like Miami and New York, with such large populations of Cubans, Puerto Ricans, Dominicans, and Colombians, seeing black people speaking Spanish in key positions wouldn't be a big deal. I thought it couldn't surprise anyone to see doctors, lawyers, mayors, and, of course, Latino anchors of color. It didn't even cross my mind I'd be the first for the second time! I saw myself more as a Colombian coming to the national news, period. And I wasn't going to be the first Colombian because Ana María Trujillo had already been an anchor at Telemundo, and that pleased me. Knowing I'd had precursors made me feel better because someone had already paved the way for my benefit.

In any case, my concerns didn't involve being first or last. What was stressing me out was moving to a completely unknown country and . . . the language! How was I going to communicate with my boss, my neighbors, and with that new world in general? My English was very basic and I could barely understand the waiters when ordering a salad. What kind of mess had I gotten myself into? This time, I was scared, and I'm proud to admit it now. Fear is part of the growth process. For a split second, I hoped the plane taking me to Miami would turn around, just like I'd hoped that double-helix plane would do when I was on my way to high school in Medellín, far from my dear Istmina. That same strange emptiness wanted to take over me again, but I didn't let it. I told myself, *I'm going to Telemundo, to a new job, a new challenge, and everything will be fine. I was denied an opportunity before, so I'm not going to let it get away now.* With this thought, I landed in my new life, in which all kinds of surprises awaited me: some sweet, some a little bitter.

As for the journalist who had organized the auditions for Telemundo in Bogotá, life brought us together years later at a wedding in Cartagena. The happy bride was none other than my former coanchor and good friend Claudia Gurisatti. The journalist in question is a renowned professional with international experience, and I don't think he's prejudiced. I suspect that, like others in charge of their first casting call in Medellín, he got carried away by the rules of marketing. I'm sure he was familiar with the profiles of the anchors and presenters who'd done well at Telemundo and probably felt I didn't meet those expectations. In Colombia, he'd prepared the perfect auditions for Telemundo executives, because they'd hired him for that. It's a phenomenon, something similar to what happens when the Pope comes to visit our countries and suddenly the streets are clean, flowers are planted, and the poor and unfortunate disappear. Likewise, this man had invited the anchors and presenters he thought would give that same image of perfection, and for some reason, I didn't fit.

"Hey, why didn't you call me for that Telemundo casting call?" I asked him, after we'd politely greeted each other. This time I didn't keep quiet. I had nothing to lose so I'd decided to break that "tasteful silence" we were so used to.

"Because I'm friends with your former boss, and how was I going to steal her talent?" he answered.

Ah, that old excuse everyone resorts to but no one believes. The world of news and TV is like soccer. No one's going to convince me a Real Madrid trainer is not going to sign, or at least consider signing, a Barça player just because he's friends with the tech coach.

That afternoon, we ended our conversation in a good mood with kind smiles and no bad feelings. By then, I'd been working as a journalist in the United States for more than a decade. What more could I ask of life?

Well, maybe I could ask that I be invited to the next audition, wherever it might be, because they say the third time's a charm.

But first, I had to pay the same dues as all newcomers to a new land. Once I arrived in Miami, I became part of another minority that doesn't have it easy either. I was an immigrant for the first time. I experienced the true meaning of the word "foreigner" and the impact of the silence that follows those of us who hail from somewhere else, those of us who are newcomers. A new silence for me, with a different texture and color, but equally harmful. Because I don't know what's more complex: to be a prophet in your own land, or in a foreign land.

10.

My New Minority

hospitality: *from the Greek* fi-lo-xe-ní-a, *literally meaning*
"love (affection or tenderness) toward strangers and foreigners"

"Where are you?" It was Joe Peyronnin, my new boss, and he sounded very upset. "Get here as soon as you can. I'm guessing you already know what's going on."

"I'll be there soon, I'm close," I replied from my cell phone; I was on my way.

Minutes before, I'd been preparing for my English classes and Jorge, a friend visiting from Colombia, had screamed at me from across the living room.

"Ilia, a plane just crashed into one of the Twin Towers!"

I never finished rinsing my mouth, just stood there in front of the TV with my toothbrush in my hand. As we watched the screen, the second plane hit the second tower.

It was so surreal, I had to make sure we were watching the news and not a movie. Once that fact was confirmed, the sunny and modern apartment where Telemundo had put me up became a heartless gray.

September 11, 2001: impossible to forget. Exactly three days before, the previous Saturday, we'd started the first Telemundo national weekend newscast, *Noticiero nacional fin de semana*, with me in the lead in this, my new city of Miami, and in my new country, the United States of America. But this morning, it was a country engulfed in fear and uncertainty. The so-called land of freedom was reeling and crumbling in real terror before my eyes, with attacks on the Twin Towers, the Pentagon, and a third plane crashed somewhere in Pennsylvania.

"I'm off!" I shouted at Jorge, wallet in hand and one foot out the door.

My gut told me this was too big to waste time on questions. I didn't understand what I'd just seen but I knew my place was in the newsroom, because of what else might happen. And so much was about to happen.

As I arrived at Telemundo, producers were whizzing by, editors hugged and cried as they watched images coming in: traces of the fourth wrecked plane. My bosses yelling orders, trying to organize the staff that just wasn't big enough for a story this intense. This wasn't the time for the new girl to ask for help; no one could offer guidance in all that shock and chaos.

Without understanding much of what the executives were talking about in English, I offered to take notes and sit in front of the camera if they needed someone to just fill the screen. For days, we barely rested. We only went home to take a shower, blink a few times, and then come back. I was covering night shifts and taking turns at dawn, relieving Pedro Sevsec and María Elvira Salazar, the station's two most veteran and best-known anchors. Between shifts, I read everything I could find on the internet about the geography of the region, about the Taliban, the politics of each state, who the key people were on the national scene, and every detail I could find on New York, a city I didn't know very well. There were endless new terms and concepts I didn't know, and that I had to learn on the air, on the fly, as is often the case in this profession.

These long and incessant hours broadcasting live during a difficult time for everyone were my baptism and initiation into journalism in my new country, the United States.

Between the tragedy and the confusion, I realized the way of working this story was so different from my country. Like a democracy, decisions were made in constant editorial meetings where everyone—reporters, producers, and on-air talent—had a voice when it came to distributing assignments and giving opinions we considered relevant to the news.

In Colombia, I was used to vertical decision-making. The chief listened to pitches from each journalist and then decided whether to pursue a story. Plus, reporters were grouped into specialties or pools of resources. I soon discovered here we all had to be prepared to cover any topic at any moment. You could report about the health status of the Tower survivors one day and interview the governor about changes to antiterrorism laws the next. The editor role was also radically different. In Colombia, it's the news director who writes all the texts the anchors read. In the United States, at Telemundo and at every other station that's big enough, there's a news writer who's dedicated exclusively to writing these scripts.

Two weeks later, as I tried to adapt to my new environment, when the nonstop broadcasting of the ravages caused by the terrorist attacks finally stopped, we were able to gradually return to our lives and our routines. It was there, alone in that apartment by the sea, where many other challenges began. It was time to face my new reality: I was in a foreign land. And I was about to get a little taste of what it really meant to be a foreigner.

It'd been a big change to go from El Chocó to Medellín, and then from Medellín to Bogotá, and from Colombia to the United States. That was like a triple jump from a trapeze without a net. Still sheltered by Telemundo, with a work permit in hand and help provided by a couple of Colombian friends residing in Miami, my big little drama was causing me real headaches. The dumbest things became complicated obstacles, hoops I had to jump through as best I could.

Without a credit history in my new country, I resorted to help from a friend of a friend to get a car lease. I soon learned my payments would be much higher because I was a newcomer. This is an economic challenge faced by thousands of families: very high interest, which in some cases makes them victims of aggressive lenders. Fortunately, I was able to pay my lease month by month, until I had established credit a year or two later. But I'm aware many other immigrants can barely establish that "good credit," which you need so desperately in this country, otherwise you're nobody. "Look, when my wife first arrived, she established credit with department store credit cards," a coworker advised me. So there I was, taking out Express and Neiman Marcus cards, and using them until my score went up, and greatly appreciating that I could pay them, little by little. As I said, millions of families have it much harder, and in some cases, this credit drama ends in truncated dreams and promises of a promised land that's never in sight.

I remember I had a credit limit of three hundred dollars a month on my first card. Welcome to my American dream, whatever it was!

Although they're not serious or critical like what other families go through, the immigrant experiences I'll recount here became a key part of my history and my way through journalism and life; that's why I must tell them. Being a foreigner is something you have to experience in order to understand. It's not that simple, even if you fly in with a work permit. Each immigrant has a different story but many of our feelings and experiences are similar, whether we carry documents or not.

For example, the most painful obstacle for me, and I'm sure for every immigrant in the world, would be the one I least expected: my family! It would take my mother six years to be able to come visit my new home. The American embassy in Bogotá denied her a visa, although I sent letters explaining I'd be responsible for all the expenses for her trip, that I was here with a work visa, and that I'd take care of her stay and subsequent return to Colombia. I didn't know that, by law, if they reject your visa application, you must wait a few years to reapply, and so we had to wait. Months passed, then years! It was neither for lack of effort or paperwork that Doña Betty didn't set foot in the United States until 2006. During those long years, I could barely travel to Colombia because of my work demands. Newcomers have almost no vacation time, we work at dawn or late at night and cover vacations and sick days for the veterans who've already paid their dues.

All along, I worried that if I got sick, if something happened to me, my mother couldn't visit me in the hospital. In fact, I had two surgeries and she couldn't be with me. Not even my sisters Lizbeth or Beatriz could come take care of me during those postoperative days, because they were also denied tourist visas, although, paradoxically, none of them had ever intended to come live in the United States.

For a mother as present as mine, not being able to see me almost consumed her. But it was that loneliness and isolation, being far from people I loved, that helped me understand part of the great tragedy suffered by millions of immigrants who cannot go home, and whose loved ones cannot come here. For many of them, it's infinitely worse! The price of being undocumented and risking going back to your country for your father's funeral or the birth of your son means you cannot reenter and you'll lose everything you've earned and accumulated in your years of hard work. The dream you came to fight for collapses the moment you cross the border. There are millions of people trying to legalize their status, but it can take up to twelve years if the request is through a family member. Others will simply never be able to fix their immigration status, which means they'll never be able to leave U.S. soil, because they have no family to sponsor them, nor a company that will hire them and is able to meet the thousand requirements for the much-desired work permit.

Those without protection may decide to leave and reenter but, if caught, they're immediately deported and punished with a minimum of five years before they can request any kind of forgiveness and reentry. Entire families feel imprisoned, trapped within this country that gives them so much: a roof, food, an education, security; but that also takes something away: freedom. The freedom to return to the land of your birth. When there's so much talk about the "border wall," I sometimes think it already exists in the minds of millions of immigrants. An invisible wall. A wall of legalities that doesn't allow them to cross the line that separates children from mothers, brothers from sisters, grandchildren from grandparents.

We see cases in places like the metal fence around the Tijuana crossing at San Ysidro, California, and other parts of the U.S.–Mexico border. Families come from both sides on Sundays to celebrate graduations, birthdays, even marriages; they shake hands, touch, feel each other for a few minutes through those thick bars that barely allow them to be seen though they're just a few feet away. Separated by a wall that provokes so many disputes and disagreements, that already divided us decades ago—an enormous, strong, impregnable wall—that keeps at least twelve million undocumented immigrants from crossing even to bury their own parents.

My personal experience didn't compare to any of this. But it meant months without seeing Doña Betty. Since neither she nor my sisters could come because they lacked visas, I tried to get to Colombia for Christmas or New Year's. We'd spend three or four days together, which we relished. The rest of the year we connected by phone or Skype, but that was harder than I expected. Ilia Calderón, the independent woman who'd left home at ten to study in the big city, was now experiencing that hollow feeling the family leaves when you can't have them by your side. It hurt. I can only say it hurt, but I can't imagine that pain multiplied if I couldn't see or hug them for five, ten, or twenty years.

Besides my family separation, I had other significant experiences and lessons to learn in my debut as an immigrant. If I thought I was part of a group that didn't have it easy in my native Colombia, I would now learn what it meant to be part of a huge and varied minority called Hispanics. How could we be considered a minority when we were officially more than 35 million by 2001 (about 40 million unofficially)? Those huge numbers, and the way we were referred to in bureaucratic language were the first things that caught my attention. In government papers those not from here were called aliens. *Aliens!* Sure, maybe that's an accurate translation of the word "foreigner" from Spanish, but "foreigner" in English might have been more successful and less dramatic. My great fortune, the one that rescued me from living in hiding, was that I was considered a "legal alien." The illegal alien had it infinitely worse than me and, through my work with the Latino community, I gradually discovered how intense it was to be undocumented and the many other hardships this entailed, aside from not being able to travel to your country of origin.

"Illegal": another word I found shocking. Where I came from, actions are illegal, products are illegal but . . . how can a person be illegal? Almost two decades later, I continue to contend with this word in daily usage. I'm constantly explaining its negative connotations and the damage it causes. I have to remain patient and clarify that your stay in this country may be irregular, but that you, the human being, are not illegal. If the person has no experience, we call them inexperienced; if they do not have immigration documents to live in a country that's their own, shouldn't we simply call them undocumented?

Without comparing my story to the real struggles and tragedies of immigration, my status as a foreigner was a bit more uncomfortable than I expected. For a woman accustomed to being in control, to moving quickly through the system, to handling language as a work tool, something as fundamental as not being able to communicate with the supermarket cashier plunged me into despair. It's a stage all newcomers suffer to a greater or lesser degree; those who've experienced it will understand me perfectly.

I made my first rookie mistake when I went to buy gas. I parked the car next to the pump and waited for a friendly employee to fill the tank and charge me. Then another driver came up—a customer like me—and smiled at me as I sat there, stiff as a board with a stunned look on my face. I stared as he took out his credit card, typed in his PIN, and picked up the hose from the spout. It was self-service. It was clear as day on a poster I hadn't understood: self-service! So, when in Rome . . . I did the same things I'd seen him do: I took out my card, slid it in the slot, put the hose in my car, pressed the button on the cheapest variant, and fuel started to pump. I felt empowered by something so simple!

Another of these situations was waiting for me when I got home.

"Miss Ilia, I don't think you've paid your light bill!" Don Félix, the building concierge, said while waving a piece of paper as soon as he saw me come through the lobby.

"What? I have to pay the electricity bill? Where?" I responded while reading the threatening notice.

"Look here." He directed me to a corner of the building entrance where there were rows of small mailboxes embedded in the wall.

He took out a master key, opened the one corresponding to my apartment, and pulled out dozens of letters, folded and pressed together. There were so many! I almost died from embarrassment. During the two months I'd been living there, I wondered why I never found mail on the floor when I opened my apartment door. I usually got home from work exhausted from the long hours at Telemundo. Nobody had told me there were mailboxes! In Colombia they delivered the mail under the door, and that's how I thought it would be here.

Among all these envelopes were, of course, the light bills, one after the other, warning me that they were going to leave me, as in my dear El Chocó, with just two candles for light—but, this time, for lack of payment.

"Don Félix, please tell me how I can fix this. Where do I go? What do I do?" I asked the concierge, feeling awkward and lost.

"Miss Ilia, this is past due, so now you have to go to the office in person. You'll have to wait in a very long line." He explained everything patiently, then gave me the address where I had to go.

At the electric company, the challenge—that word I liked so much in my professional sphere but not as much in my personal life—got trickier. The clerk spoke to me in a rapid-fire English. When I begged her to continue in Spanish, or to speak slowly, the woman—black and in her fifties—put on her glasses to get a better look at me.

"Honey, don't tell me you don't speak English," she said.

I immediately got what was happening: she thought I was a black American, like her! Or should I say "African-American"? In that moment, I realized black Americans saw me as a black American. I soon discovered that, though I felt so Colombian, I didn't look Colombian even to my own Colombian compatriots who'd been living here awhile.

"You're Colombian? Really?" they'd ask, not hiding their surprise at the store, the doctor's office, or in a restaurant. "I could've sworn you were American, that you didn't speak Spanish."

Some people would ask me if I was Dominican or Puerto Rican. Others told me my face was very typical of here or there. They always found a reason to catalog me as anything but Latina, much less Colombian. I simply didn't look like the prototype everyone saw in all those successful evening soap operas from my country. This hit me hard because, all my life, I'd felt more Colombian than coffee, than arepas, than bananas and my Chocoana jungle.

The question that always followed inquiries about my origins was: "But . . . there are black people in Colombia?" Before saying, "Yes, of course," I'd take a deep breath because I didn't want to sound rude. I soon realized we only had ourselves to blame for this line of inquiry, because we, Colombians as a nation, had been whitening our history for so long—until that day we even bleached that portrait of the illustrious Juan José Nieto Gil.

How could I blame the world for not knowing we existed if we didn't appear in our own novels, or the international marketing campaigns for Juan Valdés and his rich coffee, or anything at all we exported! How could I expect a New Jersey or Kentucky neighbor to know what color we were in El Chocó if he didn't know where El Chocó was to begin with? Even other Latinos during Miami's partying and glamorous nights would take a break from dancing to Grupo Niche and then act surprised to see me on the dance floor, with my dark skin and Colombian accent. Never mind that all the members of Grupo Niche look like me!

From the dance floor to the streets, the stories didn't stop. Even my mother, when she finally came to see me, fell right in. "Look at that black man driving that expensive car," she said. "You don't see that in Colombia!" In her head, there was no image of an Afro-descendant man with money, unless he was an athlete or an artist. But in Miami, Afro-descendant people ate at expensive restaurants, bought at fashionable stores, and no one seemed surprised. I attributed these differences between being black here and being black there to the fact that, on American soil, we could leverage the historical activism I spoke about earlier. In Colombia, we hadn't suffered official repression like in the United States, so we hadn't benefited from a civil rights movement as complex and revolutionary as the one this country—with its great achievements and great contrasts—had experienced in the 1960s.

In short, in this new world where no one could guess my nationality, at least there seemed to be more opportunities, although, obviously, it's never been and isn't yet the promised land of equality or equity, and there are still many struggles to fight for and win. Recently, what's stuck in my head is the image of two mounted police in Galveston, Texas, leading a young black man with a rope. An act of humiliation, a total lack of humanity, a vision that reminds us of the dire years of slavery. The office where the two agents were assigned offered apologies and promised to eliminate the practice so that such an outrageous act wouldn't be repeated. I couldn't even believe this was still legal and accepted in the twenty-first century on American soil!

Despite some of the patterns of discrimination sadly being repeated, the opportunities I always talk about are a little more present here compared to Colombia, where black people seem to be doomed to be poor and happy in our poverty.

In our countries, they've sold us an image, as cruel as it is false, of the black man content being poor, spending his days cheerfully singing and dancing, his feet in the sand, without a dime in his pocket. It's a great lie, created to justify the lack of opportunities affecting these communities. It's not that our people don't want to surpass themselves, or don't know how, it's simply that access to education and well-paid jobs is limited, almost null. With zero possibilities and corruption at all levels stealing monies allocated to the most disadvantaged communities, of course people are stuck in poverty! Once poor, they do the best they can. But we can't let ourselves think they'd rather be out dancing salsa instead of going to college or starting a business. That's an archaic, imperialist, and neocolonialist vision, worthy of those gentlemen who hid Nieto's portrait in a basement so no one would see a black man with a presidential sash across his chest.

Back on the streets of Miami, and despite my mother, who saw good things in my new country, doubts assailed me: Had I come to the right country? Would I have gotten further ahead personally and professionally in Colombia? The stress of September 11 and the subsequent whirlwind of information in which I was trapped on my arrival made me hesitate, especially because everything had changed.

The entire country was transformed by September 11 and its aftermath: new fears, new rules and laws, a new economic situation, and new xenophobic and anti-immigrant feelings. Everything that sounded Arabic awoke fear and distrust. Discrimination against the Islamic world joined and at times surpassed the classic and entrenched rejection of black people.

This new scenario made me reconsider my second last name, Chamat, which sometimes aroused suspicion at airports. I come from a country with a large Middle Eastern community. To talk about Colombia without including Syrian-Lebanese contributions is to refuse to see the full picture. My paternal great-grandfather was one of those thousands of so-called Turks who landed in Cartagena at the end of the nineteenth century, fleeing the Ottoman Empire. Syria, Lebanon, and Palestine remained under Turkish rule. Rumors about new and exciting countries on the other side of the Atlantic, where they could be free, gave them the courage to sign up for one-way trips. For the most part, they were enterprising young men, commercial vendors in Barranquilla, Cartagena, and Bogotá. Over the decades, they opened their first businesses selling fabrics, threads, and all kinds of things. In the mid-twentieth century, the Syrian-Lebanese community was able to scale the country's social hierarchies by sending their children to college and establishing successful businesses. So it wasn't strange to find Arabic last names among great doctors, lawyers, intellectuals, and current politicians. Don Carlos Chamat and his tiny shop in a corner of El Chocó, the son of one of those pioneering and adventurous Syrians, and of the Afro-Colombian woman who fell in love with him, was part of that wave.

Now, here I was, traveling the world with an Arabic last name and black skin. When I was questioned at immigration checkpoints and I risked speaking English, my strong accent didn't help and caused even more disorientation. I decided to answer in Spanish to make my origins clear, "Yes, I'm Colombian, of course I'm Colombian . . . Yes, there are black people in Colombia. . . Yes, how curious, true . . ." I'd have the same conversation over and over, like a scratched record.

For a few months after the terrible attacks, Arabs experienced great rejection in the most conservative parts of the country. I knew Middle Eastern blood also ran in my veins and my rebellious and defiant spirit clung to the pride of being who I am, something my mother always instilled in us.

"Immigrant," that's a word that since that 9/11 has changed dramatically. In these new political times, with the resurgence of populism and nationalism, it's been devalued even further. For many, it may sound derogatory, exclusive, or negative. For me, it's an essential part of my new life and my new passions. It was the word that opened the doors to a fascinating new job opportunity and gave me a wonderful new family whom I love. My new immigrant status, despite the more or less serious obstacles that come with it, has brought big dreams, big rewards, and led me to meet exceptional people. I'll talk about some of them in later chapters. Because with their incredible stories, they contributed so much to my personal growth and my incessant search for answers.

A year after I'd started working at Telemundo, I had no doubt I'd made the right decision. My heart was at home here, and I felt more useful than ever at the service of my big new family, the Hispanic community. I no longer cared about being a minority within a minority within another minority. From Afro-Colombian, I became an immigrant and then Hispanic, and I liked my new identity.

It was like the matryoshkas, those Russian contraptions with an infinite number of dolls inside. In this game there was one more doll: a woman. The opportunity to open that front would come years later, the result of an explosive tsunami unleashed on social media after the actions of several brave women from Hollywood and the rest of the planet. Other silences would shatter too, and cause a lot of commotion in our lives, mine included.

But just then, I was about to experience a big change in my professional family, a meeting with an exceptional person with whom I'd fall in love, and a revealing trip to a place already running through my veins.

11

A New Challenge with an Impact

Intelligence is the ability to adapt to change.
    Stephen Hawking

"Ilia, they're going to cancel the weekend edition," my producer told me sadly one night after I'd finished my live broadcast.

After four wonderful years, my work informing the entire Hispanic community of the United States every Saturday and Sunday through Telemundo was coming to an end. For budgetary reasons, the network had decided to sacrifice the show I'd anchored with Rogelio Mora-Tagle, another of my great colleagues and teachers. Roger was my first cohost on national television in the United States and, to date, he's a great friend. Originally from Mexico, he has an extraordinary sense of humor and taught me how to connect with my new audience, reminding me of the importance of good fellowship during those endless broadcasting hours when we covered, shoulder to shoulder, the invasion of Iraq, the fall of Saddam Hussein, and the death of John Paul II.

Now I had to say goodbye to the desk I'd shared with my dear friend Roger and wait for Telemundo to give me my next assignment. Although my contract was still valid and they'd promised to find me another position with the network, I felt lost. Due to the crisis, they'd also canceled Telemundo Internacional, which was distributed by cable to Latin America. As a result, dozens of colleagues and friends were left without work, without support.

Fear of losing my job overwhelmed me. I was racked by moments of uncertainty and few hours of sleep, thinking about what I would do if my contract was terminated. In this profession, once you're off the air, it can be difficult to return. That's why I was distressed trying to figure out what my next challenge in life would be. Should I go back to Colombia? Should I stay here? Should I look for other horizons, a new career?

Joe Peyronnin—my boss, my mentor, the person who'd given me the opportunity to work in the United States—was also let go once the changes were made.

Amid the chaos and confusion, I went up to talk to the new vice president of News. There was a feeling among those staying that we were all playing a game of musical chairs. Whenever the music stopped, there was a new lineup. As soon as the ratings went down, or the economy fluctuated, the first ones to go were the ones high up, but then, the next ones were us, the ones whose faces were on-screen.

In the end, the company respected the contract we had and I stayed. The new boss decided I should be the health correspondent on the new morning program, presented by the great journalist María Antonieta Collins.

I knew absolutely nothing about medicine, but had a very high sense of responsibility. So I woke up every day at three in the morning to research new developments, corroborate data, and propose stories. My participation was reduced to one minute of each of the three program hours per day.

The months went by slowly, and I wasn't particularly motivated. I didn't think this was what I was meant to do in journalism. It helped me to think about my mother's words, "You have to keep working with the same ethics and responsibility, whether you like it or not. In the end, it's TV and some other producer or director may be watching during that minute you're on the air."

A year after launching the program and my new position, María Antonieta's husband became ill with cancer, and she, as much a professional as a family person, would be absent for long periods to be with him during his treatment. On the days she was absent, I was able to participate more, replacing her as host, but always aware it was her program. That's why I had another chat about my future with that boss from whom I never knew what to expect.

During one of our meetings he asked me a question as a response to my questions and concerns.

"Ilia, where do you want to go with your career?" He knew he'd just thrown me a gauntlet.

"Here, look," I said, as I laid out the copy of *People en Español* already on his desk. María Celeste Arrarás smiled triumphantly from the cover. "I'd like to have my own show one day, like her. To go back to the world of news, because that's really my thing."

He laughed. "That's going to be pretty tough."

I understood right away that while he sat in that chair, my chances of going anywhere in the company would be null and void, and I refused to let him determine the end of my career.

Soon after, I got a hopeful call.

"Ilia, there may be something for you at Univision," said Raúl Mateu, my agent. "Verónica del Castillo is going back to Mexico and her slot on *Primer Impacto Fin de Semana* will be open. It's time. Your contract with Telemundo is expiring and we have to make a decision."

"Let's do it," I told Raúl, without a second thought. "I'm ready to go."

This time I didn't need to do an audition, nor was I denied an opportunity. As Doña Betty had predicted, "Someone's always watching," and they already knew me well at Univision from my six years on the air with Telemundo. I had participated in most of their most important global stories, I'd won the first Emmy with that team, and my news show was broadcast internationally in more than twenty countries. Within two days, and thanks to Raúl Mateu, they called me, and after a couple more meetings, the job was mine.

Univision had never had a black person as a national anchor or presenter before. I'd watched Tony Dandrades, who did a very solid job as an entertainment reporter and was the pride of Dominicans and

Hispanics everywhere, and appreciated and followed his achievements closely. In New York, Univision did have an Afro-descendant anchor but it was the local news. So history repeated itself: the first national black anchor in Colombia, and the first at Telemundo, became the first at Univision.

I was already fully settled in my new life in my new country. I felt at home, among millions of immigrants who, like me, had come here to pursue a dream, to overcome difficulties, and to offer their families something better as well as to contribute to the country that had welcomed us. More than one million of these immigrants were Afro-Latinos but we hardly ever saw a trace of our existence when we turned on the Spanish-language TV channels. That's why I felt such a great responsibility: to continue representing and opening doors.

In my mission to pave the way, there was still another step to climb, another great challenge to face, the most symbolic of all. A challenge I didn't even dare dream about, to be honest. It was like reaching the moon and looking over at Mars, yearning for the unattainable.

But while the planets lined up for my next big challenge, I'd become part of the legendary *Primer Impacto* team—they're family to me now, I'll always feel a part of it—and that was enough reason to be proud. As part of the most watched TV magazine in the United States, there would be very pleasant surprises, transformational trips, and . . . for the first time, an "impactful" love. A love that would be the second of the three great loves of my life. The first was my profession, which I continue to fall in love with every day. This second great love would bring me everything I still needed in my life.

12.

Love Isn't Blind

I don't fancy colors of the face,
I'm always attracted to colors of the brain.
   Michael Bassey Johnson

"No, thanks, I have plans," I'd respond to every invitation on my days off.

By then, I'd spent several years working for *Primer Impacto* and I'd even moved to prime time from Monday to Friday with Bárbara Bermudo, who'd been the face of the program for some time. Everything was going well but, although my friends and viewers didn't know it, I had steady weekend plans with my secret boyfriend: Mr. Netflix. In those days, we still had to send envelopes by mail with the DVDs, and now that I knew where the mailbox was, I wasn't letting up. I accompanied the movies with a pot of lentils and meat, a recipe I'd learned from my mom. With one big pot, I survived until Monday without leaving my apartment. Then it was time to go back to the newsroom. My plans were only ever interrupted by my great friends Juliana Moss, Cata Arango, and Gloria Serna, who invited me out to dinner or to have some wine.

My routine was so predictable that even the neighbors got worried if they didn't see me going to work out in the building's gym every Saturday and Sunday, only to drop back on my couch with my lentils, my Netflix, and my books.

Life in the newsroom requires a deep personal commitment and sometimes there's just not much room for fun. I, who'd always loved to party, had let my work's intense rhythm turn me into a happy hermit who left my cave only when the script required me to attend presentations, red carpet events, or community functions.

As for companions, I never liked the hunt. Phrases like "introduce me," "who is that?" or "I want to meet him" never left my mouth. I'd met my previous boyfriends because they were friends first, and then they turned into little or medium-sized romances that, by design, never ended in big commitments.

"Let's go to that singles restaurant," a friend would say, trying to convince me.

Just tell me there'd be dating possibilities and it would be enough for me not to go to the party. The rebel in me hadn't quite vanished.

"Ilia, come to dinner, someone wants to meet you," they'd insist, knowing what my answer was going to be.

"No, thanks, I'd rather keep my date with Mr. Netflix," I'd respond, kidding, and not go.

"At this rate, *mijita*, you're going to turn into a nun," Doña Betty would say. She didn't like seeing me so alone when she came to visit, once her tourist visa had been approved.

"Don't worry, Mamá, I'm fine." I tried to ease her concerns, without lying to her, because I was happy as I was, at thirty-seven!

Happy until I met true happiness, that is.

"Hey, there's a physiotherapist who moved here recently from New York," my personal trainer, Alan Angeles, told me one morning. "Can you think of a friend we can introduce him to?"

"Maybe, let me see," I said between abdominals and squats.

"Ilia, he's a very intelligent guy, from a good family, respectful, sincere." Alan really wanted to help his new friend.

"You know what? I think Normita's the one," I proposed, hoping he'd stop asking. "She's been divorced for a while, she's fun, a good person, and really smart."

"Perfect, let's set up a date for them soon."

A few days later, my colleague Teresa Rodríguez was on *Primer Impacto* to promote her exclusive interview with Father Alberto, which would be broadcast on the weekly program *Aquí y Ahora*. It was May 8, 2009, and I was wearing a yellow dress, a color that never lets me go unnoticed, and that seems to bring me good luck.

At the end of the interview with Teresa, Alan called. He was on his way to Mr. Yum, a sushi restaurant on Eighth Street some friends had just opened.

"I'll catch up with you there," I told him as I savored the thought of the restaurant's new creation: sushi topped with a ripe banana.

We were in the middle of dinner when Alan took a call.

"That was my friend, the physiotherapist I told you about. He's close and is going to stop by."

I didn't give it a second thought—that is, until the restaurant door opened and in came a perfectly combed and impeccable young man wearing a green shirt. You could tell he'd just showered, he looked fresh. *What a handsome guy!* I thought, gazing at him. He came right over and greeted us.

"Hi, I'm Eugene."

This was Alan's friend! Seeing my face, Alan talked to me in signs: he's the one I want to introduce to your friend. With just a glance, I let him know he was not to mention my friend, that I had my own eyes set on Eugene. Wordless communication can be pretty amazing.

At the end of dinner, I went to the restroom and immediately sent Alan a text, in case he hadn't gotten the message before. "He's fascinating," I wrote him. I waited ten, twenty seconds until he responded: "He just told me the same thing about you." Alone in the restroom, I couldn't help but laugh with joy and excitement.

I went back to the table and Alan gave him a little push.

"C'mon, Gene, ask her out."

"You don't need Alan to tell you to ask me out," I said, looking directly at Gene and reaching my hand across the table so he'd take it.

I just went for it! Oh my God! But as the saying goes, opportunity doesn't knock twice, or as we'd say in Colombia, *"Las oportunidades las pintan calvas."*

"Would you like to have dinner with me tomorrow?" Gene asked, taking my hand firmly.

"Of course," I said. Alan looked at me with astonishment. He'd never seen me do anything like that!

I remembered my mother and the balcony where she didn't like us to hang out and my grandmother's theories about violets and discretion. But there are times when you have to latch on tight to the possibilities. Just as I always knew how to take advantage of work opportunities and explore them with gratitude, now I had to arm myself with courage and take advantage of this opportunity the universe had offered in my personal life. It's not every day I was introduced to such an interesting man, and one who looked so good in green! His shirt was green, my dress was yellow. Everything suggested we were going to be a very odd couple as far as certain people were concerned. No problem! Plus, green and yellow are two of El Chocó's flag colors, along with the blue of the two oceans bordering our beautiful land, the only region in Colombia with coveted access to both the Atlantic and the Pacific.

On leaving the restaurant, Gene offered to drive my car and take me home. Alan followed to pick up Gene once he dropped me off. Beyoncé was playing on the radio, "Halo," as I asked where he was from, why he had moved from New York to Miami, and other typical questions. On the way, and in the middle of the conversation, we exchanged glances and nervous smiles, like school children.

I was becoming more and more interested! When we arrived at my place, he handed me the keys to my car, said goodbye with a kiss on the cheek, and climbed into Alan's car.

He called the next day. He hadn't forgotten his promise and said he'd pick me up at eight. I looked at the Netflix envelopes on the table and the pot of lentils on the stove.

"I'll be ready, of course. Just tell me where you're taking me so I know how to dress. I don't like surprises."

"You'll be fine with whatever you wear," he said, not put off by my directness.

He picked me up at eight o'clock sharp and we went straight to Baleen, an old restaurant that closed a while ago but which was very popular for its view of beautiful Biscayne Bay. He turned the car over to the valet and, as we walked toward the door, our fingers brushed. Gene took my hand, and I his, and that's how we walked in, as if we'd always been a couple.

For the first time, going hand in hand with a man gave me peace, it gave me an unspeakable sense of security. It was an overwhelming sensation, as if I'd always walked beside him, our hands intertwined.

What happened next didn't matter so much anymore, because our fate was already cast. I ordered a glass of an Argentine red wine and he asked for one to join me, although he only took one sip all night. Gene doesn't drink and never has. His parents don't either.

I remember we ordered oysters and neither one of us dared to touch them. They came au gratin and we were both suspicious of the cream sauce. We both like to eat with little or no dressings, which only obscure the real flavors. I finally decided to scrape off the sauce; he did the same and we ate. For our main course, we ordered a meat dish and a roast fish. From that day on, we've always chosen different things so we can share and try everything.

By dessert, we were in sync. We both leaned toward a wild fruit sorbet and laughed at our many coincidences. Born and raised in different countries and different cultures, of different races but with the same rules when it came to eating. At that table that night, we didn't want to look for differences—though we knew they existed—but rather focus on what we had in common. This is how we humans are: if we put our minds to it, we can find a thousand ways to connect, but if we insist otherwise, we'll only see what separates us.

On our next few dates, Gene and I continued to expand our list of things in common. We both loved discipline, punctuality (me a little more than him), sports, healthy food, and family values. In an organic and spontaneous way, we soon began to make plans every day of the week. One day we'd have dinner, another we'd watch a movie, still another we'd go for a walk. I think for the first time in my life, every-thing flowed, everything worked naturally. Gene was the perfect re-placement to the pot of lentils and Netflix. Slowly, I began to discover that he had the most wonderful heart in the world and his intelligence was the most serene I'd ever known.

In those first days of romance, I realized Gene didn't know much about my work and what this profession entails. He didn't speak Spanish and he wasn't aware of Hispanic media, so he was always surprised when people recognized me on the street or asked to take a photo. It didn't affect him or change his mind about having a relation-ship with me. I know some men are intimidated by having an inde-pendent woman by their side whose work is recognized. But Gene is self-confident, even though he can seem shy and reserved. Like me, he wasn't looking for anyone, so the relationship took him by surprise as much as it did me. Slowly, there was time to discover who I was, and who he was.

Two months after our first date, Gene invited me to go with him to a friend's wedding in New York. Before the party, he introduced me to his sister, Sue, in the simplest way, "This is Ilia, my girlfriend." With this more or less formal introduction, we became a couple. Then we had a brief lunch at a restaurant in Bryant Park, in Manhattan, near Sue's office at a prestigious bank. Calm, relaxed, and always smiling, Sue seemed to accept her brother's new girlfriend well. Once we got to the wedding, everything was easy with his friends and their partners. We had an amazing evening and enjoyed the party with the newly-weds and their families.

Six months after we met, we flew back to New York for the Jang family Thanksgiving. At Sue's house, I saw a picture up on the fridge Gene had sent of the two of us hugging. His little nephew, Jake, greeted me with, "*Hola*, tía Ilia," in Spanish, a beautiful little detail to make me feel welcome. That same afternoon, we drove to his cousins' house and, as we carved the turkey and set the table together, I knew this was my new family and that this was my new home.

When we got back to Miami, I had a suggestion: "Okay, since we spent Thanksgiving with your family, let's spend Christmas with mine."

A few weeks later, we landed in Medellín, where my cousins, uncles, sisters, and my mother gathered to celebrate New Year's Eve. Everyone was waiting for us with hugs and curious questions: "How do you pronounce his name? . . . What does he do for a living? . . . Where is he from?" Typical questions every family has of a potential new member. I told them his name was Eugene Jang, that he was a physiotherapist, and that he was from New York. No one mentioned his race. There wasn't a single comment about his eyes, the color of his skin— which some people might call yellow—or his straight and unruly black hair. And so, though he spoke no Spanish and most of my family spoke no English, we enjoyed a wonderful week of music, gatherings, and long conversations I translated, which occasionally delayed the laughter or ruined the joke but never the party.

My family has always been used to surprises and all sorts of diverse pairings, so they felt very comfortable around Gene. No one made rude jokes, the kind you often hear in other settings, because the Chamats are no more blind to race than we are to love. A difference in appearance is simply meaningless to us.

I don't know who came up with that popular but misleading phrase: "Love is blind." I fell in love with Eugene Jang, an Asian man, and everything that last name and that face revealed about him. I fell in love with his eyes, his skin, his features; they give me confidence and a sense of security. I fell in love with his strong and elegant figure, his smile and his impeccable teeth. I love the purity of his soul, his sense of peace. Gene doesn't have a smidgeon of malice in his whole being, and I fell in love with a handsome and intelligent man. Although our personalities are different, we have, as I mentioned, many things in common. And what we don't have in common, we turn it into lessons and complementary experiences.

I wasn't blind when I fell in love with him, just as he wasn't either when he fell in love with me. He loved what he saw, and not what he didn't see. Gene liked me because of my dark skin, my African hair, my big lips, and my black eyes. Gene fell in love with that hand he grabbed as we strolled into Baleen restaurant, a hand with toasty skin. We both fell in love with what we saw, and not with what we didn't want to see, because this love isn't blind.

Gradually, Gene began telling me his story and that of his family, and this made me fall in love even more. Song and Yung Jang, his parents, met and married in Seoul. Song was the first in the family to come to work in the United States. At the end of the 1960s, the Caterpillar company offered him a chance to move to Indianapolis. Soon after, he brought Yung over to their new home in Indiana. That's where Sue and Eugene were born. They then moved to Long Island, New York, when Gene was two, and they opened a fruit shop. His family told me that, as a child, Gene would do his homework under the desk at the store. The Jangs worked together surrounded by all those bananas, oranges, and apples and rarely rested. In time, they sold the greengrocer and bought a dry-cleaning business. They kept it until 2018 and now Mr. and Mrs. Jang spend their days playing golf. They retired at seventy-five, happy and satisfied to have raised two children and to have given them a college education. The American dream come true. The dream of every immigrant, the one I've connected with so much because that's also my dream.

Effort, dedication, and honesty. They are characteristics carried in the blood, in our genes. That's why, when I look at Song, I see Gene in each of his gestures and think, *This is how my husband will be when he grows older: quiet, hardworking, prudent, respectful.*

Song and Yung have always been proud Gene had a scholarship to Columbia University, and that Sue works for a major bank in the human resources department. By the way, my sister-in-law is married to an Egyptian. The Jangs, like my family, simply see human beings. As soon as I met them on that first trip to New York, I knew that, if we ever had children one day, I'd want them to be surrounded by families like ours.

Obviously, there are Asians who only marry among themselves and don't accept people from other countries, or from erroneously established social classes that are different than their own. Just as there are whites who discriminate when it comes to creating a family, and black people who only want to marry black people, and Hispanics who only want to get together with those who speak Spanish and are like them. But the Jangs aren't like that. This beautiful family, which is my family now, focuses more on what unites us than what separates us. The same thing Gene and I did on our first date.

Gene's also very American, and I like that too. Culturally, he's as American as he is Korean. He was born and educated here, after all. The United States is his country and New York his city. But being first generation in an immigrant family brought him many life lessons. Gene saw his parents work twenty hours a day and never complain. He saw them adapt to new customs without neglecting Korean culture at home. And he witnessed them struggle to make space in their new community, where they weren't always welcome.

Speaking of Korean customs, until a few years ago, every time we visited Song and Yung, they'd hand Gene a silver envelope. It's a tradition in which the oldest member of the family provides for the youngest, even if they've already become independent. For example, if we go out with his uncles, the oldest pays for everyone. After I married Gene, they started giving me little envelopes too! Now the envelopes are for the grandchildren, and the tradition continues.

Between traditions and culture, the Jangs and the Chamats began to meld with absolute ease. If anyone around us had any unkind thoughts, they didn't share them with us because they knew what our response would be.

On social media, however, some people felt emboldened, protected by distance and anonymity, and so we received several comments from people who have a hard time seeing other people happy: "She hooked up with the Chinaman LOL" . . . "Why didn't she look for a Latino like herself?" . . . "A black woman and a Chinese man, OMG." Obviously, I didn't respond to any of this, just like I'd never answered any comment I'd ever gotten about the color of my skin, stuff like: "Hispanics aren't black, YOU don't represent us on TV."

Setting aside all that social media noise, I fell in love with whom my heart chose, the man who began to appear with me in photos; the one I'd chosen to spend my life with. The people who hide behind the keyboard on their phones writing those and other cruelties don't know us, and they're blind to love. Although their eyes may see perfectly, their souls are mired in absolute darkness, because love is light, a light that illuminates everything and makes it more beautiful. Therefore, I insist, love cannot be blind.

"How do you feel when they call you Chinese?" I asked Gene one day after reading one of those messages on my Instagram.

"The same way you feel when they call you Mexican because you speak Spanish," he said, very pragmatically, and we both laughed.

I love Mexico—I think it's a rich, diverse, fascinating country, with an enviable culture. In fact, there have always been strong ties and a mutual fascination between Mexico and Colombia. Colombians love Mexican traditions, Mexican foods, and mariachi music is the highlight of any late-night holiday festivity. Getting called Mexican doesn't feel like an insult to me. On the contrary! It's a compliment. What offends me is the ignorance. The same ignorance that allows people to believe all Asians come from China—an ignorance that, unfortunately, is also deeply rooted among Latinos; I can't count how many times I've heard Latinos use Chinese generically—applying it to all Asians, whether they're Vietnamese, Japanese, Cambodian, Indonesian, or Filipino. They believe they all look the same but get angry when they're told Guatemalans and Peruvians look exactly like Mexicans. Then they must defend their identity! It's a double standard with which we like to measure things. The problem is nobody's going to respect us if we don't start by educating ourselves and respecting others. We find it hard to understand that we reap what we sow. You can't sow stones and hope to harvest delicious strawberries.

My family had introduced us to interracial love several generations ago and I got to reap the fruits of that love through my relationship with Gene. An intentional relationship entered into with eyes wide open.

Love, I'll say again to end this romantic chapter, is never blind, at least not true love. And this love would bring me even more love, although it wouldn't be easy. To complete our family, life was going to present Gene and me with a great challenge. It seemed the universe already knew how much I liked challenges, because this time it was going to make it very difficult for us. Very, very difficult.

But first, it would offer me another great opportunity: a journey that would change me and provide many revelations. Just as Jules Verne dreamed of that trip to the center of the Earth, I had already been dreaming of this adventure to the heart of my origins, my true Motherland. And the dream was going to come true, with me shouting, "Goooooal!" at the top of my lungs.

13.

Returning to Where I'd Never Been: Welcome Home!

I never knew of a morning in Africa
when I woke up that I was not happy.
   Ernest Hemingway

"Ilia, you're going to South Africa," my producer told me a few months before the 2010 World Cup.

"Africa?" I exclaimed, incredulous.

I'd always wanted to visit my ancestors' continent but I didn't expect it to be so soon and to be going for work. From my days in elementary school in El Chocó, Africa represented a mysterious place from which human beings were kidnapped and sold around the world. I'd studied what happened to them once they were forced to leave the continent but I knew little of their story before, when they were free, in control of their lands and their destinies. In my head, Africa was a magical place where black people were the majority and where all those fascinating stories I'd read and heard from voices like Nelson Mandela and Desmond Tutu came from.

"Yes, you're going to Johannesburg to report and anchor for *Primer Impacto* for several weeks, so get ready because you're leaving soon," my producer explained, making the matter crystal clear.

Africa! While most Colombians refer to Spain as the Motherland, for us, that mother is undoubtedly the African continent. I've been to Spain. Walking its streets, I always enjoy and admire its culture, cuisine, and amazing history. But I don't completely identify.

In elementary school in Istmina, we studied our other origins, which described us more accurately. Sitting at those desks, I realized many of our ancestors were brought from Africa, chained, against their will, and sold to the highest bidder as if they were cattle. They came to El Chocó to work the mines and were declared free by decree in 1851. In the mind of a child, these stories run very deep. Whenever I saw the *mazamorreras* with their turbans wrapped around their heads, whenever I listened to their songs and their laughter, I wondered why anyone could think we weren't people, but merchandise. How did they determine a black-skinned human was worth less than a white-skinned person? Who decided, and why?

During my time in Istmina, Africa didn't extend much beyond our classrooms and what certain professors and academics researched in their effort to not let our cultural heritage die. Outside of school, we also moved to the rhythms of salsa, pop culture, and dressed in seventies and eighties fashions. Perhaps there was always a desperate attempt to fit in with the rest of the country and the world, while we showed our black pride more privately, only among ourselves.

Once we entered the twenty-first century, and now that I live far away from Istmina, the opposite phenomenon seems to be taking place, thanks to globalization and social media. Much more connected to the world now, and with more access to information, my Chocoana people strive to rescue African musical traditions beyond the books. Dance groups proliferate, showcasing the steps of our ancestors. Girls wear braided hairstyles or turbans and strut. Shop windows from Quibdó to Acandí display gowns, skirts, and necklaces in Mandingo, Bantu, or Lucumí styles. During my absence, El Chocó had returned to the Motherland but I hadn't. At least, not yet.

"I'm going, but I feel like I'm not going, more like I'm returning," I told Gene as we said goodbye and I headed to the World Cup. We'd been together for a year, seeing each other every day, and this was the first time we'd be apart for so long.

"Call me every day, I want to know how you're doing, how you feel," he said, understanding the strange feeling I was having about my journey.

Gene was born on American soil but something similar had happened to him when he visited Korea for the first time. Walking through a place where everyone is like you, where everyone smiles like you and walks like you, it had to be an incredible experience—and I was about to have it. Although in Istmina the number of Afro-Colombians far exceeded that of whites or indigenous people, it wasn't the same. On TV, in movies, in government, in positions of power, and even in sports, there were few like us. The same happened in Miami Dade County, where I lived. Its residents are 70 percent white, and the figure is even greater in the rest of the state of Florida. The images promoted via music and tourism may make it seem like there's a lot of brown skin in the famous 305, but there's not. Now, for the first time, I was going to immerse myself in a world where 80 percent of the residents were black, almost 10 percent were mixed, and only 9 percent belonged to the white or Caucasian race. I imagined a sea of passersby with African faces in the streets of Johannesburg, and the feeling this produced was, I insist, inexplicable.

"Home" was the word that accompanied me throughout the flight, making our way across the sky over the Atlantic with my producers and camera people. The other word in my heart was "return." But how can you return to a place you've never been? My head was spinning with unknowns. I had no idea what I'd feel when we arrived.

Part of me was ready. I'd spent long weeks preparing myself for this great adventure. I read tirelessly, I read everything I could about South Africa, its precolonial history, its ethnicities, its official languages, and, of course, its most recent history, the most painful, the infamous apartheid era.

Once we landed in Johannesburg, the city that welcomed me was not exactly the same as the one the encyclopedias and books had described: the whole country was decked out and partying amid all the World Cup uproar. Yet, in spite of the crowds of tourists in town for the 2010 World Cup, I didn't feel strange. It was just as I had imagined: for the first time, I was treading on soil I felt I already knew. The markets were jammed with brightly colored clothes, there was always someone singing and playing the drums, the sidewalks were crowded and the parks were full of families enjoying themselves and playing ball. Everything was so different from El Chocó, but so familiar at the same time! It was a feeling as unique as it was strange.

Under a spell, I wanted to walk around the city by myself so I left my colleagues at the hotel. My eyes met those of other pedestrians and those quick glances confirmed what I suspected: nobody thought I was different, even though I saw very few mixed-race people like me. Colored is what they call us. Still, I fit perfectly into that crowd. Thousands of black faces, and no two alike. I'm no expert but I could sense they came from countless different tribes and that their cheekbones, their stature, and even their smiles could tell me where they were born and where they lived before coming to the city. Suddenly, I realized I was one more in that range of colors and shades, and I couldn't hide my fascination.

When I got back to the hotel, I was impressed by the sweetness with which everyone spoke English, despite the strong accents from their diverse communities of origin. The cleaning ladies, the manager, all addressed us with friendly and respectful expressions.

"Good morning, sesi," one of the employees said, greeting me as I walked down the hall from my room. I would hear that same greeting every day for the rest of my stay.

I asked why they called me "sesi." "It means sister, sister, that's how we greet each other." That made me melt. I was part of that "we." I felt seen, counted, a sister, although not necessarily a blood relative. I could finally confirm that feeling black isn't a matter of skin or last names, but of identity. Like in my much beloved El Chocó, I had cousins and friends with absolutely white skin who felt as black as me and, like many other Chocoanos, now I felt as black as they did, and they looked as black as the rest of those born here. Faced with their funny looks when they heard my accent, I told them that in Colombia we were almost five million Afro-descendants, or maybe more, and this intrigued and surprised them. Not even the Motherland knew where her children had gone, those who'd been snatched from her arms with impunity.

"Today we're going to Yeoville, a mountain where people go to pray," Ivanna, my producer for this assignment, told me.

Ivanna had shared my excitement and joy about this trip, so different from all the work travel we'd done together.

On the way to the prayer mountain we passed several suburbs full of unpaved labyrinthine streets with no power lines, unfinished brick buildings with unframed windows and simple curtains for doors. The only noise in those neighborhoods was the hundreds of children running around every corner. They played with balls made from plastic bags skillfully rolled into the shape of a skein. Some of those homemade balls were amazing engineering works!

"Wait a minute, let's stop here," I told Ivanna as we went by a small park where two teams jumped and sweated, brimming with energy as they tried to put their handmade ball between the two stones that served as the goal. "We should do a story about them. I've seen those kids all my life play in El Chocó, in the San Agustín neighborhood in my town, just behind where I lived. I have to tell their story!"

"Let's do it!" Ivanna was as excited as I was and called Miami to let the other producers know about our plan.

While she coordinated the details with the rest of the *Primer Impacto* team, I set out to carefully observe the small and very closely set houses, obviously constructed without any specific design. Each one raised its roof in whatever way was possible. The lucky ones had an added layer of cement on the facades. The others left the bricks exposed. As a whole, it was a cheerful poverty, like the one I had lived in during my childhood, and the children confirmed it with their huge smiles. These were smiles that said you don't miss what you've never had.

Obviously, the city had cleaned up every corner in preparation for the World Cup. There was no question this bucolic picture we saw was not what this square was like the rest of the year. The same thing happens when the Pope comes to Latin America: we wash, perfume, and comb the city as if it's a schoolgirl on her first day of class. But, still, those thousand-watt smiles weren't faked. The joy in those kids' faces was authentic. Poverty can be sordid but it can also have small brushstrokes of color, and this one was definitely colored. Their instinct was to put on their best face to deal with the situations they had to live.

"I have an idea," I said, interrupting Ivanna's calls. "Let's not do the story right now. Let's come back later with Pibe Valderrama. He's here working with a few Colombian stations and it would be wonderful to bring him and give them real balls."

That same afternoon we went looking for the already retired soccer legend at the press center, where foreign media was broadcasting. He said yes before we'd even finished explaining what we wanted to do. For those who don't know him, this is Carlos Alberto Valderrama Palacio, known as El Pibe, a simple man, generous and dedicated to good causes.

In a matter of hours, we'd bought all the balls we could find in the stores near the hotel and went straight to the neighborhood to see our future soccer aces. When we got out of the van and faced the flood of kids, we realized the real challenge of the day would be communication, because each kid spoke a different language! Some shouted cheers in Afrikaans, others in Zulu and in other languages that not even our guide could decipher. But everyone played together in peace.

Some of the kids understood English, so we explained who Pibe was to them. I don't know who got more excited about this, the children or Pibe himself.

"When I was a kid, I played with these kinds of homemade balls too, Ilia," said the master, our legendary number 10 who set up the most famous Colombian team goals, the man who thrilled us in more than one World Cup.

"Me too!" I said, and we burst into laughter, recalling happy childhood memories.

While we were giving away brand-new balls in this little patch of stones and dirt, we couldn't stop laughing from excitement. In the middle of all that, I remembered a game we had played in Istmina. We called it Yeimi. We would use one of our handmade balls to knock out bottle caps arranged in a huge triangle. The opposing team had to run and fix the triangle, putting the caps back, without getting hit by the ball. If you got hit, you were out. If I'd had bottle caps on me, I would've taught them how to play right then and there!

When we finished giving away the balls, Pibe improvised a game with the kids. Afterward, he talked to me about opportunities—that word continued to come up again and again in my path and in my search for answers. He described how his father gave him his first opportunity. Back then, his father played for the Unión Magdalena in his native Santa Marta. What would have happened to his talent and vocation if he hadn't had the best teacher and guide at home? Pibe explained that the most difficult thing in the world of soccer wasn't to be born with skills. The most difficult thing was making sure opportunities for these children were made equally available, because there were many aces in these hidden neighborhoods and unattended villages, which no coach ever visited.

The problem was always the same: a lack of opportunities. It seemed to be the mother of all problems. From an audition to a scholarship, to a coach seeing you play one day on the side of the road. If silence is added to this lack of opportunities, we already know the result: we become more and more and more invisible, until we disappear from the world's view.

That afternoon, in that Johannesburg neighborhood, opportunity came in the shape of leather balls manufactured in China. We broke the silence for a few minutes with the two teams shouting and later with the story that would be seen by millions of viewers through Univision. What that little opportunity triggered, we'll never know. Maybe, in ten years, we'll hear the new AC Milan star talk about how one day some strangers gave him and his neighborhood friends some real balls and, after that, he never stopped practicing, even for one day. Or how a famous coach came to see him after he saw him on TV and offered him a scholarship. Why not?

Another story I felt we needed to do during the long hours of coverage from South Africa, even if it wasn't as fun and colorful as our little soccer players, was Soweto. We couldn't ignore this important part of the country's history, we had to share it with our viewers, even if it was sad and dark. In two days it would be the anniversary of the city's uprising, a symbol of the fight against apartheid. On the same day of the commemoration, June 16, we would air our story.

Soweto's an urban settlement southwest of old Johannesburg, and the neighborhood designated by white authorities as an all-black area. South West Township, or Soweto, for short, was the perfect place to separate the races, because the area also had so-called sanitary cords, or urban barriers, such as rivers, railroads, and highways that kept black people "at bay," just as the white rulers wanted. At bay and in silence. During the day, they allowed the black population to leave to work for the Europeans in Johannesburg. But, at night, they were forced to return under strong surveillance. This consolidated the largest official ghetto of the twentieth century. It was not until June 16, 1976, that the world began to pay attention to the atrocities that were happening there. That deadly and cruel silence ended the day Soweto made international headlines: thousands of very young students, mostly from high school, protested in the streets, and those voices echoed throughout the rest of the planet. The white government had just imposed a law requiring all schools to teach only in Afrikaans, eliminating other ethnic languages. That was the last straw. Young people decided to demand their rights and say "Enough is enough." During the uprising, law enforcement hit hard against thousands of students, leaving a terrible official tally of 176 dead and one thousand injured and an unofficial balance that claimed more than seven hundred were executed. During the next two decades, riots and clashes continued in the precarious and repressed streets of Soweto, and this name became the standard for the struggle against the apartheid regime.

At the time of the so-called youth uprising, I was four years old and running free in my peaceful and forgotten Istmina, safe in our Macondo, oblivious to these types of injustices, even though we experienced and suffered others.

When my producer, my cameraperson, and I finally got to Soweto and saw those streets with so many stories to tell, I felt an indescribable torrent of emotions. During a moment of silence in a park where the dead are remembered today, I transported myself in time and saw myself among the thousands of young people shouting, demanding freedom and air to breathe. I saw myself running through those streets with a rebel hustle, committed to the cause against injustice with every fiber of my being. I understood that, if instead of a little girl, if I'd been a teenager, and instead of Istmina, I'd grown up here, I would've probably been there, in the fight.

What I saw and learned that day digging deeper, imagining, and dreaming about those historic corners, was the true value of youth. That message got even clearer when we went to the great Nelson Mandela's house. Young people are the ones who give voice to the weariness of parents and grandparents, and always have. It's young people all over the world leading the charge to end the silence, unleashing change in the face of injustice. They are strong and vigorous and have ideas about how to fix what's not working. I'd have the same clear and definite feeling again in Puerto Rico nine years later and I'll talk about that later too. That feeling repeated itself when I reported on the students at Marjory Stoneman Douglas High School in Parkland, Florida, the survivors of one of the bloodiest gun massacres in American history, when they took to the streets of Washington, DC, followed by almost half a million people protesting in favor of stricter gun control.

But, back to my journey of discovery. While we all learned a little more from our host country and continent for the 2010 World Cup, in every report Univision offered, the background music was none other than "Waka Waka." Shakira, when recording the official World Cup theme, had masterfully combined Afro-Colombian rhythms and instruments with African guitars. The Barranquilla native, who also has Arab roots like the Chamats, hadn't forgotten our other half, black Colombia, and included us and brought us with her art to the Motherland.

At the end of our assignments for *Primer Impacto*, we were exhausted from two weeks without rest. But Ivanna and I decided to spend our last day making a very special visit. This time we would go without cameras. I couldn't leave my newly found home without seeing more of how my people had lived and suffered, which was all documented at the Apartheid Museum, just three miles from the capital.

It's true that in El Chocó we were segregated for centuries and confined to oblivion, lacking opportunities, services, and resources, but we were never legally repressed as aggressively and violently as people were in South Africa. Although it's also true that in El Chocó, the punishment for our blackness was applied through abandonment, by stealing our natural resources and opportunities to prosper and leaving us on our own in the middle of the jungle, far out where they didn't have to deal much with us and where silence enveloped us. Nobody heard us protest. And we stayed there, unheard.

Abandonment is a cruel tactic. I remember seeing children on the verge of death due to malnutrition among some of the ravine families in Istmina and other nearby towns. Apathy and institutional neglect were such that some families had neither a banana to eat nor a vaccine with which to protect their babies. This was and continues to be a kind of segregation that produces fewer headlines, but is equally harmful. As time goes by, this forgetfulness on behalf of the authorities is the difference between a world with or without resources, and without resources it becomes more and more abysmal, and hunger, poverty, and crime run rampant. Thinking about my beloved El Chocó, it was time to learn about the real apartheid that had been practiced in South Africa, which never tried to pass itself off as abandonment and was up front about some of its killings.

The museum, located next to huge chimneys from an old gold mine, is impressively austere. There are only two narrow doors to pass through its concrete walls. One is labeled WHITE; the other, simply NOT WHITE. As a tourist, you can choose which door you want to walk through. Ivanna picked hers and I, logically, went through the one assigned to my race. Throughout the tour, it felt like we were in a real prison, surrounded by threatening metal rails. The photo galleries narrated, step by step, the cruel ways in which black Africans had been treated for decades. In one room, ropes hung from the ceiling. There was an array of tools used to impart the death penalty to people of color who rebelled and/or violated those inhuman laws. When I got to the videos and testimonials about the mass killings, I cried. I cried a lot, alone, in silence, in front of the images of these "legal" and institutionalized massacres that went on until 1994, when Nelson Mandela, with his movement, managed to oust the Pretoria regime in a presidential election in which the black people of South Africa voted and decided their future for the first time.

One photograph in particular caught my attention. It was a portrait of several frightened bare-chested men with their hands tied behind their backs. A uniformed white man is raising a menacing whip in front of them. Their torsos bear scars from previous punishments and open wounds from more recent blows. I remembered the fake whipping inflicted on an Afro-Colombian character in a period soap opera I watched when I was little. It was called *La pezuña del diablo* (*The Devil's Hoof*). I'll never forget the dialogue from one scene: "Who will bid the highest for this slave? Let's see, who's gonna bid the highest?" But what was depicted in that museum thousands of miles from Colombian TV stations and homes had been real. This wasn't a story recreated on film or TV. This was as real as the looks of suffering worn by all those human beings in the photo. Those looks said they'd done nothing wrong and didn't understand why they were being condemned. Mouths closed, eyes revealing true terror in total silence. Silence. The photographs and the dead do not speak; they have no voice. The enslaved never had it. They were all wrapped in a silence that became impenetrable, black, very black, even blacker than their skin.

Next to that specific photo of the whipping, there was a larger one in which another row of men equally hog-tied and totally naked waited to be shot. That's the other image I haven't managed to get out of my head even years later; I don't think I ever will. Those men, naked in the face of death, trapped in their only sin: being born with that skin. And enveloped in that jet-black silence.

Silence has a negritude; it's the negritude of those muzzled by history's beatings and abuse. Maybe that's why, standing there, staring at this huge photograph, each beat of my heart echoed the word "responsibility." All the black people in the world—and the non-black people too, and those who are mixed, which, at the end of the day is all of us— we have the responsibility of reclaiming those who suffered in silence, those who fought and died in silence. We have a responsibility to honor and remember those who broke the silence and made changes, large and small. Every battle, regardless of size, helped us move forward, however slowly. We can say it: just recently, the United States elected its first black president, which would've been impossible if an enslaved person had not first rebelled against his "master," and thousands of Americans had not offered their own skins in a bloody civil war. Martin Luther King Jr. came later, as did Rosa Parks and the four NASA human "computers" whose lives were portrayed in the popular book *Hidden Figures*: Katherine Johnson, Dorothy Vaughan, Mary Jackson, and Christine Darden. Each of these individuals we study built their success on a previous struggle. The hero manages to be a hero because another hero before him dared to raise his voice.

Ivanna and I finished our tours through the lugubrious museum at almost the same time. We were equally shocked by what we'd just seen. Outside, the hot July sun in Igoli was waiting for us. "Igoli" is Johannesburg in the Zulu language and means "place of gold," because the city was founded around the mines and deposits of the precious mineral discovered in the nearby hills. Just like my Istmina! How was it possible that in regions so rich and blessed by Mother Nature, so much poverty, so many shortages, and so much suffering could also be so prevalent? Gold is always at the center of discord, the driving force of greed, an excuse to enslave whoever's nearby.

"We couldn't even have peace and prosperity in our own land," I said when we got back to the hotel. "South Africans weren't strangers to this land! This is their home, their land! The Europeans were the interlopers in this story. Can you imagine that nine percent of the population—a recently arrived nine percent—dominated, subjugated, and segregated ninety-one percent of the native population? It's surreal, but it happened!"

Ivanna didn't respond. She just nodded to let me know she agreed. She understood what I needed right then was for someone to listen and nothing more so I could vent and ease my rage and indignation. I had to pack in less than an hour and I had to find a way to make peace with history and with the past so I could carry the better memories of this land which had welcomed us with such warmth.

That afternoon we said goodbye to the friends we'd made during our three-week stay. We said farewell to Patrick, the receptionist, who'd just become a father in our last days but never stopped tending to us between visits to the hospital to see his son and beloved wife. Every night I'd been there, Patrick would go looking for me, no matter the hour, so I could take Gene's calls.

We also said goodbye to our sesis, the cleaning women, who traded their jokes and smiles for tears and hugs.

But what hit me hardest was when we got in the van to go to the airport. That strange hollow feeling—the same sensation I'd had when I first left Istmina, when my grandfather died, and when I left Colombia—was back again. It was a terrible hollow feeling in my chest knowing I was leaving home and wouldn't be back for many years. I would've given anything as we drove those few miles to find a reason, an excuse, to stay. But, obviously, Gene, my commitments to my job, and my immigrant family in the United States were plenty of reasons to get on the plane and return to my world.

So, with the same anguish in my soul with which I used to climb into those little planes that flew over the Chocoana jungle, I left the Motherland. My home country. The place in the world where I'd most felt like I was in the womb, the place where my story and my heritage were already flowering even before there was light in my dear El Chocó.

It's been many years since that journey and I still dream about going back. But in my dreams now I have different traveling companions. I want to go back with my daughter, Anna, and with Gene. I want to show them this other home where they've never been. Back in Miami, the three of us went over a map together and I pointed out South Africa, Kenya, Zambia, The Gambia . . . who knows where fate will take us! All I know for sure is that Anna will feel the same way I did when she sets foot on our continent. We'll disembark and she'll know we're home. Gene will know too because Africa belongs to those who know how to feel it.

But that's a future trip. The end of this one took me home to Miami, where a wedding and in vitro treatments awaited me because, in order to take Anna back to Africa, our girl had to be born first!

14.

One Hundred Percent Anna

You name the sky, girl,
And the clouds war with the wind.
    Octavio Paz, "Niña"

I'd always wanted to be a mother and I always knew one day I would be. I'd dreamed about it since I was a young girl. But in those dreams, I never saw myself pregnant; I simply appeared alone with a baby in my arms, as if I'd always known about the obstacles I'd have to overcome to conceive. What I wasn't sure about was when or how it would happen. I never had a plan in my head, nor a timetable, like so many of my friends, who said: "I'll get married before I'm twenty-five, and have one, two, or three babies before I turn thirty." My only plan was to work hard and enjoy my family whenever I could escape to Colombia for a couple of days. Gene hadn't shown up in my life yet.

At thirty-three, without a partner, much less wedding plans in sight, I got the news.

"Ilia, you have endometriosis and intrauterine fibroids," my gynecologist told me after a routine checkup.

"Now I get why I've had such discomfort for years before and during my period . . . Is it dangerous? What does that mean, exactly? Is there anything I can do?" I imagined myself hospitalized and thought the worst.

"No, no, you're very young, you still have time to fix it," he said. "Let's treat this." He encouraged me and explained my options, although they didn't make my decisions any easier.

After the final tests, I underwent my first surgery to remove the biggest fibroids. But, as is usually the case, the fibroids returned, and with them intense pain, profuse periods, skin changes, and serious hormonal imbalances. The medications to relieve these symptoms only made things worse. I know this can sound banal but I felt bloated, and when you work for the public in a medium as demanding as TV, it can be torture. When I stopped taking the meds, I lost tons of weight. That was a good excuse for some to say my face had changed because I'd had cosmetic surgery. Who knows what other rumors were out there? I had a second surgery at thirty-five and a third a year later. The problem persisted; the fibroids kept coming back.

"Doctor, do you think I can still be a mother someday?" I asked without much hope after so many procedures.

"Yes, but the sooner the better," he said. "With your condition, you can't risk being a miracle mom after forty."

Fortunately, Gene showed up just in time and the plan I'd never made began to emerge all by itself. Suddenly, endless afternoons began to run together, future projects, conversations about buying a house and where to spend the holidays: With your family or mine? We became a couple seamlessly, organically. And, naturally, I confessed I wanted to be a mom someday but that it wasn't going to be easy. The news didn't seem to discourage Gene and we decided we would first try to get pregnant without medical assistance. The clock and the calendar were working against us. I had just turned thirty-nine and three other fibroids threatened to become the final obstacle to our desires.

"Talk to Gene," my doctor, Larry Spiegelman, advised. "We can do in vitro. I think it might be your last chance to be a mom."

When I got home, I went straight to my copy of *In Search of Emma*, the book in which my friend Armando Correa narrates what he went through with his partner to parent his little girl. I'd already read it, but I read the last pages again. I couldn't hold back my tears. I started sobbing. Gene held me and asked me what I wanted to do. We had to decide.

"I don't know, we can always adopt, or look for a surrogate mother.

If I can't carry it, another woman could . . ." I was extremely confused, and terrified of the possibility of not being able to conceive.

"We'll do what you want, what you and your body feel is safe." Gene couldn't have been more understanding.

The other problem we had to face—drumroll please!—was that my left fallopian tube was blocked. If we'd been trying to get pregnant naturally for a year, the probability of success would've been about half. Every time it was my left ovary's turn, it would have been a missed opportunity.

"Let's try in vitro. I'm ready, let's do it," Gene said, taking the reins and encouraging me to call the clinic.

We went ahead and did the genetic testing and everything was fine. We started treatment that same month, with injections and more injections to raise my fertility rate. For three weeks, I'd go every morning to have my ovaries monitored at the clinic. Eventually, the doctor okayed the procedure.

"The eggs are mature enough, let's extract them," he said.

I called Gene and we made an appointment for the next day. After sedation, they proceeded to the extraction. A day later, things got harder still. I was told I had eight ovules, of which only two were of optimum quality. A very low rate.

"Let's do it, doctor. Let's try with what we have," I said. Gene approved. And so I was back to "defying the challenge" once more.

It's curious how possibilities, opportunities, mark us even before birth. Those two little eggs only needed one chance. Exactly as in life.

Two days later, I returned to have two embryos implanted, those two already fertilized eggs. I will never forget the date: February 24, 2012, my mother's birthday. What better gift for Doña Betty! I spent the whole weekend in bed, aware I was carrying those two tiny possible lives inside me. I felt like the most fragile glass in the world. I barely moved, I didn't use perfume or soap, I didn't cough, and I only got up to go to the bathroom. Gene took all the electronic devices out of the room. We weren't sure if that could have an effect but we weren't taking any chances with our two little embryos. Or rather, singular, because in the end we only had one. During our second ultrasound, we found out one of the two fertilized eggs hadn't survived. The other, the survivor, was tiny. And that brave survivor struggling to cling to my being became our only hope.

Throughout this odyssey, the only people who knew about each step of this treatment were my mother and my sisters. I didn't miss work one single day, although I was on an increased dose of progester-one so my body wouldn't reject that tiny being hanging on for dear life. This was the biggest opportunity yet!

That year I was anchoring the Univision evening news, *Noticiero Univision Edición Nocturna*, with Enrique Acevedo. *Primer Impacto* and all the great experiences I'd had on the popular and beloved magazine were behind me. My new nightly challenge kept me busy and dis-tracted me from the struggle I fought every day to make Gene's and my dream come true. Every night, four and a half hours before I went on the air, I got in my car, drove home from Univision, and Gene injected me with progesterone. Then I came back, nerves on edge, thinking an important story might have broken and that I'd missed it, unable to respond to the breaking news. My sense of duty haunted me every sec-ond and when I stepped into the newsroom again, I breathed a sigh of relief. In the end, Gene trained me so I could inject these new hormone doses myself. I never thought I'd be able to inject myself with that thick substance that caused me so much pain but also brought me so much hope. This would leave a scar because, as I am right-handed, I could only apply them to my right side. But every sacrifice was worth it, and nothing and no one was going to stop us. Not even the president of the United States, literally!

It was during those critical months that María Martínez told me there was a possibility of an interview with Barack Obama, who'd just started his second term in the White House. Since the 2008 elections, interviewing the first black president of the United States had been one of my professional goals. But the stars had not lined up.

"The interview is a go, Ilia! I got you an interview with Barack Obama and, to top it off, in Colombia!" María told me.

"At the Summit of the Americas? In Cartagena?" For a second I got really excited but soon my spirits came crashing down. "Oh . . . ah . . . I can't. I'm sorry, María."

Oh, María's face! No journalist in their right mind would say no to an opportunity of this caliber, but I think she sensed something was up with me. Trying to keep my secret, I explained the real reason for my refusal to our news director, Daniel Coronell, in private. I didn't want the rest of the team to know. I also didn't want to announce this pregnancy just yet, because it was high risk and anything could happen.

Daniel supported my decision not to endanger the only chance Gene and I had in our delicate game of life and instead sent my coanchor, Enrique Acevedo, who had just joined me on the evening news.

I won't deny it: it hurt to not be able to interview President Barack Obama. I'd witnessed his victory from my anchor chair, the headlines filled with hope and optimism for many. Obama's win was a triumph for a whole people cornered and oppressed by the history of this country. The first African-American to reach the presidency of the world's greatest power was the American dream come true: anything could happen! Everything sold to us in the movies, music, and in speeches by leaders like Martin Luther King Jr. and César Chávez was true: Yes, we can! Even if your skin is black and your father is an immigrant from Africa, yes, we can! If one day I was the first anchor of color in one country, and then the first in the Hispanic market of another, I couldn't even imagine what it would feel like to sit in front of the first African-American to reach the presidency of this great country. My professional and personal lifetime dream had always been to interview Nelson Mandela, and I hadn't been able to pull it off. The great Madiba's health was deteriorating and it was impossible. Then Barack Obama emerged as a representative of everything that could be achieved but that had been denied us for centuries. Conversing with Obama would have been, for me, an opportunity to feel closer to the legacy of great historical figures, like my admired Mandela, or the tireless abolitionist Harriet Tubman.

Since I'd heard his inauguration speech in January 2009, I'd begun to mentally prepare the questions I'd ask our young new president if the opportunity ever presented itself. There was one I was especially focused on: How had he handled racial discrimination in his life, by shutting up or confronting it? We all take risks when it comes to silence: some for being too quiet and others for making too much noise and inconveniencing the system.

Just like Obama risked his entire career in one election, Gene and I risked our big dream on a single bet: that of being parents. Obviously, the dream of interviewing the president would have to wait. On this great occasion, I'd stay at home and my news partner would go to the presidential interview.

Without delay, Enrique flew to Colombia and interviewed Barack Obama. Meanwhile, I secretly clung to my divine dream of being a mother.

In the sixteenth week of my pregnancy I got the news: everything was fine. The tests indicated the baby was in good condition. "The baby?" I screamed when I heard my doctor talk like that. In fact, they could verify she was going to be a girl. What incredible joy!

"Ava or Eva." Gene had been thinking about names.

"Okay, something short, yes, I like it, something your parents and my family can pronounce easily and can't be bent into a nickname or diminutive," I said.

That's how we came up with Anna. My mother's full name is Ana Beatriz but she was never called by her first name. She was always just Betty. Now we'd have another Anna in the family. Gene and I wanted to give this to her as a gift, because of how much she'd done for us, for her daughters. Ana Beatriz Chamat made me who I am today. She gave me courage, taught me how to take on responsibilities, how to be strong, prudent, generous, loyal, and instilled in me a social conscience. For that reason, our daughter would be named Anna.

We now knew her name and that she was healthy, but everything else was a mystery. On the ultrasound, she never showed her face. She'd playfully cover her features with her hands, something she still does at bedtime, with Pepe, her doll, always snuggled up close. We knew the first time we saw her would be a total surprise.

With calendar in hand, we slated a date for the C-section. High-risk pregnancies like ours rarely end in a natural birth, and even a C-section doesn't guarantee there won't be complications. Anna switched positions after the last ultrasound and I ended up taking sedatives because it was so incredibly painful to turn her back again and get her out successfully.

The moments just before her birth were very emotional. In the midst of all my anxiety, all I wanted was to see Gene. Minutes later, they brought him into the operating room and he took my hands and looked at me. I was trembling and crying just from laying eyes on him, like when you're facing your first great love. Dr. Spiegelman looked on with satisfaction and that was my sign that everything was all right.

"She's coming," Gene said, narrating every moment as he recorded everything with his cell phone. "Soon you'll have her in your arms." And suddenly, I saw her. Her back, her little head, her black hair . . . the doctor was holding her by her feet. I didn't know what to do or say or feel! A staggering happiness, like nothing ever before, overwhelmed me from head to toe. It was total ecstasy. Gene's face reflected his own sense of fortune and fascination. He had stopped in his tracks when he saw her.

Patricia, a Colombian nurse who'd assisted the doctor, wrapped her in a blanket and put her on my chest. I felt her shivering, barely able to open her eyes. But open them she did, as if she were staring back at me. Newborns can barely see but she was also looking at my face for the first time after so many months together.

I cried, hugged her, kissed her. Gene took pictures and put his arms around us both, promising to always protect us. *I'm a mother; there's a baby in my arms and I'm a mom, like in my dreams!* I thought, dazed by so many emotions.

"So what are you going to name the baby?" Patricia asked.

"Anna Jang-Calderón," I replied, firmly.

I wasn't planning on taking my husband's name. I use Ilia Calderón professionally. But I wanted our daughter to have both, to represent the union of our two families forever. Anna would be both a Jang and a Calderón.

In fact, Anna would have the genetic tools to connect with the Chamats and those eyes and marvelous cheeks that are so much a part of the Jangs. Time, and only time, would determine how she wanted to define herself and her many ethnicities. She had so much to choose from! She'd been born rich in heritage. She was a lucky baby, with many possibilities, and with many magical opportunities we'd provide with love.

I spent the first few hours in the hospital just staring at her as if I were hypnotized. I'd been a very involved aunt with my nieces and nephew and my friends' children. I was the aunt who visited, hugged them, and played with them. But this was an entirely different sensation: this little being was mine . . . ours, and I was completely awestruck by her. Anna was from Miami, where she was born, and from Asia, from where she'd always carry her special essence, and from my beloved El Chocó, where the color of her skin—like coffee and wood— came from; her roots were deep, like those of the guaiacum trees that held up my childhood home. During all those hours just staring at her, never once checking the clock or caring about the outside world, I considered I was looking at the face of the future and it gave me a certain peace to think that, with an Afro-descendant president in the White House, the world was turning in the right direction for thousands of Annas to be able to aspire to great adventures. All those Annas who aren't that well-known yet, but who are already here, becoming increasingly more visible.

The fact that a country with a history of slavery and discrimination like the United States could democratically elect a minority as president filled me with hopes and dreams about a diverse world in which our physical features don't determine how we're treated or how far we can go. Our little Anna would reach the stars, if that's what she desired.

Years after this magical period in my life, that grotesque and surreal scene with Chris Barker would take place in the middle of nowhere in North Carolina. "I'm one hundred percent white," he'd said over and over with a strange pride and without making too much sense. You can be proud of your roots, I get that. You can be proud of your traditions, of your family, of your country, and even of your soccer team. But you don't belong just to one family, because you have two parents. You don't belong to just one city, because you've probably moved at least once in your life. So your traditions aren't so pure either. Some of us have double citizenship, and it's no big deal. You can be both Colombian and Peruvian at once, black and white, cheer for both Boca and Milán. Why not?

What good is it to cling to just one race or nationality? As if we could choose before birth the color of our skin and the country where we'll be born. As if any of that would make us cleverer, handsomer, more joyful, or healthier. Poor Chris Barker, bragging about a purity that only exists in his dreams. Purity limits human beings if they interpret it as a weapon to look down on others. Only children are pure, only good intentions and love and tolerance are pure. Everything else is more beautiful when mixed.

In the meantime, the Annas of this world, and the Annas to come, are already building a rich and diverse planet, inclusive and empathic, where everyone is welcome. It's a natural evolution, which won't be stopped by stupid prejudices. Anyone who clings to the past so they can hold on to what they believe is theirs by rights or genetics will suffer greatly because the wave of love, of equality and equity the Annas are bringing is unstoppable.

That first night in the hospital in my new role as a mother, I imagined that tiny wrinkled creature saying, "I'm one hundred percent Anna, one hundred percent human."

Of course, this original and special 100 percent wouldn't be easy to manage. A multiracial girl like the one life had just gifted us would have to face great challenges, as would we. Only those who've experienced it know what will happen with our descendants. I—who'd always thought facing discrimination with silence was a dignified response so as not to allow anyone to make a victim out of me—was soon going to learn, thanks to this newly arrived person in my life, that, because of her, and for all the new generations to come, keeping quiet no longer made sense. It was no longer valid, at least not for me.

15.

The Day I Blew Up

Either be quiet or say something that's better than being quiet.
Pedro Calderón de la Barca

"Like this or a little shinier on the lips? You don't like it?" the makeup artist asked minutes before I had to sit down to read the news that Wednesday night.

"No, sorry, I didn't make that face because of the lipstick, I love it, it was because of this, look." I showed him what I'd just read on Twitter.

"Rodner Figueroa compared Michelle Obama to one of the monkeys from *Planet of the Apes*. What's wrong with him?!" tweeted a viewer.

In seconds, one of our colleagues came into the makeup room and explained what had happened. He was worried, because he could see the repercussions and they weren't going to be pleasant for anyone.

"He was asked about a photo depicting an actor made up to look like the First Lady. Rodner said he didn't like it, that she looked like a character from the *Planet of the Apes,*" our friend told us. "The other anchors tried to soften the comment, but he repeated it. I don't understand, I don't understand anything."

What? How? What I'd just heard made no sense at all. My stomach turned. When you hear a racist comment aimed at someone like you, you immediately put yourself in their place—it's inevitable that you'll feel the offense was against you. I took it all in in that moment. Regardless of her status as a public figure, which we can all talk and opine about, Michelle Obama is a mother like me, like all of us, and she has daughters like ours who could one day have something equally degrading said about them. Sitting there in front of that huge mirror in

143

the makeup room, I stared at myself, at my features, and thought, *Do people see me as a monkey? And what about my sisters, my nephew?*

Rodner worked for the same network I did, and although we almost never coincided because I'd been on the evening news for a while, I knew his father had African blood. In fact, when we saw each other in the halls, we often talked about our rebellious and hard-to-handle nappy hair. It made no sense that he would have said that now.

I left the makeup room to read the news but I was full of doubts. Later, I saw an excerpt of what had happened on *El Gordo y la Flaca*. And I still couldn't understand: Rodner compared the actor's look to an ape, but the actor was made up to look like Michelle Obama, so his words ricocheted back on her.

Perhaps it was the pressure that's part of these kinds of programs, in which talking off the cuff about fashion, appearances, and other people's work can turn into quicksand. Or perhaps it was the pace of live television. Or maybe it was simply a quick dose of unfiltered honesty in a society in which even those of us with African roots have been brainwashed to believe, by sheer force of repetition, that certain traits are uglier than others by decision of the one race in control of trends. It's the same race that regulates fashion, culture, politics, the world economy, social rules, and, therefore, the definition of beauty. It's a beauty so stereotyped that it took us decades to fashion clothes tailored to our curves, and makeup that took our skin tones into account. How many times at the beginning of my career did I have to go on-screen with a foundation that was too light or too dark due to a lack of skin tone variety?

Driving home that night, I took stock of what had happened. The responsibility for what comes out of our mouths, especially as communicators, is enormous. Regardless of whether we work in news or variety shows, the public expects us to be professional, but, above all, to have respect and express compassion. What we say, for better or worse, instantly becomes solid and palpable, even if we're just making it up. Words have weight and meaning, magic when thousands or millions are listening to us. They repeat what we say until it comes true. This left me terrified: that same night, how many viewers turned their gaze to Michelle and saw an ape because of what they'd heard?

When I got home, Gene was already asleep. This is what life is like for a mother and wife who works until midnight: I get home when the lights are out and there's no one awake with whom to talk about my day. I climbed the stairs to Anna's room. Our girl was going to be three years old and, seeing her sleep so peacefully, I thought about what she would hear and see when she was older. That responsibility is definitely ours, as adults. We have to be consistent and model tolerance and respect and turn away from this culture, these customs and behaviors in which it's okay to make fun of everything that's different from us. We have to nip this in the bud, I told myself as I settled into bed.

As I tossed and turned, I remembered the words I myself had heard during my school days in Medellín: "Ugh, not even my horse is black!" I recalled how I chose not to react. I remembered furtive glances on the bus on the way to college, people surprised because I was carrying school books. At the time, I'd thought, *What's wrong with these people?* It was as if they'd never seen a black student. I remembered that in my house we minimized what assaulted us, we refused to be labeled as victims. I finally fell asleep, but only for a few hours.

Like always, I woke up early and went to the gym, thinking it would help me disconnect for a couple of hours. But my head was still spinning, like the bicycle wheel during my forty-five minutes of cardio. That second night, I published a brief tweet: "Unacceptable." Two days later, a bomb exploded like thunder in my chest. The detonator was a call from my sister, her voice anguished.

"Ilia, listen, Samuel came home from school and told us he doesn't want to be black, he said 'Mommy, I don't want to be brown,'" Beatriz told me, as hurt as any mother could be.

Beatriz lives in New Zealand, where she works as a public health dentist. She'd married Juan Carlos Patiño, also Colombian, and the two had decided to start a family in that faraway place because it offered them many good opportunities. My nephew, Samuel, was born there, among the white population descended from settlers and a large number of Maori, the island's original inhabitants and the real owners of that land. But now, Samu, only four years old, had discovered his tanned skin, from his Afro-Colombian mother and white Colombian father, could cause him to be rejected even though the Maori (which means: common, authentic, real) have dark skin.

"They tell him the brown and black people do bad things, that he doesn't want to be bad." My sister was inconsolable. I cried with her.

We cried out of love, because we love our nieces and nephews as much as our own children. We cried together because we knew that, even though we didn't want it, it would soon happen to Anna too, and she'd have to come to terms with that moment, to face the cruel world outside the little paradise we'd created, surrounded by good friends who don't see them as different. Homes like the one my mother and grandfather forged for us. The little Chocós or Istminas we carry with us wherever we go, regardless of country or continent.

Together, we remembered when, before becoming mothers, I'd visited New Zealand. We got on a tour bus to Cape Reinga, a beautiful national park on the North Island where the waters of the Pacific meet the Tasman Sea. On that bus, a group of white girls looked at us and began to make gestures like monkeys, clearly mocking us, not caring that we spoke English and understood them. The *Planet of the Apes* was also a popular and despicable joke in the Southern Hemisphere.

"I always thought we were going to have this conversation when our children turned fourteen or fifteen, during the typically turbulent teenage years, but never so soon," I said to Beatriz, feeling her so far away, on the other side of the world. "It didn't happen to me until I was eleven, when that girl insulted me at the nun's school."

"Age doesn't matter anymore, Ilia. Look at Luciana in Medellín." My sister reminded me what a classmate once told our niece Luciana, our sister Lizbeth's daughter: "You're ugly because you're black." With the strength of our Chamat lineage and all the wisdom of a seven-year-old girl, she'd replied: "Then your heart is the color of my skin." How could this have happened in a city as multiracial as Medellín, the same city that opened its doors and accepted me in their homes through the TV?

On that occasion there wasn't any crying. Lizbeth called to tell us how proud she was of her daughter's response. "She's a lot like you, Ilia, and she takes after your strong personality," she said. "It's undeniable. She's like you even when it comes to her hobbies and obsessions about food and smells."

"No, Luciana isn't like me," I said. "She's braver than me. I never confronted anyone who discriminated against me with such fortitude."

I never had . . . until that night. Because Beatriz's call from New Zealand was the straw that broke the camel's back. I had to let go of that silence, to stop keeping quiet about matters concerning my race and skin color. My time had come to open up. That silence with which we grew several generations of Afro-Colombians, that scarred us more than we wanted to admit, made no sense. At this point, to ignore the racism I always knew existed would be to perpetuate the behavior of some and the suffering of others. In a few months Anna would enter prekindergarten, with new classmates from all kinds of families and environments. Like it or not, someone was going to puncture her bubble, and I couldn't ignore that.

A letter poured out of me, breathlessly, without pausing for a grammar check. It came straight from my soul. After talking with my sister, I sat down, still hot, and wrote it, addressed to all of us, to the world, to whomever wanted to read it. The first person I read it to was Enrique Acevedo, my coanchor.

"You have to publish it," he said. "For you, for me, for the children of the future, because this is part of the answer you're going to give Anna when she asks what you did to help change what's not right; you have to." That was his response after I read him every sentence and every paragraph.

"I'll think about it," I said. "I've never talked about being black or about race before so directly." I hesitated, remembering thousands of images in my life which I'd tried to minimize. How I played down the looks the moneyed ladies in Bogotá gave me when I went to high-end hairdressers. "What is she doing here?" their eyes said.

Somewhat tormented, I talked to Gene. Who better to understand me? He'd grown up facing the same challenges as me, or even bigger, because he never had a magical El Chocó to protect him in his early years. Gene was born in Indianapolis, Indiana, and grew up on the streets of Long Island, where Asians weren't so common. After listening to me, my always judicious husband made me see that silence and pretending nothing had happened had ceased to be an option. Everything happening around me was nothing more and nothing less than one of those wonderful opportunities. The opportunity to blow up. My turn! And why not? Without reading it over, I uploaded the entire letter to my Twitter account, without changing a single tilde. If I published it directly, nobody could modify it.

In the letter, I expressed why I was concerned about the world we live in, but more concerned about the world Anna will inherit. I said something I'd never expressed before, with my habit of hiding unpleasant things: A few years ago, the daughter of one of the executives of one of the companies I worked at said to me: "Don't touch me, you're black." And her father, ashamed, apologized: "Sorry, children are cruel." No! What a way to excuse our sins as a society! Children are not cruel, they're like blank cassettes on which every sound around them is recorded, and which they then automatically play back. And I continued the letter with the following:

> As Dr. Maya Angelou rightly said, "People will forget what you do. People will forget what you say. But they'll never forget how you made them feel." And it happens every day, at all times, and without us noticing.
>
> How often does an entire family in a car, with their children, pass by an accident in which a woman is involved. The father says: "Of course, it had to be a woman, they don't know how to drive." And you, the woman by his

side, do you do something to correct an attitude that discriminates against your gender?

How many times in your life have you pulled your eyes back with your fingers to make fun of Asians? Or used a banana to make fun of blacks? Or judged Indians by their smell? By the way, have you asked any of them what you smell like?

How many times have Hispanics discriminated against Hispanics from other countries calling them "Indians"? (As if it was an insult, as if we all didn't descend from indigenous communities.)

But when an American somehow discriminates against a Hispanic, they all come to put their chest out, to criticize, to say they are racist and demand justice.

Also, it's grievous when someone expresses contempt for those who love someone of the same sex. Or to believe that all Muslims are terrorists, or to keep pointing to the Jews.

I worry that we live among all these comments, so common in the hallways, at gatherings of family, friends, and work. And nobody says anything. There is a double standard.

There is a fine line, which can often be crossed, between criticism and satire, and the offense to someone who did not choose to be how he is.

My daughter is not guilty of having slanted eyes, dark skin, and curly hair. She is the product of the love between two people who decided to bring her into the world against all odds. That should be enough. Why would her physical characteristics be important?

Every day I confirm why I also have to teach her how to respond with dignity to those who want to hurt her because of what they see on the outside. Double duty. Prepare her to be an exemplary person and prepare her to confront those who are not.

I ask you: As parents, have we taken the time to talk to our children about respect and learn from our differences? Have we explained that a child with two dads or two moms, or a dad or a mom, are like them, the product of love?

Have we explained that neither weight, nor color, nor abilities, nor disabilities, make someone a better or worse person? Have we told them to approach the child everyone rejects in school? Because it is better to be next to him, than beside those who mock him.

Have we explained that "little pain" you feel in your heart, when you see someone helpless, is called compassion? And that it is a good and noble sentiment?

Let's focus on the real difference, which is making a difference in the new generations. It is everyone's job.

And you, how do you prefer your child's heart? Black, white, or gray? Children are not born discriminating. Teach them not to discriminate.

It was less than an hour after I pressed the send button that various media contacted me, asking if they could publish it. Of course! If silence wasn't an option, then I couldn't back off. After *People en Español* and journalist Mandy Friedman, the first to reprint my message, other magazines and platforms followed. Most of my colleagues also shared it on their networks. It turned into an unstoppable avalanche and responses of all sorts came in.

Human beings and the inexhaustible ways we have to react to the obvious and the undeniable will never cease to amaze me. Ninety-five percent of the comments were words of support, solidarity, understanding, and respect. Thousands told me about their own experiences and ordeals similar to those I'd narrated in my letter. They were with me: words have power, what we say, what our children hear, is extremely important, and we're responsible if we want to change the tone.

Then came the other 5 percent, sadly also in the thousands. They took my letter as a direct attack on my former colleague, Rodner Figueroa. These people interpreted my words as criticism of what he'd done. They didn't realize my words went beyond what happened for thirty seconds on an entertainment program. The core of my intention was that each and every one of us on this planet perpetuates abuse and discrimination through what we say, or in my case, what we don't say. I'd been silent so long, wanting to ignore so much for so many years.

My letter was attacked and mocked and photos of my daughter made to look like a monkey were posted. They also uploaded a picture of me with Anna in my arms in which I'm looking distractedly to the side because the flash bothered me, but as a caption they wrote: "Even she doesn't want her black daughter, see how she looks at her . . ." And to complete the trinity, there was a third photo with my husband, this one captioned: "She married a Chinese man, and they're pigs."

Did this affect me? Well, no. To me, it's clear social media draws all kinds of comments when people vent their frustrations. But somewhere in the world there's a black woman, or a mom, reading those comments and feeling that those attacks on me were also an aggression against her, just like what happened to me with Michelle Obama. Social media, which in the case of Trayvon Martin helped raise awareness, and even brought wonderful people to join me by supporting my letter, is also home to poisonous languages and ignorance. But that shouldn't discourage us. "You deal with the insults depending who they come from," my mother used to tell me.

What those who attacked or insulted me didn't understand was that the purpose of my letter was to constructively use a situation to invite our audience to reconsider an issue, to establish a dialogue, to provoke self-analysis, and to rethink our role in the community. Because a civilization's progress isn't measured by technological discoveries, nor by its economy or its weapons capacity, but by advances in humanitarian issues, in civil rights, and in something that I love the sound of in English: equal opportunities. Same opportunities for everyone. That's progress, and that's the future.

And speaking of the future, ours was about to change dramatically.

When I published the letter in March 2015, decorum still prevailed. Little could we have imagined that, exactly ten months later, the world was going to turn upside down and all the rules of decorum would go down the drain with the emergence of a new leader on the world stage, through the subsequent tweet-storms and responses this person would trigger. Soon, the only thing that mattered would be scandals to feed an electoral base he knew was dormant but not extinguished. The trend had begun years before, with a revolution in TV networks that had discovered countless reality shows in which the most grotesque characters were applauded for their supposed honesty, for "saying what they thought," and for boasting of going through life with "no filter," although that attitude would only lead to bad consequences and erratic results.

I think that, without realizing it, we were witnessing an awakening of egocentrism that nobody could have predicted. The more controversy came out of the mouths of politicians, celebrities, artists, and other communicators, the more followers and more success they got. It was crazy! The more hurtful the message, the more famous they became, and it no longer seemed to matter if such fame was good or bad, as long as it was fame.

In my case, two specific people would introduce me to this new no-filter, crazy trend: a candidate I just referred to and an artist, both new, with hardly any experience in their respective fields. Both were going to show me this new way of operating that defies all the rules of good communication. The rules that had been instilled in my profession since I first sat in front of a camera were now out the window. "Connect the tongue with the brain," a boss had told us before we read the day's news. Today, it would be the opposite: disconnect the tongue from the brain, and the mouth from the heart, and get ready to say whatever spills out.

Today my letter, which I wrote to connect years of personal experiences with a tone of total respect and consideration, would have remained floating in the immense digital ocean. But Anna will read it someday, when she's older, and she'll know that at least I didn't keep quiet, that I finally broke my silence . . . and that I did it for her.

16.

What Offends Sells

Words are like coins: one may be worth many,
while many are worth nothing at all.
Francisco de Quevedo

To shut up or not to shut up, to confront and denounce or avoid. Something in me had changed both in my professional and personal life. I was now focused on the weight of words: Is it better to speak or not? Because there are times when words do as much or more damage than silence itself. This came up in an interview with a singer from the new trap, hip-hop, rap, and reggaeton scene, where incendiary lyrics please millions but are also a sales strategy.

"Why do you think I'm such a hit? *A mí me ha trabajao* (It has worked for me)," the successful artist told me.

With that simple "*A mí me ha trabajao,*" it became clear to me: what's disturbing is also compelling, what scandalizes attracts, and what offends sells. That's what we've become: scandals for sale.

I instantly realized I knew someone else who was an expert at offending to sell. Only this person didn't have the excuse of making music for young people to back his behavior. I'm referring to the president of the United States of America.

We cannot blame the person who sits in the White House for people's musical and cultural tastes, but we can draw a parallel. After all, we choose the person sitting in that chair, and we also choose what songs we consume, as well as our values and morals. And if what offends sells in music, it seems it's even more true in circles of power.

Up until now, I hadn't wanted to mention Donald J. Trump in

these pages because this is not a book about politics. It's a book about my experiences as an Afro-Latina, mother, and immigrant, and how the decision to speak or keep silent can push us to the top or cruelly stunt our growth and limit our achievements. Unfortunately, when I take stock of words and their impact, I have to resort to his name, but I'll do it briefly.

In this moment, President Trump likely couldn't have given me a greater lesson than this: Speaking without a filter, raising our voice without measuring its impact, defies silence in a way that produces toxic noise.

Like every good reality TV show performer, Donald J. Trump knows that if he shocks, he'll get followers. It's the new order imposed by social media, which, as I've said before, is as positive as it is annoying. Trump's aware that each controversial tweet feeds his electoral base and those who applaud him at his events, in the same way artists' fans do.

From the president to the rapper, to the famous YouTubers, influencers, and the protagonists of those programs of alleged reality, all these people shield themselves, paradoxically, by proclaiming they're not hypocrites, that at least they say what they feel, and they boast about being very "real." We already know the result: talking without a filter seems to be the excuse used to attack, hurt, divide, separate, and sow fear. "Oh, well, at least, I don't lie . . . I'm direct, I'm honest . . . this is who I am, it's my way of being, I'm sorry . . . I don't pretend." These are some of the explanations people give to defend the indefensible and keep spouting hurtful words.

Trump's first attack, when he was just a candidate, was aimed at our Mexican brothers, when he accused them of being criminals with those sadly legendary words: "When Mexico sends its people, they're not sending their best . . . They're bringing drugs, they're bringing crime. They're rapists. And some, I assume, are good people."

Then came the wall, his electoral workhorse, and with the wall came more offenses. He lashed out at all immigrants, at women, at

Muslims, at war veterans, and then we lost count. And, to top it off, now from the White House, he said the now famous phrase, "There are very fine people on both sides," to spread the blame between white supremacists and protesters in Charlottesville, Virginia, where a confrontation ended with the death of a young woman mowed down by one of the supremacists who rammed his car against a group that had come to peacefully protest the extremists.

Like a rapper seeking to be number one on the Billboard charts, Trump seems to write his refrains against every living thing. He pops the trigger and shoots on Twitter, and sees who falls. This is how we spent a year and a half of the election campaign and almost all his time in office, nearly four years. In just his first twelve months in the White House, Trump published 2,568 tweets. It would be useless to try to list each offense, so I'll only mention one more: the one about shithole countries.

"Why are we having all these people from shithole countries come here?" the president exclaimed in an important meeting in which protections for immigrants from some countries in Africa, Haiti, and El Salvador were being discussed. "Shithole" literally means shit hole. You can tell me if it lends itself to misunderstanding, if the media misinterpreted the president's words, or if . . . "What he meant to say is not what he said when he said what he meant to say" and it was us, the "evil journalists," as he calls us, who gave this matter such an ugly turn.

But like the urban music artist who claims to tell the truth or the reality TV star who speaks like he's sitting in a confessional, President Trump emerged unscathed from this and many more situations. Nothing affects what they say, much less what they do.

At the height of "selling by offending," another phenomenon emerged that would divide us and make us hate each other even more: "fake news."

"Fake news" is not a term coined by Donald Trump, although we owe him its current popularity and its transformation into partisan and political ammunition. Trump invented nothing, not even lying as a strategy—that has existed since human beings took their first steps on earth. But the candidate, and later president, took advantage of his moment in the spotlight better than anyone. In his first 869 days of office, the *Washington Post* noted through its Fact Checker section that Trump spewed 10,796 false or misleading statements. His master stroke to avoid dealing with his lies is to accuse others, which in this case means to disseminate false information in order to divert attention from his own fake news. This phenomenon, or smokescreen, is a technique commonly used by people with narcissistic profiles. It consists of generating drama and accusations from all sides, then pointing fingers and accusing accusers of the same thing to distract attention. Brilliant!

As an example of how effective and obvious this technique can be, I'll mention the undocumented immigrant who shot a weapon that was found and ended up causing the death of a girl in San Francisco. Donald Trump immediately used the case to justify his xenophobic policies, and even lied, claiming José Inez García Zárate, an undocumented immigrant, had intentionally shot Kate Steinle. During the trial, witnesses confirmed only one bullet was fired, randomly, and that it bounced off the concrete, hitting the young woman. José García, whose previous crimes were possession of a small amount of drugs and having returned to this country numerous times after being deported, was acquitted after it was verified the weapon used wasn't his, that he hadn't stolen it, and that he'd found it under a bench. Curious (and using very poor judgment), he was just playing around with it. The victim's own family accused Trump of misrepresenting the facts to accommodate his rhetoric and of using the family's misfortune for the benefit of his election campaign without first having the courtesy to call them or ask for their opinion.

Trump used this incident to inflate the number of murders committed by undocumented immigrants, and blew up the statistics concerning people crossing the border without papers. He failed to mention the number of immigrants who die facing the border patrol, or perish in their custody, like the many Central American minors who died while they were in immigration detention centers. These inconvenient figures were left out of his equation.

Given how well offenses sell and how fake news reports are impossible to keep track of, life and routines in every newsroom in the country took a strong hit. Serious journalists, of impeccable reputation, and with solid and admired trajectories, were the protagonists of a tweet, a joke, or an insult, with which he hoped to damage their credibility.

We got directly caught up in this drama at Univision because our audience is primarily made up of immigrants. The first one of us to run up against Trump was my colleague Jorge Ramos when he was thrown out of a press conference in Iowa because of direct orders from the then candidate. Jorge wanted to ask him about his immigration policies. Trump told him, "Sit down . . . go back to Univision." The tense scene turned into front page headlines across the country and the world, and Univision was permanently tagged as "fake news" to Trump followers.

Our boss, Daniel Coronell, made the point: "We have to keep reporting and working with rigor." And that's what we do.

Of course, the president's attacks on us don't compare with what our audience began to experience with increasing intensity and frequency on the streets, where now anyone emboldened by the GOP's campaign can scream insults at anyone speaking Spanish or anyone who looks Hispanic.

In the midst of the campaign storm, some networks decided to tone down their coverage so they wouldn't be seen as anti-Trump. Others decided to praise the future president, to coddle him and let him be right about everything, obfuscating his lies and unjustified attacks so they could win over the audience who defended him. Many newsrooms debated how many minutes of coverage should be dedicated to the president each day. But we remain firm and haven't allowed ourselves to be frightened by the trauma of fake news, nor have we let this distract from our purpose of reporting.

Almost four years after the start of this nightmare, or five, if we count the election campaign, I can say with some pride that this is a great time to be a journalist and a part of this trade that has brought me so much satisfaction. In fact, I see everything that's happened as an opportunity—blessed word! The opportunity to motivate our team more than ever, with a greater desire to lift the mantle of fear our community is experiencing, and provide our audience with the necessary tools. I feel with all my soul that the moment to tell our stories is now, more than ever, because if we don't tell them, who will, and how?

Amid these turbulent waters and this historic chance for a real information revolution, I could hardly imagine another wonderful opportunity would come my way, the biggest one yet. An opportunity I didn't expect and never dreamed of. It would be an important step in my career, but it came about in a racist, anti-immigrant, and hostile context toward women and minorities. And, as an Afro-Colombian woman, I seemed to check off all the boxes!

Against all odds, I needed to face my fate with gratitude and forget about the rants and the new beats with offensive lyrics. Because, at the end of the day, not everything that offends sells, and, to the rhythm of the most classic and elegant salsa, one can dance better, one can succeed, and we can even talk about our truths and break those oppressive silences without having to hurt anyone.

17.

The First, but Not the Only One

Be that flame of fate, that torch of truth to guide our young people
toward a better future for themselves and for this country.
  Michelle Obama

"María Elena Salinas is leaving and we're considering you but first we want to know if you're interested," my boss told me, without preamble, in the middle of lunch. He followed with a detailed explanation. "Ilia, the nightly news anchor slot requires a greater commitment, more travel, events in our community, special programs, and all this means more of your time. I want you to talk to your husband and tell me if you'd be willing to do this."

I was filled with emotion from head to toe, because I hadn't been expecting it. Suddenly, a door opened to a wonderful opportunity, to anchor the Spanish-language news most watched by Hispanics in the United States, the main source of information for our community. My heart beat hard for a few seconds, and then again my pragmatic side brought me back down to earth. The position wasn't mine yet. Daniel was just telling me I was among those being considered and they'd later make a decision.

"Boss, I have nothing to think about and nothing to discuss with Gene," I said. "My husband will say yes. I feel honored and I thank you for considering me, knowing there are candidates inside and outside Univision."

As far as Gene was concerned, I wasn't worried. He and I have talked about the nature of my work and my career from the moment we decided to start a life together. My profession always requires changes to which we have to constantly adapt. Gene's aware of this and supports me in everything, as I support him in his business and career.

Since 2011, I'd worked the evening edition of the Univision news. In 2012 Enrique joined us as coanchor and over the years we managed to build a solid team. My family was already used to me working nights. I took care of Anna in the mornings, gave her breakfast, took her to school, took care of meetings and school activities, and Gene relieved me in the afternoon, for homework and dinner, to read a story and get her to bed every night. On a personal level, it was difficult to know that when other families gathered around the table for dinner and shared their day, my colleagues at work and I couldn't have those moments, moments which I'd dreamed of so much. Every afternoon when I went to work, Anna asked me if I was going to sleep at home or not. Today it makes me laugh to remember her asking that at the door as she watched me leave, but she was absolutely right: her mother left the house and she didn't see her until the next day, when she woke up.

Now things might be different. As if I sensed it, I began to prepare for this new challenge. My restless nature was asking for a change. The rebel girl from El Chocó had woken up with her boss's proposal on the brain and it had reignited the desire to be challenged that had always driven me.

"Okay, we'll let you know," my boss said.

I've never lost sleep over "maybe" or "we'll see." I'm as pragmatic as Doña Betty and I didn't waste time analyzing anything beyond what Daniel had just told me, nor had I paid attention to the rumors circulating for months about María Elena's possible departure. For me it was unimaginable that a woman who had been at the head of the country's biggest newscast for thirty-five years, who worked with such passion for her people and her profession, who was making history, would retire at the top of her game. I'd also never considered I might be her replacement. It was as simple as that.

"They're going to pick you, they're going to pick you," said Catriel, one of the makeup artists and a close friend, enthusiastically.

"Sure, María Elena's leaving, that's a fact, but that doesn't mean they'll give me the job," I replied with my usual dose of realism. "The good thing is that, this time, there won't be any auditions to get left out of because, at least, I was already at the dance."

We laughed and continued without giving it any more importance. Whether they chose me or not, they'd already considered me as a candidate and that was a great honor. After that, Univision was free to choose whomever they wanted and it didn't have to be me. They could opt for any of the anchors who'd been with the company for years, or they could choose to bring in a journalist from outside. They could even leave Jorge as the only one. Other American networks use just one anchor for their national news.

Whatever they decided, I was at peace. This time, I didn't feel that my Afro-descendant profile was a deciding factor, for better or worse. First, Univision was my home, since 2007, and neither my race nor my native country was an issue. Second, our audience was ready to see diversity on their screens. Who knew! They could hire a Salvadoran, a Honduran, or a Peruvian, or someone from any other country. Our audience is still mainly of Mexican origin, but it's so diverse that what's important is that there be on-screen representation of what it means to be Latino in the United States.

During those months waiting for Univision to make a decision, all sorts of events happened: hurricanes, earthquakes, and floods. I remember the summer and fall of 2017 with sadness and gratitude at the same time, for everything I experienced and learned, for how much we worked from sunrise to sunset, seven days a week, and always on a plane. That's why, one afternoon, when Daniel Coronell saw me walking through the newsroom between different trips, he grabbed the opportunity to talk to me before I took off again on my next assignment. He came up and told me with a smile but without making much of a fuss because he knows I don't like drama or big celebrations.

"It's you, you're the chosen one," he said, congratulating me and tapping me on the shoulder. "Let's talk about the details when you get back from your trip."

I think my response was even briefer. I just thanked him and kept walking to the elevator, feeling that my chest was going to burst with excitement, but trying to keep my cool. I knew I had to keep it a secret until the company made the official announcement. Even though it was a well-known secret, I gave no answers to the constant questions.

The new position meant a lot to me. It represented a great leap professionally and the possibility of becoming the first person of my race in that role. It meant telling new generations that it's still worth dreaming, regardless of Trump's speeches and policies, the way they reject minorities. I could become an example of the opposite: that there are doors still open to us.

Immediately, someone suggested celebrating my promotion but I just wanted a simple written statement, as companies do when they promote or hire someone. A note in a newsletter, and everyone could keep on working.

It may seem strange that I've chosen a profession in which I have to sit in front of a camera every day, while not enjoying the attention. But when I read the day's news, or when I'm out reporting and interviewing, I feel like that's what a journalist should be: a link, an instrument, not the focus. But now, with my new position, it'd be impossible to avoid making headlines, at least for a couple of days. Like it or not, the camera's focus would point directly at me and my phone would start ringing. I'm always so embarrassed when I'm being congratulated!

Gene reacted like me, without any impulse to ring bells. It's not that we weren't happy, it's just that we both prefer not to make a fuss, always thinking about what has to get done rather than what has been accomplished. There's a reason I married him—he just fits perfectly with my way of being. Of course, I called my sisters and my mom to share the news, but they didn't make a big deal out of it either. Naturally, they were happy and told me how proud they were to see my work being recognized this way. They congratulated me, excited, with infinite joy, but then, back to work, as my mom had taught us.

"Congratulations, Ilia," María Elena Salinas said, surprising me. She was one of the few people who knew about my promotion. "The higher-ups said we can talk about you being my successor now. I was dying to say something but Daniel asked me for confidentiality until the company announced it, so only my closest circle knew."

María Elena asked me to follow her to her office to continue our conversation. There we hugged excitedly and it was in that exact moment I finally reacted and felt the impact. It was a fact, I'd been appointed the next coanchor of our signature newscast.

"Ilia, you've worked so hard, you deserve it, and I want you to know you have my support," she said. "I'm very happy it's you, that it's someone from our team who's been working and making her way up Univision. I won't lie, you'll have many difficulties, especially being a woman, but you can handle it. Your strong personality and firm character will help you overcome and focus on continuing to grow."

I just listened, attentive and excited.

"I'll leave the office clean and tidy for you," she said, joking a bit. "I promise all these messy papers will disappear and you'll see this place has very good energy."

Of course that little room had good vibes! They were the same good vibes she'd radiated in our newsroom for so many years. The audience knows this great journalist, I don't have to describe her here. What they may not know about this determined, intelligent, firm, and honest Mexican-American is that she's warm, maternal, generous, and supportive. And that was the legacy she left me when she decided to leave to work on her personal projects, travel, and devote more time to her daughters.

Interestingly, this special hug in her magical office was the beginning of a whole new relationship. For years, we both worked at different times and only saw each other briefly in the hallways or in the makeup room. I came in to start my night shift as María Elena was leaving. We barely spent time together. We got along but we weren't close. But from that day on, after she congratulated me, María Elena made sure that I was included in all the meetings, in all the plans, and set out to bravely defend me on Twitter when the trolls began to complain about the change, which they didn't like. We're still friends and keep in touch constantly. If I need to ask her something, her response is there, on text or the phone, and whenever there's time, in person. There's one piece of advice I keep especially close. She shared it on one of her last days at Univision.

"Ilia, this job is very demanding, but sometimes you have to know how to say no, especially when you're a mom," she told me with some nostalgia. "We have a great responsibility to our audience, but you also have a responsibility to your daughter and how she grows up. Her special moments should be special for you too."

She didn't need to say more. It was a message from one mother to another. I understood María Elena had gone through those moments and experienced the same pain I feel every time I have to leave home on a trip or I'm working on a long project. Millions of working moms go through this. We know we're going to miss the moment when the first tooth falls out, or when our child takes their first step, or spends the night with a fever, or sheds their first tears over a boy they like. María Elena is an exemplary mother, always involved in her daughters' lives; all her coworkers have witnessed it. Even so, great moments were still lost and I had to prepare myself to be strong and decide which chapters of Anna's life I could compromise or negotiate, and which I couldn't. But I've always thought that my work, my sacrifice, and my long hours away from home are also a tool to show Anna that I pursued a dream, that I enjoy my work, that it fulfills me, that I have my own life and goals outside the home and that I want her to someday also feel fulfilled as a human being and as a professional. If I don't see my daughter every day because I'm on an assignment, it's precisely to teach her to be free, to follow suit, but not because I like being away from her. If you only knew how much it hurts every time I have to grab my suitcase!

Fortunately, I had the support of other great women and colleagues in this new challenge. I wasn't alone. Lori Montenegro was one of the first to call me with words of encouragement—the same words she'd welcomed me with when I arrived to the United States sixteen years earlier. The well-known and prestigious Telemundo Washington correspondent was my guide and mentor from the moment I was hired by the network. Lori gave me my first tour of the White House, a master class on my new country's politics, and patiently explained how things worked here. Another one of the few Afro-Latinas in Hispanic journalism, Lori became my best friend and adviser: "Ilia, those glasses are too big for you, get something else . . . That report was too long and sounded like something was missing, you could have interviewed someone else, you want more . . ." Or: "Congratulations, Ilia, that went very well." With each call, visit, or text, Lori has been present in my life and part of all my great moments. She even taught Anna to walk! On one of her trips to Miami, she came by and when she saw my ten-and-a-half-month-old daughter trying to stand, she took her by her little arms, helped her up, and said, "Look, she's ready for her first steps." And Anna proceeded to move, one foot in front of the other, before my mother's and my stunned looks.

Lori was not the only colleague who offered support. From different bureaus, congratulations continued to pour in, making me anxious, although deep down I thanked them with all my heart. Friends called from Argentina, Peru, Spain, and, of course, from my dear Colombia. Yamid Amat sent me a beautiful message: "My dear, you never fail me, I'm proud, we miss you."

Joe Peyronnin, my first boss in the United States—the person who'd offered me my first contract in this new land—called me between classes. He now spends much of his time teaching at New York University. Joe offered me heartfelt congratulations and reminded me of the advice he gave me when I first arrived in Miami: "Your job is to serve the Hispanic community. What you owe them is to tell their stories and show their best side. Remember we're their main source of information and they believe what you tell them. Always act responsibly and report with rigor. If you have the opportunity to interview influential leaders or politicians, always question them. You must question power. That's why we live in a democracy. And finally: follow your heart, listen to your heart." Joe always emphasized my origins and reminded me that the shortcomings and difficulties of the land where I was born were very similar to those that many of our viewers experienced. That's why he asked me to never lose my essence as a girl from El Chocó, because that was my connection with my work, and what would always put me at the service of our audience.

When Univision finally made the announcement on November 8, 2017, I was in Sutherland Springs, Texas, covering a story about a massacre where twenty-six people were killed and another twenty wounded while attending Sunday service. The story was, sadly, not new: A man rushed in carrying a semiautomatic rifle, shot the parishioners, and then took his life with a single shot.

At the time the statement was released, the only two companions who had traveled with me, David Romo, producer, and Andrés Sánchez, camera operator, hugged me and congratulated me but there were no more celebrations. We didn't feel like celebrating, surrounded by a whole community mourning their dead in the same setting of the terrible massacre. The sadness that flooded us was indescribable.

When we got back from this assignment—one we'll never forget—my colleagues were waiting for me with applause in the newsroom and a giant image of me on the set's background screen. We briefly toasted with champagne but, like in all newsrooms, the parties are short because you have to keep working.

In the following weeks I traveled to different cities to meet the local news teams and community organization leaders who work for the rights of our beloved audience. It was nonstop, and then María Elena's last day was upon us. I wanted to be present and she wanted me there too. I had even imagined how she would hand me the chair and we laughed! But terrible forest fires broke out in California, so

I was sent, last minute, to cover them and I ended up presenting my report at a distance for Jorge and María Elena's last newscast together. I said goodbye to her via satellite. Sometime later, we had the opportunity to celebrate with a group of her closest companions, and we danced to the rhythm of one of her favorite songs: ABBA's "Dancing Queen." From that moment—and those who follow us both on social media can confirm it—I call her Queen and she returns the compliment.

A few days later, I sat for the first time next to Jorge Ramos on *Noticiero Nacional de Univision*, the national news. I would keep in mind Joe Peyronnin's wise words and go where my heart dictated.

That first newscast came sooner than expected. It was December 11, 2017. For this very significant date, we decided I'd be accompanied by my mother and daughter. Gene and I agreed he'd stay home, because we both wanted it to be an intimate moment for our three generations of women. Above all, we wanted to give Doña Betty the spotlight. My new position was the culmination of the work Doña Ana Beatriz Chamat had done for her daughters for many years. It was time to appreciate what she'd invested in her eldest; it was time to reward her for all the gray hairs I'd caused her—me, the craziest and most rebellious daughter.

That afternoon the three Chamat women arrived determined to write our little chapter in the history of Univision. Doña Betty was the most nervous of all, seeing her daughter achieve her dreams, which had also become the dream of all of El Chocó.

Surrounded by loved ones and good wishes, I sat next to Jorge and the news intro music began to play.

"Ready?" my new partner asked, seconds before going on air.

"Ready," I responded, with a thumbs-up, unable to hide my joy.

I won't deny that my immense happiness was combined with a lot of anxiety from the pressure and the expectations I'd been subjected to during the last few days. I was delighted to see my mother sitting in a corner of the set, holding her breath. I thought, *Oh, do I just like to make her suffer?* Poor thing, she wanted everything to be perfect; her nerves filled me with a strange joy.

In thirty minutes flat, Doña Betty's daughter finished her work on set and everyone moved to the conference room to take pictures and continue celebrating. That's when I realized my mother had taken the floor and was giving the most emotional thank-you speech I'd ever heard from this strong and usually reserved woman. "I'm always there, I've always been there, supporting her, letting her fly as far as she wanted." She finished by thanking our Univision family for the great opportunity, and for the support they had given me.

The party was short-lived because, as I've said before, in a newsroom time is money and obligations can't wait. Everyone went back to their jobs. I sat in my new office to attend to pending matters.

From that day forward, that's where I've been, with that great team of professionals, and with Jorge, whom I admire deeply and who serves as a pillar and teacher. Like a good working couple, we share tasks and roles equally, selflessly. Jorge is generous and is always poking fun at himself or playing jokes on me, just before the broadcast, to get everyone in the studio to relax and start the news with a smile. In addition, he's on top of my work, making suggestions if he sees something can be improved and suggesting stories that might interest me. Between assignments, we talk about children, trips, restaurants, and recommend books, series, and movies to each other. He's a very funny and sweet guy. Jorge also likes to do good work quietly. This legendary Mexican is a great example of journalism in the United States and Latin America, and I continue to learn from him every day.

In this regard, I've been very fortunate. Throughout my career, I've coincided with great coanchors who end up being my best teachers. In addition, in our news, and in the rest of Univision's newsroom, there's room for everyone. There are many of us, and no one feels overlooked. Everyone brings their own sensibility and tone to the news, and no doubt, their own color.

Precisely on this occasion, it was important we celebrate our colors and our diversity. That's why I didn't say no when Univision decided to make a big statement about my appointment, underlining that I was the first Afro-Latina to anchor such a stellar newscast in U.S.-Hispanic media. In the past, I would've preferred not to do this, but considering the times we live in, I thought the celebration was simply necessary.

I understand certain voices will question my company's decision to mention this fact and say: Why does the network have to highlight that she's black and celebrate it as if it were an achievement? Why does it matter that she's black? Why celebrate it as if it were a moon landing just because she's black? For the first time in my life, I wanted to answer those voices with exclamations and questions: Why celebrate me? Because when you create a new opportunity you have to shout it with a loudspeaker so more will come! Because thousands and thousands of dark-skinned Latinos will see someone like them sitting in that chair for the first time. Because if we make noise around my appointment, we can inspire boys and girls of all colors, traits, and nationalities. Stay quiet and not mention my roots? As I said the day I tweeted that letter because I couldn't take it anymore, that was no longer an option.

When I was appointed anchor on the national news in Colombia, I didn't celebrate my African blood and kept a low profile about it because, as I said in past chapters, I felt the focus shouldn't be on me but on my work. I reacted in the same way when I first arrived as an anchor for Telemundo in the United States.

But I no longer keep quiet, and I no longer pretend nothing happens, because it does. With these achievements, appointments, and goals reached, there's great power, the power felt by whom you reflect and represent. The mere fact that you see yourself represented on-screen can confirm you exist, that you're worthy. Every day, minority girls and boys are left out of auditions, not included in the list of candidates for a job, and denied access to scholarships. I'm not asking to be given anything just because I'm a black person, or a Hispanic, or any other minority. I only ask, through my own experience as the "first," to give us a chance. And not just a chance, but as many chances as are given to other people who are hardworking, fighters, and have the same abilities.

I'm infinitely grateful for the opportunity Univision offered me, and that goes beyond what I ever imagined. But at the same time, I have to be realistic: being the first is not enough. The first must be followed by a second and a third. I've been the only national news anchor of African descent in U.S.-Spanish media for eighteen years and I don't like that, because I'm not the only Afro-Latin person prepared to do this job. The issues we—this minority within a minority—bring to the table are invaluable. It's crucial there be voices in editorial meetings that talk to these issues because we've experienced them in the flesh. It's the same as when Hispanic journalists who work in English media participate in editorial meetings and fight for more truthful and respectful coverage of topics such as immigration.

We have great Afro-descendant producers, publishers, and writers in Hispanic media, and among the correspondents, we have real legends, like my dear Lori Montenegro, Isolda Peguero, and my partner Tony Dandrades. There are also excellent Afro-Latin professionals locally and in other kinds of programs. But, in total, they're so few I can count them on the fingers of my hands. In national news, presenting nationwide, the counting begins and ends with me. Therefore, part of my mission is to make sure that the day I leave—or even sooner—someone else will be there to honor and represent the diversity of our community.

Just because the doors opened for me in the almost twenty years I've been in the United States doesn't mean we've overcome our prejudices.

When Yalitza Aparicio was nominated for an Oscar as best lead actress, Salma Hayek shared a post on her Instagram noting she was the first Mexican to be included in this category and how she now wished wholeheartedly Aparicio would win it for her work in *Roma*. Some people misinterpreted her words, accusing Salma of wanting to rob Yalitza of her moment of glory. But others understood. Since 2002,

Salma had been the first and only Mexican on that privileged list of nominees. Of course, Salma was happy and celebrated that a second Mexican woman would come now, and soon a third, and that one day we'll stop counting because it won't be necessary anymore. That same opportunity has to keep coming and being passed down.

The task of every person who gets there first is to pave the way for those who come later. I feel that, by celebrating my assignment on the biggest Spanish-language news program—much more modest than an Oscar, of course—we might accelerate the arrival of the second Afro-Latin anchor at an important media outlet. My story and my words can generate new opportunities for somebody else. It's clear keeping quiet won't help those who come later.

Silence is no longer an option in my life. But beware! There are all kinds of silences. Among them, a kind of silence that must be respected. Some silences are much more painful and delicate and were about to be uncovered in an unprecedented revolution, silences broken that would transform the present and affect even our private lives.

From my new Univision News anchor chair, I would soon have to set personal celebrations aside and start analyzing what it means for me to be a woman in this position, at this juncture, in today's world. And the key question would be: Me too . . . or #MeToo?

18.

Silences That Heal and Silences That Kill

And it bends foreheads
down toward the ground.
　　Federico García Lorca

It all started with a column written by a brave colleague and sister journalist in which she mentioned respecting silence. And, without my asking, my name would remain trapped in the middle of the storm that was about to break out.

It was the beginning of 2018. The shock of the first wave of complaints of sexual harassment and abuse against the famous Hollywood producer Harvey Weinstein had awakened something unexpected and unprecedented: the #MeToo movement. Since actress Alyssa Milano launched her first tweet with the label, more women brought new cases to light.

First it was the great Hollywood celebrities who raised their voices: from Gwyneth Paltrow to Uma Thurman, to our own Salma Hayek. They all told about their experiences of sexual harassment in a resounding tone. Then heartbreaking confessions from college students followed; later, denunciations came from the worlds of finance, politics, even the Pentagon. Prestigious and legendary congressmen had to resign from their positions, professors and academics were suspended, and, as expected, this unprecedented revolution also shook the media world. One of the first cases was NBC's famous presenter Matt Lauer, after strong accusations of inappropriate behavior with several employees.

And in the Hispanic world? Nothing. We were in shock, witnessing the collapse of male power in such high places; we didn't see ourselves reflected in any way. But soon our own cases would begin to emerge, many of them in our countries of origin. That's when, on January 19, 2018, having just started my new position fronting Univision's national news, I read the words Claudia Morales published and I cried.

Claudia is a wonderful human being, great journalist, friend, and Colombian colleague, committed to good journalism. When I arrived in Bogotá, she was one of the people who offered to guide me; she treated me with love. In those years, Claudia was the correspondent who covered the Colombian presidency for *CM&,* then my new company. I attended editorial meetings with Claudia where I listened to her very attentively, wanting to learn from one of the best.

Over the years and after my move to Miami, we lost contact but I saw her again on one of my work trips to Colombia to interview President Álvaro Uribe on the first anniversary of his election. Claudia was working in the new president's press office at that time and she'd helped me get the interview. In the few hours we saw each other, she treated me with the same affection as always and I saw her with the same sense of responsibility.

Almost fifteen years later, my eyes filled with tears as I read her column in *El Espectador,* entitled "A Defense of Silence." Claudia confessed for the first time that she had been raped by a supervisor and that she chose to keep quiet, heal privately, and turn that page in her life. Claudia didn't reveal the identity of her attacker and her reasons are perfectly understandable. Fear for her safety and that of her family. To this day, that man equals danger. Claudia asked us to respect the decisions of people who have been abused who, like her, prefer not to name the abuser. She wants us to understand some people will speak up as soon as it happens, others will be silent for years or decades, or perhaps forever. But that we shouldn't judge or question the timing and terms of the complaint. In doing so, we will only get more people to keep quiet for fear of rejection, of being branded liars or provocateurs.

Simply put, the message in her column was: each person has her reasons and her fears, let's respect them.

Fear! That word alarmed me. Knowing Claudia, she must have felt real terror to keep quiet for so many years. I was even more horrified when I realized this had happened to a strong woman with character. We tend to imagine the abused person as weak, fragile, someone who has no one to turn to for help. But there's nothing further from the truth! They say abusers choose those who can't defend themselves, shy young girls, easy to intimidate, but this isn't always the case. They can attack anyone, whomever they think they can corner quickest, because of the surprise factor, economic or family needs, or any other crisis the person might be going through which makes them vulnerable.

The response some Colombians gave Claudia when she published her brave column also hurt. Although there was a lot of solidarity and understanding, the unpleasant phenomenon of "Why now?" "Why doesn't she say his name?" and the morbid intrigues that distort the purpose and message of such a valuable effort was also on full display. Instead of focusing on Claudia's wise words, which asked us to respect the silence of those who choose to keep quiet, some began pointing fingers, shuffling names, and wondering restlessly, *Who was it?* while comparing dates with her positions at work.

But after reading Claudia's piece, I was more concerned with another question: What if I'd had a run-in with an individual like that? What kind of luck would I have had? I consider myself a direct, resourceful, and independent woman, like Claudia. What makes me think I'd have reacted differently if a man snuck into my hotel room, flaunting his power, and pushed me onto the bed? I can't put myself in those delicate shoes and say, "Oh, I would've screamed, I would've kicked him, I would've run." I don't know if the terror would've paralyzed me, or if I would've frozen in surprise. I don't know what good a kick or a scream is when the aggressor, with his gaze and his body language, lets you know he has all the power, in and out of that room, and you're the one who has everything to lose. My duty is to listen to those who, like Claudia, want to tell us as much as they want to share, and ask us not to judge beyond that, because instead of judging the predator, we end up questioning the victim.

Consider the response to Salma Hayek after she published her impressive opinion column in the *New York Times*; she was eaten alive. "Why was she quiet for so many years? . . . She probably did it out of self-interest . . . Because it'll help her career . . . Because surely she had to open her legs on more than one occasion to get where she is."

Forgive me, but machismo in our societies makes us even crueler among Latinos and Latinas. Our first impulse is to question the woman and safeguard the man, the untouchable patriarch. And then we wonder why these women didn't talk before? Precisely for this reason! Because of the derision, the doubt, the stigma with which the public would regard them!

Our patriarchal society creeps into our souls and, even today, it's hard to shake. If in our families we grow up with the idea that for a man to be "man" he has to harass girls at a party, and if he corners you at the bar, it's because he likes you, then we're screwed. Really screwed. These little boys—who could one day become abusers and perpetuate this cycle of pain and injustice—grow up in our family circles. It's up to us, at home, to stop the cycle right now.

It would be precisely another woman, Paola Ochoa, who'd question Claudia and her defense of silence. She'd respond with a column of her own, titled "Breaking the Silence." Life is so full of ironies! It seemed as if reality was being written by the best Hollywood screenwriters. And I got dragged into this complicated script.

Paola wrote her challenging words in the newspaper *El Tiempo* and, although I want to think her intentions were good, she involved more than one woman, and a few men, by openly wondering about the experiences possibly had by other well-known Colombian journalists, such as Claudia Gurisatti, Ángela Patricia Janiot, María Elvira Arango, Adriana Vargas, and me, Ilia Calderón. She wondered if we'd ever been harassed and chose to keep quiet. I understand she wanted to motivate more women to talk and report, and thus stop the abusers. But, I repeat, in my opinion, this was not the way.

After reading her column, a lot of the public retained only the lurid aspects. Readers were left wanting to know who Claudia's attacker was, and they focused on the intrigue about other journalists: whether Ángela Patricia, another Claudia, María Elvira, and I had ever experienced anything like what had happened to Claudia. Perhaps it had happened to us and we were just keeping our mouths shut. And if it happened to me, Ilia Calderón, then the tyrant had to have been one of my supervisors. Since I've only worked for a few bosses throughout my career, who was it? Tom, Dick, or Harry? It was terrible. Paola had wanted to open a space for frankness but she'd skipped over the key person in this story, Claudia, and brought in others who had nothing to do with the scandal.

And, with my new attitude of no longer remaining silent (although I respect those who choose to do so), I turned to Twitter. By then, my phone was blowing up and I kept getting emails from everywhere asking if anyone had ever abused me, and how, when, and where. I went on social media and wrote: "I support victims of abuse and/or harassment. I condemn those responsible. But I can't allow even a smidgeon of doubt (in my case) about my supervisors, from whom I've received support and respect."

In my twenty-five-year career, I've never been abused nor forced to maintain a relationship I didn't want in exchange for moving up or for anything else. No one has harassed or attacked me sexually. No one has ever locked me in an office to say inappropriate things to me and no one has made me feel uncomfortable. Never? Well, I suddenly remembered the only time I'd ever felt vulnerable and I'm going to talk about it here. It didn't go beyond a horrible moment, but it could have been a sexual assault.

A very important man from Colombia's political world asked a friend to dinner at his house. My friend invited me, assuring me "a group of media colleagues will be present." Since I was already working in news and, since the man in question lived very close to my apartment, I decided to go. Surely I'd see familiar faces and colleagues at that dinner. When I arrived, his assistant received me very kindly. But after I'd arrived, my friend called and told me she couldn't make it. I didn't like that, and warning signs flashed on in my head.

Once in the living room, I noticed I was the first guest to arrive and that the man was the only one there. "Maybe they're all running late," he said, seeing the surprised look on my face, perhaps trying to make sure I wasn't worried. Attempting to behave charmingly, politely, he offered me a glass of wine. I said no. He insisted. "Let's have a little wine." I said no again. His assistant poured it anyway and I kindly took it and put it on a table. At that moment, as if everything was calculated, his assistant left the room, closed the door behind him, and the man slid skillfully from his side of the sofa to mine and glued himself to me. Without a trace of the gallantry with which he'd welcomed me, he passed his arm over my shoulders, and squeezed my left shoulder tightly. "You know I like you very much, don't you?" he asked. I was scared to death. "Well, but I don't like you," I responded and immediately jumped up. "No, sit down, the others will be here soon," he insisted, regaining his composure and realizing things weren't turning out as he'd planned. "You know what? Thank you, but I'm leaving," I said, already at the door as I grabbed my coat and purse and left, trembling. I took the elevator down, past the doorman who opened the door, skipped a few steps, and got into my car, which I'd parked right across the street. I locked the doors, took a deep breath, and drove those four blocks between his apartment and mine as fast as I could.

I never found out if the other guests showed up or if it was a vile trap. I couldn't imagine what would've happened if, out of fear, or shame, or pressure if he'd been my boss, I'd have remained on that dangerous sofa for five more minutes. Fear floods my chest sometimes and that fear is what confuses you, clouds your mind, and makes you lose your clarity. The man didn't work in my industry but he was powerful enough in other fields to ruin my career if he'd wanted to. By the way,

I saw him again at a public event a few months later and then at a wedding. On both occasions he greeted me very casually and even seemed happy to see me. Because of this, I realized the annoying scene meant nothing to him and that he'd immediately set his eyes on other targets.

Could I have been exposed to something horrible that night in that apartment? I admit it. I fell into the lion's den and got away unharmed by sheer luck. That's why I have no right to judge anyone who's had worse luck than me.

Claudia is an intelligent woman, raised impeccably, who doesn't give in, who has firm convictions and a clear mind, and still she couldn't help what happened to her. That door closed behind her boss and nobody saw anything, nobody heard anything. Just silence.

Silence that we must respect. But then there's that other kind: the silence that kills. It literally kills. And my job was going to give me front row seats. On one of my trips, I was going to shake hands that had possibly strangled a life while that other harmful silence protected him.

With my sister Lizbeth sitting in the hallway of my grandfather Carlos's stationery shop, 1976 (*Betty Chamat*)

Sitting on the steps of the Jesús Pobre nursing home with all of my childhood friends. We spent hours playing on those steps. Istmina, El Chocó, 1978. (*Betty Chamat*)

The day I turned fifteen, Medellín, 1987. It was a party I did not want and from which I escaped. I went to another simple party with friends. I've never liked to be celebrated. (*Betty Chamat*)

My sister Lizbeth's quinceañera; she's in pink, flanked by my grandfather Carlos and my mom. I'm on the left in yellow, and my youngest sister, Beatriz, is next to me. Istmina, El Chocó, 1989. (*Betty Chamat*)

On the cover of *Aló* magazine.
CLOCKWISE FROM TOP LEFT: Me, Inés María "Ine" Zabaraín, María Cristina "Tata" Uribe, and María Helena Doering. Bogotá, circa 1998–1999. (*Aló* magazine)

Viernes magazine cover with Pilar Vélez. Thanks to her speaking up and saying I was missing from the casting, to which I had not been invited, I got to work at *CM&*, circa 1998–1999. (*Viernes* magazine)

With Carlos Alberto "El Pibe" Valderrama handing out
balls to children in a Johannesburg neighborhood
during the World Cup, 2010 (*Yvanna Jijena*)

Visiting a hill in Johannesburg where religious groups
go to pray, 2010 (*Yvanna Jijena*)

Had the opportunity to visit the Apartheid Museum with my producer
Yvanna Jijena during our World Cup coverage, 2010 (*Yvanna Jijena*)

One of the photos that had the greatest impact on me at the
Apartheid Museum, portraying the punishment and humiliation
of the black people of South Africa, 2010 (*Yvanna Jijena*)

The day I made my mom's dream of visiting New York City come true, 2010 (*Eugene Jang*)

The day I became a U.S. citizen, Miami, 2011

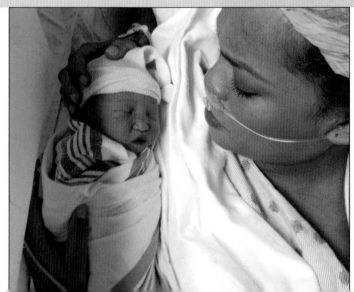

The happiest day of my life: Anna was born on October 26, 2012 (*Eugene Jang*)

With my husband, Eugene, in San Miguel de Allende, Mexico, at my colleague Enrique Acevedo's wedding to Florentina Romo, November 2014

My family. TOP ROW, FROM LEFT TO RIGHT: Juan Carlos Patiño, husband of my sister Beatriz; Beatriz; Luis Guillermo "Memo" Quintana, husband of my sister Lizbeth; Lizbeth; my mom, Betty Chamat; me; and my husband, Eugene Jang. BOTTOM ROW, FROM LEFT TO RIGHT: Luciana, Liz and Memo's daughter; Samuel, Beatriz and Juan's son; Valeria, Liz and Memo's daughter; and my Anna, 2014. (*Courtesy of Betty Chamat*)

I try to bring Anna to work once in a while so she can see where I go and what I do when I leave home. Here with my colleague Enrique Acevedo, 2016.

Covering the Democratic National Convention with Jorge Ramos and María Elena Salinas, Philadelphia, 2016 (*Evelyn Baker*)

The day I met Génesis, a young eighteen-year-old woman who joined the migrant caravan with her month-and-a-half-old baby, César, Puebla, Mexico, 2018 (*Paola Byron*)

My first day anchoring *Noticiero Univision* next to Jorge Ramos, December 11, 2017 (David Maris, *Univision Noticias*)

Covering the earthquake that shook Mexico City with Enrique Acevedo, September 2017

Finding strength and hope in the children of the migrant caravan deeply affected me. Despite all those days spent walking and sleeping on the streets, their spirit and dream of a better future were bigger than their afflictions, 2018. *(Evelyn Baker)*

Gene, Anna, and I in front of the Eiffel Tower in Paris, October 2019

19

The High Price of Silence

femicide: *from "femina," woman, and "cide," act of killing*
The killing of a woman at the hands of a man because of
machismo or misogyny.
(Three decades after its appearance in English, the Real Academia
Española decides to officially accept the term at the end of 2014.)

"Ilia, we have to do a story about this murder. El Salvador has one of the highest femicide rates in the world," Evelyn Baker, my new producer, told me while she showed me a portrait of a young woman on the front page of several newspapers.

It was this that had brought us to El Salvador: the murder of a young journalist, Karla Turcios.

Her body had been found a few days before on a road outside San Salvador, strangled, her head wrapped in plastic bags. My heart froze for a moment thinking about how vulnerable we can be.

"I got an interview for this afternoon with her father, her brother, and her partner," Evelyn said after a couple of calls. "We'll interview them in your hotel room, but first we're going to the newsroom where she worked."

On our way, I read up some more on the development of this investigation, a case that had deeply affected the small Central American country.

Karla was thirty-three years old and worked as a reporter for *La Prensa Gráfica*. She had a six-year-old boy with her partner, Mario Huezo. The three lived with Karla's father. Mario wasn't working.

Although he said he'd planned to open a cybercafe soon, Karla was the one responsible for putting bread on the table.

On Friday night, April 13, 2018, Karla went to work to update the paper's website. As she left later that night, she playfully threw a kiss at the security cameras, happy to be going home. She got in the car with Mario, who had come for her. The next day, Mario called the police to report her disappearance. According to his version of events, he took their son to the park at noon on Saturday and then shopping. He said that when they returned, Karla was no longer at home. That same day, a passerby discovered a woman's body on the side of a road. Twenty-four hours later, the police called Mario to come identify it. At first, Mario avoided going, but in the end, he agreed and, in fact, confirmed it was his partner.

When we arrived at *La Prensa Gráfica*'s newsroom, we found Karla's desk intact, with her flowers, family photos, papers, and computer. Her colleagues were anxious, wanting to share how wonderful Karla was: an excellent journalist, serious and committed to her work while also very warm, affectionate, and something of a kidder. Everyone agreed Karla had a beautiful and contagious smile that made her stand out in a crowd. At the end of the visit, we made a call to the authorities to confirm an interview with the attorney general who would tell us more about the case. But our contact warned us, "In the next few hours, there's going to be a new development in the story."

"They're going to arrest the partner," I said to Evelyn as we got in the car and headed back to our hotel. "Let's move the interview up to today."

"Yes," she replied. She'd had the same hunch. "Look at what they're saying on social media: nobody forced the door; Karla didn't have a lover. Plus, they say Mario didn't work, that he spent all his time in cell phone chats."

In ancient Kabbalah, this phenomenon is called the bread of shame. It happens when a person gives you everything, saves you, and treats you better than you deserve. Gradually, you're consumed by the fact that you can't live up to it. You're tortured by the idea that the other person has more decision and acting power because they're the provider. Instead of thanking them for everything they do for you, you end up resenting and hating them.

With a single call, my producer convinced Karla's father and Mario to come as soon as possible and not wait until the following day. Suddenly, and somewhat mysteriously, Karla's brother refused to meet us. But her father and partner agreed to see us in half an hour, and even said they'd come together.

When we got back to the hotel, I sensed we were being watched. There were strange goings-on around us.

"Something's happening here," I told Evelyn, sharing my suspicions. "I'm seeing both plain-clothed and uniformed police."

"Ilia, don't be silly, no need to be afraid," she said, knowing I can be very distrustful. She paid no attention to me and we went up to the room to prepare the cameras.

A few minutes later, our guests arrived. Mario was the first to sit with me. He looked emaciated, his eyes red, and he was fidgety. He began to cry when he showed me pictures of Karla, smiling, happy, full of life. He insisted, without my having asked, that he never mistreated her, that he never hurt her, that he'd never laid a finger on her. No matter what I asked him, Mario defended himself: "She never filed a complaint . . . never complained to her family that I mistreated her . . . nobody saw her bruised . . . But, of course, I'm nobody, people think it's me . . . I know they're following me." He wouldn't stop crying, but I felt it was more a cry of despair than of mourning. He kept saying people thought it was him and wondered about him.

When he calmed down a bit, he began to direct his attention elsewhere. He told us Karla complained about alleged bullying from her colleagues because of her weight. Every so often during our conversation, he'd say, "I'd never hurt her." His eyes sought compassion and solidarity. "I wanted to save up to take her to Paris . . . It was her dream," he said between sighs.

At the end of the interview, I reached out to shake his hand, the hand that had so often touched Karla in the name of love. Although they say there's a thin line between love and hate . . .

After Mario, I interviewed Don Demetrio Antonio Turcios, Karla's father, who was utterly dismayed. His tears were authentic. It broke my heart. On the verge of retirement, the elderly lawyer felt very guilty because his daughter had disappeared while he was out shopping and, if he'd stayed home, he repeated endlessly, maybe it would never have happened.

"Mario's a good man, people are being very unfair to him. I lived with them and I never saw anything strange, he's a good dad, a good partner," said Don Demetrio, a sweet and sensitive man determined to see the good around him.

Throughout the interview, I was overcome by a lump in my throat and just wanted to burst into tears. His last words on camera were asking for justice, for help in finding the murderer. He even wanted to bring in the FBI, which was very unlikely, but Don Demetrio wasn't about to give up.

We said goodbye with a hug that reminded me of my own grandfather, Don Carlos Chamat. Both men were very dignified, courteous, and warm and had taken care of their daughters and grandchildren all their lives. What an injustice to see him so shattered!

In the lobby, Evelyn accompanied our two guests to the hotel door, turned around, and, at the precise moment as they crossed the street to their car, Mario Huezo was arrested by the National Civil Police. Neither Evelyn nor I saw any of it.

Early the next morning, we got a call from *La Prensa Gráfica*.

"Do you know what happened? They arrested him! And you have Mario's last interview as a free man, his last words."

I was outraged that the person who claimed to love her most, to want to take her to Paris and buy her flowers and a ring, was the man suspected of taking her life.

The next morning, we edited the interview and it aired on our newscasts across the United States. Great exclusive! But I was still uneasy. No matter how many years I do this job, there are things I'll never get used to, and don't want to. I refuse. No matter how many misfortunes and injustices I cover, I can never lose my sensitivity and compassion. There are stories that affect me, that touch my heart, and that's perfectly fine. We're journalists but, above all, we're human beings.

The next day, our phones rang nonstop. As so happens in some cases, the story behind the story was bigger than previously thought. Karla's friends knew she was tired of the relationship and that Mario didn't work. They also told us Karla threatened to leave him and Mario refused to end the relationship.

Over the next few hours we learned details the National Civil Police had kept secret so as not to jeopardize the case. An anonymous note had been found in the garage which said: "Say goodbye to your daughter, dirty dog," implying it was a settling of accounts by someone displeased with Don Demetrio's work. There was also a second, almost identical note that fell from Mario's pocket at the coroner's office the day he went to identify the body. From that moment on, the prosecutors had put him under surveillance. And then there was this piece of evidence: both Mario's and Karla's cell phones triangulated signals on the same road where the body was discovered. That meant Mario was there and left, possibly taking Karla's cell phone, which he would then discard elsewhere. Someone found it later and turned it on. This person changed the phone card but the old chip was intact, which meant it could be located by the authorities. As a result, they were able to trace his movements in the last hours in detail.

The most chilling part of the case was that, according to the prosecutor's office, cameras at several gas stations along the road that leads to where they found Karla's body had captured images of their son in the car with Mario. According to the young mother's friends, the boy kept repeating during the wake, "Everything will be fine, everything will be fine . . . something terrible happened but everything will be fine." The boy is on the autism spectrum and can only repeat what he hears. He couldn't explain what he saw but his reaction clearly indicated stress.

Finally, police found blood in the house, the last piece of evidence corroborating what they had feared: Karla was beaten and strangled in her room. The perpetrator had wrapped two plastic bags around her head, tying the ends with one of her panties, the killer's final signature showing pride in his femicide—a spine-chilling detail that betrayed sexual tension, possession, and absolute control.

Back in Miami, I couldn't shake Karla's smiling face from my mind. In the United States, the #MeToo movement continued to make headlines and, in my head, everything came together: harassment, silence, abuse, aggression, and, as the ultimate expression of submission and discrimination, femicide. An evil that's everywhere. If you're a woman, there's no El Chocó, no Istmina, no river house where you can seek refuge from the blows. There's no country in the world that's spared gender violence and in which women don't end up dead at the hands of their partners or ex-partners.

In honor of Karla and all the women who have lost their lives in the same circumstances, I kept reading and inquiring. I learned that in El Salvador, laws that punish crimes against women are much tougher and more advanced than what we have in the United States. Ironically, in one of the countries where more women die at the hands of men in proportion to the population, there's a law that recognizes and penalizes suicide or induction suicide as femicides, a modality in which the abuser psychologically and physically corners his prey until she takes her own life, putting an end to the abuse and the ordeal to which she's been subjected.

In Colombia, for example, the case of Rosa Elvira Cely, who was raped and murdered, prompted the approval of a new law in her name: The Rosa Elvira Cely Law. Since 2015, this new law targets femicide and toughens penalties. The Yuliana Samboní case, another aberrant murder, shook the foundations of Colombian society with a great intensity and mobilized it. But none of these well-known and outrageous stories, nor these tougher laws, has put a halt to this evil. All over the world, women continue to be killed because they are women.

Laws, statistics, and that picture of Karla smiling. I wanted to go back and follow up on that story, because there's no need to stop talking about this. It's necessary to open spaces so the subject of femicide can go from conversations in the hallways to legislators' desks, so we can push for tougher laws. We have to tell each of these stories, make them visible. Both the stories of those who survive and of the heroines who carried that grief inside, who fought against this prejudice in our sexist societies, a prejudice which didn't let them report their abuse on time, which allowed them to lose their lives at the hands of those who said they loved them. We have to claim our rights. When we tell these stories, thousands of women are reflected, they know they're not alone and that someone is listening. And that might give them the impulse to report their suffering.

"Evelyn, we have to go back and follow up on Karla's case," I said to my tireless companion. "It's our duty to continue working on this issue."

"Yes, perfect, we're approved for a special on femicide for *Aquí y Ahora*, so we'll go back to El Salvador and find other cases, talk to a survivor, and then we'll go to Mexico for other interviews." Evelyn didn't want to let go of these stories either.

When we got to San Salvador the second time, we discovered the legal machinery was moving slowly. Nine months had passed since Mario Huezo's arrest and the trials, appeals, appearances before the judge, and other bureaucratic procedures were still ongoing. (In January 2020, Mario was found guilty of femicide and sentenced to fifty years in prison, the maximum for the crime.)

On this follow-up visit, the first thing we asked was to meet Karla's son. I had the opportunity to spend time with him, to hug him, to see how loving he is. His little face is identical to Mario's and his eyes are like Karla's, sweet, always seeming to smile. Looking at those eyes, I couldn't help but wonder how much they must have seen that Saturday in April when his life changed forever. It's difficult to know to what extent he's aware of what happened to his mother, but there's no doubt he misses her, and now, he also misses his father. The grandfather, Don Demetrio, and the grandmother, Mrs. Dolores de Turcios, are his new family nucleus.

I found Don Demetrio sunken, morally shattered. He still couldn't get over the idea that he had defended Mario at the beginning and now he's the main suspect.

Once we finished the new interviews with Karla's family, we went to other parts of the city for more reporting, which we'd include in our special program.

In this next case, our heroine was Rosa María Bonilla, another professional woman. A medical doctor, she was divorced from her son's father; she was a Christian, a strong believer. A few years ago, she'd met Denys Suárez Mejía and they'd started a relationship. Because he didn't get along with the rest of her family, Rosa María moved to Santa Ana, about two hours from San Salvador, to try to avoid family friction. Like Mario Huezo, Denys didn't work either, and the pattern repeated itself: an independent woman with financial control trapped in an abusive psychological cage by a man with less education and professional success than her.

In time, and with a loan from Rosa María's family, Denys opened a juice place. He completely controlled the income from the business. By then, he also managed the salary Rosa María earned at the medical center. With that money, Denys paid support for his children from a previous relationship and gave Rosa María a small allowance to cover her personal expenses.

The story had other similarities to Karla's: Denys was accused of assaulting Rosa María and then strangling her. Rosa María's sixteen-year-old son was also present in the house during the attack, though he says he didn't hear anything because it was late at night.

When I sat down to interview him that afternoon, so full of memories and tears, the boy broke his long silence for the first time.

"No, I didn't hear anything. God saved me—that's how he wanted it, because we could have both been dead," he said, his eyes full of tears, revealing both courage and pain.

Denys's explanation was that Rosa María had slipped and fallen down the stairs because she'd just gotten out of the shower and was still wet. The prosecution's version was totally different: she woke up early to bathe and go to work and he attacked her, then strangled her. Afterward, he dragged her to the stairs and let her fall, hoping to create a different kind of scenario.

Rosa María's son ran out of the house screaming for help from the neighbors, who came over immediately and helped Denys carry the bloody woman into a car and drive her to the hospital. She was still alive when they arrived, but died moments later. To the doctors who attended her, it was obvious Denys's story didn't make sense. The marks on Rosa María's neck gave away what had really happened in that house; the bruises on her body didn't match those of someone who'd fallen down the stairs. To make matters worse, Denys's arms and neck were full of scratches, indicating Rosa María had fought for her life to the bitter end.

Denys was arrested within a few hours and a year later he was found guilty and sentenced to the maximum penalty for femicide in El Salvador: fifty years in jail.

After sharing very emotional experiences for hours with Rosa María's family, we returned to our hotel feeling utterly helpless. We felt impotent because even Salvadoran laws, which are so progressive, had failed to discourage femicides. Why? The answer lies in society, in the implementation of those laws, and in the atrocious silence that surrounds these crimes and their victims.

If society itself in everyday life doesn't speak, doesn't protest and condemn acts of abuse against women, the collective mentality won't change. If the collective mentality about women, their role, and their value as human beings doesn't change, abusers will continue to attack and commit crimes. If the laws are severe but they aren't applied properly, they're useless. It's an endless cycle in which silence prevails at all levels: family, society, and legal institutions.

According to the Salvadoran Institute for the Development of Women (ISDEMU), of the 1,519 murdered women from 2015 to 2017 in El Salvador, 258 were classified as femicide, and those were the only cases where the murderers were found guilty.

It's obvious laws will not stop them. Only education will succeed. Educating them from the time they're children to value women. If the cycle isn't broken from the beginning and the victims aren't given a voice, this will just keep happening.

Our third protagonist is alive. She lived to tell her story. We didn't want to end our report without hope; we wanted to show it's possible to emerge victorious even from the worst misfortunes.

Brenda Vásquez was waiting for us in one of San Salvador's suburbs and she sincerely told us her story. She suffered physical abuse from an early age at the hands of her parents, who constantly beat her. Her mother despised her and blamed her for all the evils that happened to them, subjecting her to constant psychological abuse. Then Brenda got married and her husband took over and continued to torture her. After the birth of her first daughter, he beat her because he didn't want girls. When a boy was born, Brenda learned to take the girl out of the house with the baby in her arms every time her husband came home drunk. This prevented him from hitting them. The girl, with her little brother wrapped in a blanket, would ask the neighbors for help finding a place to sleep.

Brenda knew what was happening in her home wasn't right, that she didn't deserve it, that it wasn't fair, but she couldn't find a way out. Fear paralyzed her from head to toe and plunged her into the most terrible silence every time her husband threatened to cut her to pieces. From time to time, Brenda would get the courage to file a police report, but the officers just said, "Be a good girl and you'll see nothing will happen to you . . . If he comes home drunk, don't confront him and you'll see, he'll get over it." Her neighbors were on her as well: "Be quiet, it happens to us too; just take it easy, don't make him angrier."

One day, Brenda got fed up with being a good girl and keeping quiet. After imagining herself dead, she asked for help from a women's organization. Guided by experts and social workers, she managed to get out of that hell and got a divorce. Today, this brave mom is a financially independent seamstress. Most important, she's here to tell us her story.

In her limited spare time, this strong, savvy, and proud peasant, who loves to read and learn about health and legal matters, is dedicated to sharing what she experienced as a child with other women and to helping other Salvadorans in the countryside open the doors to a freedom that it took her thirty-three years to attain. It was the door to opportunity, to staying alive.

With all of these and other stories we filmed in El Salvador, and others in Mexico, the femicide special for our weekly show, *Aquí y Ahora,* was complete. I understand a whole program dedicated to this subject may sound painful, but in fact it was a song of hope. Especially the way we edited and produced it. We hope this program isn't the only one. We have other countries to visit, like Colombia, the rest of South America, Central America, and Spain, where unfortunately, they continue to kill us, and, for all of them, we also need to raise our voices.

Amid this revolution about what it means to be a woman, we have to tell these stories more than ever to transform the so-called victims into heroines, even though they may have lost their last battle. We have to honor the Karlas and the Rosa Marías, and include the Brendas, those who are still alive, to change the focus and rename them survivors.

I want these painful and uncomfortable interviews to be my contribution to this overwhelming worldwide problem. I wish I could change the end of these stories in the tabloids and the crime chronicles and give them a different outcome, an ending with a battle and revindication.

By telling the lives of these women, I want to generate the opportunity in our society for dialogue and denunciation, because what kills us is silence, the shame of speaking about and reporting abuse, worrying about what people will say, because these women don't want to be seen as victims, because it's more dignified to erase or ignore what happened, and thus make it small and store it away at the bottom of a drawer, just like I used to do as a young girl in the face of any affront.

With these interviews and specials, I want to give voice to those who survived and those who left us, and somehow bring about a change, because that's what we need: change, to re-educate the current generation, and the ones that follow. If we manage to change the global vision of what it means to be a man and what it means to be a woman, we'll see these statistics drop rapidly. Only by uprooting the concept that women are inferior to men can we eradicate this scourge.

The scourge and burden that we've been carrying since forever, since we were considered a piece of man, a rib, an extension, and not the center, the foundation, the uterus, which is what we are biologically, without the intention of adding any connotation of superiority in this metaphor of life. We're simply the origin, physiologically speaking. So, to all those who have stolen a woman's last breath, I say: You're a piece of the flesh and blood of a woman, your mother. She produced your hair, your nails, your skin, your bones with her fluids, her molecules, her organs, working in the most perfect alchemy ever imagined. You come from the bowels of a woman and it was a woman's heart that first pumped blood and oxygen into your veins. It was a woman who gave you your first great opportunity in this life: that of being born, that of being alive.

At a time when everyone's shouting: Black Lives Matter; Yes, We Can; *Je Suis Paris*; or We Are Charlie, why not add one more? After all, femicide has already been declared a pandemic by the United Nations due to the high numbers that already exceed many other rates of violent deaths.

If you ask me today what makes me most vulnerable in the world, it's not being an immigrant, or having black skin, or my religion, or my political inclination. What exposes me most to being raped, to being killed, to being robbed on a deserted street, to being exploited at work, to being denied a promotion in many professions, to being paid less, to being insulted in a bar, or to being humiliated for my looks on Instagram, and to have to prove every day what I'm capable of, is the fact that I'm a woman. As if that were our fate from the moment of birth.

It would be destiny itself that would now take me to meet different kinds of heroes, leaders, and survivors, whose stories are equally worthy and deserve to be told. Heroes and heroines whose voices will help put an end to the harmful silence that suffocates us in many aspects of our lives. They say the best teachers are born from misfortune, and I was about to meet some brave beings who refused to give in to any kind of silence.

20.

Until the Last Breath

Misfortune is the heart's closest bond.
Jean de La Fontaine, French poet and writer

They say that, after the storm, there comes a calm. I would add that Mother Nature's fury, always alive and alert, brings out the best in us. Heroes are born from great disasters and misfortunes; they bloom and shine brightly when they raise their voices. These are the tireless voices I want to talk about now, the ones that taught me life lessons. It would be two very intense journalistic assignments that would remind me that, while there's breath, there's no room for silence.

"While we're in Phoenix, we have interviews with Dreamers for our special; from there you fly to New York for your breakfast with Malala Yousafzai," Bea Guerra, my producer, said as she read my itinerary. We were sitting at the airport waiting for our plane to Arizona. "Then you go to Los Angeles for a conference led by actor and activist America Ferrera."

While the plane taxied before takeoff, and I noted how I'd zigzag the country in three days, I got an alert on my Twitter account: Mexico had just shaken. A 7.1 earthquake!

Inevitably, the plane took off. Midflight, Bea managed to connect to the internet; her mailbox was chock-full of messages from our bosses.

"Forget about New York and Los Angeles," she said. "I've just been informed we're going to Mexico City."

We landed in Phoenix, took a flight back to Miami, and finally managed to reach Mexico City, where chaos and uncertainty reigned.

The information coming through email and social media was discouraging: dozens of deaths that could soon become hundreds.

We were still in the first twenty-four hours of confusion. My colleague Jorge Ramos arrived at the same time and they were already reporting, as well as our colleagues from the Mexico bureau: María Elena Salinas, Enrique Acevedo, María Antonieta Collins, and a team of reporters who'd come in from different parts of the United States.

As we made our way through the streets of the capital, my eyes were lost in the rubble of hundreds of fallen facades. We got out of the car in front of one of the collapsed buildings where rescue teams were working arduously, and I stayed a few minutes, watching the scene unfold.

Women came with bottles of water and clean clothes for volunteers. Men improvised a food stall in a corner. They pulled huge pots of tamales from the trunks of their cars to feed the firefighters and neighbors. A group of friends in a pickup towed a piece of cement wall off public roads to make way for the ambulances. Everyone was doing something to help. Most surprising of all: no one was giving orders, no one was directing the crowd that was so eager to help. Everyone moved in sync without explanation. I thought about the ants I see when I take Anna to the park, all working together to drag a piece of bread back to the colony.

They say ants have a collective identity and intelligence that makes them act like that, as if they were a single being. It's mistakenly believed the queen ant gives orders and governs, but the truth is that, in a colony, where more than half a million ants might coexist, there's no boss or hierarchy. The queen simply lays the eggs to continue reproducing and the rest of the ants, called workers, already know what they have to do. They don't need a boss, or manager, or guide, or police; only "teachers" know how to fulfill their role. United by an instinct that tells them "we are all one," they create bridges entwining their bodies so they can pass over a small torrent of water, or form a raft in which all can float, one on top of the other, in case of flood.

In the Roma neighborhood, there were wonderful people who seemed to know what to do and where to go at all times, barely uttering a word. Hundreds of people ran from here to there. Above the "organized chaos," we could hear Karina's voice tirelessly calling to her brother, Erick Gaona, through a megaphone.

"Resist, hold on, you can do it, Erick!" Without pausing to breathe or even taking her finger off the on button, Karina spoke to a mountain of debris at the corner of Medellín and San Luis Potosí streets. "I love you, your family is here, and we won't move until we have you with us." Her voice traveled around the world on internet videos.

The morning of the quake, Erick had escaped from his office safely. But once the tremors passed and everything seemed to have settled down, he went back in to gather his belongings from the third floor. That's when everything collapsed. Erick was trapped inside.

Twelve hours later, Karina wasn't giving up, insisting that words of encouragement could keep his hopes up until rescuers found him. Karina didn't let go of that megaphone, a device that can give us a voice when we feel no one can hear us, that pierces the silence that sometimes others, or life itself, impose on us.

Twelve hours went by and then two nights. The dawn's strange calm on those almost deserted streets was interrupted by the barking of a handful of dogs and the sound of the generators and other equipment the rescuers were using. From time to time, the Mexican volunteers and the volunteers from all over the world would silently raise their fists in the air. Everyone froze, holding their breaths. The rule of silence was understood. The gesture meant they'd heard possible signs of life and needed absolute quiet. And so, in that almost sepulchral silence, Karina saw two or three wounded people on stretchers, but alive, and her hopes were revived.

"You know I love you. I won't move from here until you leave with me. Have faith, may God take care of you," she continued, voicing her love and hope into the megaphone with even greater urgency.

At exactly fifty hours, when fatigue had already disfigured the young woman's face, the rescuers raised their fists again. Another silence descended on the popular intersection. And Karina knew: it was Erick. She watched as they lowered him, a sheet covering him from head to toe. According to forensic reports, Erick had died instantly, buried by tumbling concrete after the collapse. No one will ever know for sure if he ever heard any of the words of love and encouragement Karina cried out to him with such passion and devotion. Then Karina turned off the megaphone forever and the lights went out for this wonderful family.

Within a few hours, I experienced one of the most painful moments of my career as a journalist. It wasn't the first time I'd sat with someone who'd just lost a loved one and, sadly, it wouldn't be the last. Interviewing Karina, the sister, and Carmen Maravilla, Erick's wife, hurt me terribly after all those hours of anguish in the rubble while their voices held steady and kept hope alive.

At the Gaona home, the first to sit with me was the young widow, Carmen, who told me Erick was thirty-five, he worked as a driver, and that morning he'd been assigned to that office. She said they had two beautiful children and then she couldn't continue. Carmen broke down, asked to stop, went to another room, came back after a breather, and then locked herself in the other room again to scream her heart out, asking "Why? Why Erick?" Eventually, she opened the door and begged me to continue with the interview, that she wanted to do it in honor of her husband, because this interview would be his tribute. But her tears got the better of her again and she asked to stop.

Some say journalists shouldn't get emotionally involved with their stories, and that makes sense because we're not a part of them. But it's also true that compassion, the ability to identify with the pain of others, is a professional virtue. And sometimes crying is inevitable, and I cried, I couldn't hold back the tears. I cried because I could feel their pain.

"Let's keep going, let's go on, I don't want to be quiet, I want to talk," the young widow begged every time we stopped recording. "I need to tell the world who Erick was, why he was the man I chose."

She wanted to talk, not opting for silence, even after losing all hope and losing him, her beloved husband. That urgent desire Carmen had to say what was in her heart is something I still carry with me, and I don't think I'll ever forget it. Every word of pain and courage she said will be with me always.

Karina, the brave sister, could only sit with me for a couple of minutes, exhausted and trying to find a way to accept the finality of her efforts. "Did he hear me when I talked to him, did he hear me at least during the first hours? I want to believe he did," she said.

My soul was shattered after we said goodbye to the Gaona family. I left Mexico after five difficult days, but I held on to a mental picture of that perfectly synchronized dance of people helping, of brave survivors amid the shock of collapsed buildings, of a country willing to stand up because it can and always has. If they could do it in 1985, they were going to do it this time too. They weren't going to give up, they weren't going to shut up. Silence isn't an option either when you're fighting with your last breath.

And, gasping for air, we kept going all summer and fall of 2017. I don't remember another time in my career as a journalist when I covered so many natural disasters and so much destruction. Tragedy after merciless tragedy struck our communities in the United States and in several of our countries. The next one was waiting for us after we left Mexico. Another assignment, another great life lesson.

"Ilia, when you get to Miami, please pack again and go straight to San Juan," a producer from the Univision operations center told me. "The situation in Puerto Rico due to Hurricane Maria is serious, and we need to distribute our team. You're going to the island."

"Count on me, but let me call Gene and Anna to let them know I'm only stopping by to repack my suitcase," I said, resigned and helpless before the onslaught of disasters.

Hurricane Maria touched down in Puerto Rico on September 20. In my head, I tried to make sense of the sequence of events: First it was Hurricane Harvey in Houston and the Gulf coasts. Then Hurricane

Irma hit a large part of the Caribbean, passing through South Florida. Hurricane Jose deviated from the larger islands but left heavy rains. Puerto Rico was still recovering from all these when Maria began to form, a phenomenon that would reach Category 5.

But only when we left Luis Muñoz Marín International Airport, next to the Puerto Rican capital, did I understand we were facing what would soon be classified as the second deadliest and most destructive hurricane in history.

On the way to downtown San Juan, I was stunned by the desolate landscape, the hot temperatures, and the lack of electricity. This island is always full of music and people in the streets, always cheerful, but now it looked almost deserted. All we could see were long lines of cars trying to get gas.

At the hotel, only a few rooms had electricity. We needed power to edit our reports and transmit them so the whole world could know the magnitude of the tragedy.

As soon as we left our bags, we went out to explore different corners of the island and collect the images hundreds of thousands of Puerto Ricans in the United States and other countries longed to see. There was spotty cell phone and internet coverage, and in some areas, our viewers relied more than ever on us to see if their parents' town was still standing and to send and receive messages reconnecting them with their loved ones.

I felt that our presence as journalists was very necessary. But, after Hurricane Maria, with our stories, our connections with people, and our cameras sending images to the outside world, we became one of the few voices of hope for many and a way to demand help, to press for the necessary assistance. As we say in Spanish, "A heart can't feel what an eye can't see." Wallets remained unopened. The squeaky wheel gets the grease, and the person who doesn't have the means can barely raise his or her voice of despair for the rest of the world to listen. Without phone antennas or Wi-Fi on 96 percent of the island, without access to social media or texts from family members, Puerto Rico was going to need our voice more than ever. Our reports would be the megaphone, like Karina's in Mexico, to keep hope alive and let everyone know what was happening. This time the ones to help break the silence would be us, the journalists, the communication channel for a people pleading not to be forgotten.

At the beginning, when we first arrived on the island, the authorities confirmed about fifteen to twenty deaths. Within months, the truth would come out in a gush of gruesome statistics like I'd never seen before. While the government of Puerto Rico calculated sixty-four fatalities, a Harvard University study claimed a minimum of 4,600 deaths, warning that there could be thousands more. Those of us in Puerto Rico who had witnessed the destruction the hurricane had already caused sensed the island would discover thousands more to mourn. The first to call attention to the issue were the invaluable reporters at the island's Center for Investigative Journalism (Centro de Periodismo Investigativo). There I met Omaya Sosa Pascual, a colleague already working on verifying reports of people burying their dead in courtyards and funeral homes in small towns that weren't included in the government's figures. Omaya told me from the beginning, "There are more, many more."

From town to town, my heart sank before such a bleak landscape. I'd been to this beautiful Caribbean island before, once for work and once as a tourist. To Chocoanos, Puerto Rico has always seemed close, familiar. In my dear Istmina, I grew up to the rhythm of the best Puerto Rican salsa. When I think of another culture apart from Colombian that influenced my childhood and youth, it's Puerto Rican culture. Menudo, El Gran Combo de Puerto Rico, and the Sonora Ponceña— this was the soundtrack of my life. My favorite song, the one I always request at parties, is "Isla del encanto" by the great maestro Gene Hernández, performed by Orquesta Broadway: "You're the beautiful dream of the best poet, who died dreaming inspired by you . . ."

Seeing the island in these conditions, I felt so close to its people and their suffering; it hit me hard. Extremely hard! It was as if I'd just come to my own El Chocó in ruins. Lymaris Marrero-Deya, a journalist working for the Department of Veterans Affairs, was my guide to these isolated villages and crumbled roads as I dealt with my emotions. Her mission was to find each veteran on her list, verify they were still alive, and provide them with assistance.

"We're opposites," I said to Lymaris when we were introduced. "I studied social work and work as a journalist, and you studied journalism and work as a social worker."

These two professions always intertwine. To inform is to educate, to help. Thousands of social workers, far from the glamour and media attention, perform very similar tasks.

On our first outing, we were joined by another colleague and a volunteer nurse from the United States. When Lymaris took us to a building impacted by the hurricane, we had to climb sixteen floors, just like the residents who'd been left without electricity. When we arrived at our designated floor, we found ourselves in an apartment where strong winds had shattered the windows. Doris Valentín was waiting for us, a retired and elderly veteran with diabetes who had suffered a stroke just after the hurricane. Every morning and afternoon, her neighbor's youngest children brought water, food, and ice to keep her insulin refrigerated.

The same neighbors had collected the broken glass and swept the floor. Now, a sticky heat hung in the empty room, which had only one recliner where Doris sat all day. Her daughter lived in the United States and they could only speak when one of the neighbors went down and then back up hundreds of steps after charging the cell phone, which sometimes had enough coverage to get through.

"I'm fine, I don't want to be taken to the veterans' hospital," she said. "There are few beds left and there are people who are worse off than me." Though she looked small and weak, she'd decided not to accept the offer to be moved. "Look, my walls are standing. My neighbors take care of me. I'll be fine."

I was struck by her response. I imagined her as a young woman, solid as a rock or an oak tree that couldn't be brought down, and my heart fell apart. It reminded me that we're often called the "weaker sex" and how they've made us believe women can do this but not that. And then, at times like this, an older woman like Doris shows us not only her great strength and courage but an enormous sense of generosity and solidarity, which we use to help others in need.

There we were, ready to rescue her with all our equipment so she could be treated at a medical center and rest with air conditioning, have light and food, and Doris gave it up for those worse off than her. She preferred to offer that opportunity to whomever needed it most.

After saying goodbye to Doris, I walked down those sixteen floors with a singular thought: no windows, no furniture, no place to charge a phone, and just a little ice to keep her insulin cold, and the determined veteran felt she had more than others.

Our next stop was in Toa Baja, a small town less than half an hour from San Juan. We had to leave the truck parked in the middle of the road and walk by dozens of fallen trees with the small camera equipment and the couple of lights we could carry before we reached William's house. His children in the United States had asked Lymaris to help him and explained his situation. Between uprooted tree trunks and weeds, the house William had built with his own hands for his retirement years had been half destroyed. Only the second floor appeared habitable. But the old veteran welcomed us singing at the bottom of the stairs. William had been a professional musician in a Puerto Rican bar and had the soul of a beautiful bolero performer.

"I remember you!" Lymaris exclaimed. "Of course, I've seen you sing."

"My musical spirit and military training saved me and kept me alive through the hurricane," he said, while stroking his two dogs, which were lying at his feet.

William had been sharing cans of food with his pets for several days on that second floor. Part of the roof had been blown away by the hurricane. Like Doris, this stubborn and strong old man refused to occupy a bed in a hospital, and asked that others take that opportunity.

The rescue team left enough food and medications for a week and agreed they'd come back in a few days.

"Don't worry about me. I can give up my bed. There are people worse off than me. I'll stay here." He said goodbye, waving his hand while singing his favorite bolero by Tito Enríquez:

And I thank the Lord for letting me
be born on this beautiful land.

The next day, another song was waiting for us, from the most tender of voices. A school had decided to open its doors, although it wasn't ready to resume classes. They just wanted to provide the children with the stability of their routine and offer them a hot plate of food. Their homes destroyed, the teachers came to take care of their students. One of the kids told me how the roof of his house had disappeared. Crying, the little boy dropped into my arms and I hugged him, as he recalled that his world, his home, had been demolished. When you're mother to one, you're mother to all.

With the few supplies they had left in their classrooms, the children drew stories on paper of what they'd experienced. Fallen houses, lots of rain and wind. With pencils, they told us everything. As we said goodbye, they clapped and chanted to the beat of cheery children's songs, convinced their beautiful island would rise again.

Our wandering around the island in search of images and stories that could help the outside world understand and measure the disaster took us to the José Miguel Agrelot Coliseum. Outside the popular site, Carmen Yulín Cruz, the mayor of the capital, was waiting for us, surrounded by a handful of volunteers and members of her team who had improvised their headquarters there, and from which they worked twenty-four hours a day without rest.

I was struck by how determined she seemed in spite of the uncertainty and the many needs of the people, of her people. Despite her short stature, she moved with great confidence. When she greeted us, I noticed her voice was hoarse from talking so much. Talking, not shutting up, telling the world how they were suffering, and emphasizing the lack of help. Ten days had passed since the catastrophe and ships with food, water, and machinery to remove trees and rebuild roads had not yet arrived. The mayor, with what voice she had left, explained in blunt terms that they had been left alone; she reminded everyone that Puerto Rico is part of the United States, but that a lack of coordination between different government entities was costing lives. In the absence of help, the humiliating words President Donald Trump aimed at the island would soon add insult to the island's injuries. The most painful and serious issue for her was that the president had denied the number of victims again and again. "My people are dying for lack of help," Yulín said as we finished our short but intense interview.

When I left the Coliseum, I looked back and saw the mayor's diminutive figure in the distance, restless, always on the move, and remembered Karina in Mexico, with her megaphone. The two shouting their sadness, their discontent, until they had no voice left. The two fighting the silences that do no good and kill all hope.

The images newscasts like ours transmitted to everyone in different languages began to raise a sense of urgency among political layers and also nongovernmental organizations.

Months later, Carmen Yulín had mostly recovered her voice and she sounded clear and alive. This brave woman took her complaints and demands to the highest levels and was named one of *Time* magazine's one hundred most influential people. Every time I saw her protest, it became clearer that to be silent before an injustice will never be a solution if we want peace, equality, and prosperity. Silence is neither a solution nor an option when Mother Nature hits and help is absent.

Still on assignment on the island, we returned to our hotel and I found myself overwhelmed by voices so capable of challenging the worst of silences. After tough months when U.S. policy only sent messages filled with hate and insult aimed at immigrants and minorities, when multiple hurricanes were followed by earthquakes, my faith in humanity, in solidarity, in the future, and in the world I'm going to leave as Anna's inheritance was returning. It's undeniable: we're heard the loudest during the worst of times.

It was with their voices that these survivors I'd just met among the rubble and fallen trees also confirmed we humans are creatures of love, of dialogue and connection, and that hate, selfishness, and all those other mean feelings are derived from fear. People are born interconnected, like intelligent ants, and not separate from each other. That separation, the theory that we aren't equal, that some are more equal than others, and that we can't work together for a common good arises when fear overcomes us.

It's fear that makes us believe that to earn our daily bread we have to snatch it away from our neighbors, that for us to ascend, someone else has to descend. And that for us to reach our goal, someone else must fail. That for us to live, others have to die. All evil is derived from the selfish competition fostered by petty fear: racism, sexism, xenophobia, and even femicide. It's no secret: fear is the father of hate. I would add that fear is also born of the silence that extinguishes voices and stifles hope for survival.

"We've barely eaten all day," said Andrés, one of Univision's cameramen. It was almost midnight after a long day of interviews and reporting all over the island.

Luckily, we found a pizzeria across the street from the hotel that, with the help of a generator, had opened its doors and started serving again. Together with David Romo, our producer, and my colleague Pamela Silva, we sat down and ordered the only dish they had. Suddenly, someone connected a pair of speakers, just like we used to do in Istmina during the holidays, and music flooded the place.

"My song, my song!" I exclaimed like a little girl when "Isla del encanto" came on.

Singing along with those beautiful verses, the Puerto Ricans around us seemed to be shouting out at the world: "We have to recover our island, and we'll do it! Although nobody is helping us from Washington, even if the ships with food never come, even if they just throw rolls of paper towels at us and ignore how many have really died, even if they don't invest in our infrastructure and in repairing our telecommunications, Puerto Rico will once again be Puerto Rico."

Days later, I got on a plane back to Miami with the song still in my head and the certainty that this sister country would know how to heal. More than three years after María, what still resonates in my mind is the federal government's racism and the corruption at different levels that has left this beautiful island so bereft.

From the sixty-four initial deaths the government reported, the official statistic then jumped to 2,975. This was based on a study prepared by the University of Washington. Meanwhile, Harvard University, in a parallel study, claimed 4,645 lives had been lost. According to the National Oceanic and Atmospheric Administration, María is among the six most deadly hurricanes that have hit the Americas since 1900.

Despite so many loved ones buried and mourned, and despite the discriminatory treatment Puerto Rico endured from Washington, the island didn't lose its magic and, even without the federal aid other places affected by disasters received, Puerto Ricans made their island slowly come back to life. Despite the indifference from the outside, and the corruption that lurked inside, people tried to return to normal. The megaphones sounding off alerts and denunciations faded, but didn't quite stop.

Puerto Rico would still have a surprise for us that would leave the world amazed. An event that would have me returning to those streets and plazas, to witness and hear the last word. That word hadn't been pronounced yet in this story about fighting until the last breath.

21

Inconvenient Caravans

A long day awaits you,
to get where you imagine.

    Guilver Salazar, Guatemalan writer

Silences kill and silences save lives. Silences that offend and dignified silences. The black silence of our skin and of the injustices committed in its name. The red silence of those who die without voice or justice. So far, I'd directly experienced life in my skin, or indirectly through my profession, and the many silences in our world.

But I still had to add one more: the transparent silence, colorless, that immigrants use to render themselves invisible when they leave their home and take the path to uncertainty. Silent: that's how I met many undocumented immigrants when I moved to the United States. A silence interrupted by a phenomenon as controversial as real. I mean caravans. Those processions that travel from Central America to the southern U.S. border and have generated headlines and political skirmishes, together with the minors crossing alone and the separation of families, with the inhumane imprisonment of children and babies in cold cages and cells.

For many decades, immigrants to American soil walked through borders without making noise, through shadows, wrapped in silence, with extreme humility, practically without complaining so as not to be perceived as demanding. Throughout the last decades, some groups of immigrants were gutsy enough to claim benefits, but, fearful of being discovered, arrested, and deported, many were unable to raise their voices.

But now, with this phenomenon unfolding on the southern border, the silence was going to end, for better or worse, and the whole world was going to listen to them as they continued their journey, giving interviews and using their real first and last names. They weren't going to be invisible anymore and that would bother and surprise many. Even I was caught by surprise when a young girl greeted me from among the crowd.

"Hello, Ilia," she said in the sweetest voice. "How are you? Look what I have."

I was in a makeshift migrant camp in Tijuana and there was a tiny, happy, bright little girl showing me her stuffed animal. Martica, from Honduras, was eight years old and already had more life experiences than most of us.

"How wonderful to see you again, come give me a hug!" I said while also greeting her mother, two older brothers, and her dad.

Martica smiled at me with the same intensity as the first time we'd crossed paths in Puebla, weeks before, when the first migrant caravan of 2018 stopped along the way. Since that moment, she had been filled with cheer while I interviewed her, laughing with her playful eyes.

"I want to go to the United States," she said.

"Oh yeah? How come?" I asked, amused.

"To achieve big things, to learn English." Her answer was precise and enthusiastic.

Now in Tijuana three weeks later, Martica seemed firmer, more mature, yet with the same innocence and sweetness. As if these rough thirty-five days running from her native Honduras and the thousands of miles traveled on foot and in trucks had not touched her soul or changed her spirit.

Watching her play with the other children from the caravan, I saw how everyone followed her and obeyed her lead. Even older children gravitated around her. Several adults asked about the girl, just like I did at first, and I realized I wasn't the only one who had been taken by Martica's spell. A network of love, honesty, and strength was growing around her. There is no doubt leaders are born, but it's life that shapes them.

Martica perfectly sums up the intention, nature, and spirit of these migratory manifestations—phenomena that managed to strip away the silence from the thousands of walkers and put them squarely in the public eye.

"I'm ready, Miss Ilia," said Martica's mother as she showed me a folder she clung on to for dear life. "The documents for our request: birth certificates, everything. Tomorrow we'll turn ourselves in at the immigration station and see if they'll process the asylum application."

Asylum. A completely legal option that makes appearances in both American federal laws and in the international laws the American nation respects and observes. The Immigration and Nationalization Act, revised and expanded with the 1980 Refugee Act, determines that every foreigner can apply for asylum if he considers that in his country of origin he is subject to persecution or violence. The United States government commits, by said law, to providing assistance, asylum, and protection to those who can prove their case is credible.

Martica's family, along with thousands of other migrants advised by the nonprofit organization Pueblo Sin Fronteras, was seeking to exercise a recognized international law. Others, as so happens with these phenomena in other parts of the world, may use the circumstances to present tangled misrepresentations of their situation, all part of the political opportunism of our day. But the people I saw walking in this caravan in the spring of 2018 were seeking asylum legally.

During the time I shared with the Way of the Cross Caravan, I heard their own testimonies of how these men, women, and children left everything behind to achieve a dream so longed for: a safe home, without violence, with work and an education for their children. After spending time with them, and with Martica and her family in mind, I feel confident affirming that the vast majority are good people, normal people, like you and me. They're tired of being looted, raped, robbed, and killed. Tired of their children living in neighborhoods without resources, among gang members who constantly harass them, under the yoke of corrupt leaders who steal all their opportunities.

"Miss, the land doesn't provide; it just doesn't provide like before," they kept telling me when I asked why they'd left their country and joined the caravan. "With what we grew, we used to survive, my wife and two children. Now, it's not enough to feed one mouth."

It's undeniable that the countryside, from Mexico to Patagonia, has changed due to global warming, international treaties, deforestation, and our lack of awareness. The best phrase to describe those agricultural microeconomics that used to feed millions of families is: "the land no longer provides."

But even before the countryside changed, Hispanic communities had been coming and going from the United States for decades. It used to be primarily a solo trip, because the routes weren't particularly dangerous. Children were left with grandmothers, since ranches and small towns may have been poor but safe. Once settled in the promised land, kids were then brought safely up to Chicago, San Antonio, Los Angeles, or wherever. Today, it's different, and we must accept it. The American dream is no longer a dream but a nightmare that begins the day they start their journey to the border. Along the way they may be intercepted by gangs, drug traffickers, and people with political interests. These lifelong migrants, tired of being abused, assaulted, and murdered on their way, formed these Way of the Cross caravans to travel northward, slowly, in an organic and natural way. In small groups of fifty or one hundred, they feel safer. Waiting for good weather, they always set out on their trips in spring, around Easter, which is the reason behind the group's name.

Like I said, the caravans are nothing new. They're a phenomenon that has been going on for more than eight years. The recent controversies arose when—for geopolitical and economic reasons, and helped by social media and their convening power—the number of migrants increased and overflowed. Before the avalanche, the president of the United States, an expert in "what offends sells" and in instilling fear, took advantage of the situation to alarm voters, and to demand construction of the border wall, Trump's foundational election promise. Trump began to talk about an "invasion," and that incredibly misleading term managed to convince many and they sided in his favor.

Suddenly, "organizers" who'd never been there before appeared out of nowhere. Dozens of conspiracy theories sprang up. Gangs, criminals, and rioters infiltrated the caravans, attracted by media attention and opportunism. Suspicious characters popped up, encouraging the masses to complain, shout, and break down the barriers so they could continue on their way to the next country. Two to three thousand tired and desperate people are easy to manipulate, and they succeeded—to a certain degree and while facing the enemies of migratory movements— to distort this social phenomenon's message that reflected a reality: the unsustainable situation of an entire region on the continent that needs an immediate solution, the urgency of many migrants to protect themselves from crime once they decide to take the road north.

Martica's family didn't leave everything to embark on this trek on a whim, exposing the girl and her two little brothers to terrible circumstances. People who judge them ignore the details in each of the personal stories these fathers and mothers tell. From our couches in our comfortable homes, it's relatively easy to criticize and say something like, "I'd never do that to my children."

After sitting down to talk with another young girl in the same caravan and listening to her story, I confirmed we should never say never.

Génesis, also from Honduras, was eighteen years old and another protagonist on this pilgrimage, who our cameras followed for several days. She would show me what it takes to carry a child in your arms, and would remind me we're no one to judge the decisions made by a mother who is desperately trying to save her child.

Génesis told me she escaped the misery in Honduras after a childhood marked by an absent father and a mother who beat her and blamed her for all her misfortunes. At fourteen, she arrived in Tapachula, in southern Mexico, where another teenager she introduced me to as her cousin Wilmer took her in. Together they earned a few pesos working retail, transporting blocks for construction, and cooking quesadillas. It was enough for them to eat. As an inexperienced young girl who'd never been loved or cared for, Génesis trusted a boy who made her feel loved and protected and got pregnant in the blink of an eye. The young man left as soon as he heard the news. Then, according to Génesis, a gang member showed up, fell in love with her, and began to court her. When he realized she was pregnant with another man's baby, he was blunt: "When your son is born, I'm going to get rid of him. If you're going to be mine, you can't have someone else's children."

Terrified, Génesis continued working until the day little César decided to come into the world and her contractions began. Her employer didn't believe her and she had to give birth in the warehouse restroom. She then had to wait an hour until a doctor arrived to properly cut the umbilical cord. Her main concern, seeing César's tender and pure face, wasn't the bathroom full of germs and bacteria. Her fear was the gang member, out there somewhere, who'd soon hear the news. To top it off, her boss told her she'd have to cut her pay from that day forward because with a baby in tow, she would no longer be able to do the same kind of work.

Still suffering postpartum pains, her baby wrapped in the only blanket she had, the young mother spoke with Wilmer and the two decided to join the caravan that was about to leave. Migrants from countries all over Central America meet in Tapachula to begin their Way of the Cross.

"What I want is to stop suffering, for my family to stop suffering; they're my inspiration and I want to be able to help them," Wilmer said while carrying Génesis's five-week-old baby.

"We're not terrorists," she added. "I'm going to the United States because I want my son to live, so that in the future he won't have a need to ask for anything, so he won't need things like this."

After twelve hours on a bus, and with the baby always in their arms, Génesis and Wilmer were welcomed at a church in Puebla's central square, where they slept on a thin mat on the floor. The next day, they resumed their journey under the intense sun, afraid to stumble due to fatigue and worried César could tumble from their arms. Without sunscreen, covered only with a blanket, the baby already had a sunburned forehead.

Sadly, a year later, the caravans would be packed with children among the walkers. The rumor had reached Central American countries: presenting a minor when requesting asylum at the border was a kind of passport to guarantee entry into the United States. The truth is this wasn't always the case, and Génesis was about to experience it.

At this point, with my heart shattered by so many painful stories, I had to go back to Miami for other assignments with Univision. At least, we managed to get a cell phone for Génesis so we could contact them once they arrived in Tijuana with the rest of the caravan. We agreed to see each other there, at their final destination, before the great moment: the request for asylum.

Exactly nineteen days later, I returned to Mexico to continue monitoring the caravan that had reached Tijuana. We landed in San Diego, California, and drove to the other side of the border.

Dialing the number I had for Génesis, I managed to reconnect with the sweet and naive young mother, now in a makeshift migrant camp next to the border gate.

"When are you going to surrender to the immigration agents?" I asked, anxious to know the plan.

"No, I can't. My cousin already crossed. They won't let me through because my baby doesn't have a birth certificate." She was sobbing.

This is how laws work. César is undocumented in the United States, in Honduras, and even in Mexico, the country in which he came into the world. He wasn't born in a hospital and, in her inexperience, Génesis never registered him as her son with the authorities. Because of this, her request for asylum couldn't be processed.

"I'm going back to Tapachula, I don't know anyone here in Tijuana," she said. "I'm going to work a little, get my son a birth certificate, and then I'll try again with another caravan." But she didn't sound very sure of this new plan.

I told her not to lose her phone, that I wanted to stay in contact with her. Perhaps there was some organizer or a member of Pueblo Sin Fronteras that could offer another solution to the problem she was facing.

The next morning, I set out to look for Martica first because I was scheduled to tell her story on *Al Punto*. A few acquaintances told me the whole family had already surrendered, had already officially requested asylum earlier at the San Ysidro checkpoint. I never got a chance to say goodbye!

I called Génesis and managed to communicate with her a couple of times, until her prepaid phone stopped ringing. I felt a stab in my heart. Génesis is a girl raising a baby! She's a good soul but I'm not sure she'll survive this hard journey a second time, or if she'll run into that gang member again who swore he'd kill her baby. I don't know if one day she'll be able to reconcile with her mother, whom she still loves and misses. I don't know if life will give her a break, and let her sleep without fear or need.

Génesis never got the chance to request asylum, to ask for peace. And these types of opportunities don't always knock twice.

I returned to Miami having finished my assignments at the border. Despite a feeling of helplessness, I carried with me other thoughts about this controversial caravan which made headlines around the world. Through stories such as those of Génesis, César, Wilmer, and Martica, I reconfirmed there's a genuine need for those who escape violence and persecution in their countries. We're not perfect, but we're better when we organize. Situations like these bring out and forge great leaders. A mother or father's power in the face of adversity is infinite. And there are more things that unite us than separate us, although some may use the public pulpit to lecture otherwise for their own political benefit.

These caravans, which some people view as desperate acts by the neediest, or desperate acts by the most calculating, are nothing more than acts of hope. They are one more way to break silences of all colors, and to shout to the world: look, this is our Way of the Cross!

Five months later, I received an email from Martica's dad. He told me he was still in Mexico, that he couldn't take advantage of the asylum laws but that his wife, Ana, Martica, and the two boys were already on the other side; that, at least, they were never separated from their mother, contrary to what happened to other families; that Martica and her brothers were not put in cold cages, as was happening to hundreds of children under Trump's inhuman zero tolerance policy. His wife and children were very lucky and were soon allowed to go to New Orleans, home to one of the children's grandmothers.

When I finished reading this email, I answered and asked for a phone number. I wanted to hear Martica's voice again.

"Hello, surprise! Do you remember me?" I asked when her mother put her on the cell phone.

"Hi, Ilia, how are you?" she answered, in English, with her usual joy, now in a more decisive and mature tone than the last time we'd met. "You see? I'm already learning to speak English, like I promised you."

While listening to her stories about her new school, her grandmother, and her brothers, I imagined her twenty years into the future, as a congresswoman from Louisiana, or as the first Latina governor of that beautiful and diverse state, or as a great leader who, with her voice, represents those who fear to use their own.

When I hung up, but not before promising we'd keep in touch, I couldn't help but think about Génesis. I dialed her number again, although I didn't hold much hope. No one answered. It was a missed call.

Génesis had fallen again under the mantle of silence; she was invisible once more. At least, under the sun and during the caravan, we could see her, we could hear her, even if it was only for a few hours. She existed, she was real. The whole world knew about her odyssey, and it knew her first and last name: Génesis Martínez.

Almost two years after having walked with Génesis, the separation of minors from their parents at the border has become official protocol. No one is spared anymore. There are thousands of children, even babies, who have not been reunited with their parents. With constant reports of sexual harassment, and their lives in cages or at centers lacking the most basic resources, sometimes I think maybe baby César is better off wherever he is, in Génesis's arms. Because this young mother's American dream has been reduced today to a cage with cold bars.

22

Law-Abiding Silences

Where there's little justice, it's dangerous to be right.
Francisco de Quevedo

"*Turning Pages: My Life Story*," a friend suggested while I was looking for a book to buy for Anna. "It's the new book by Justice Sonia Sotomayor."

"But is it appropriate for children? Her other book is for older readers," I asked, making sure Anna, now that she had just turned five, could read and enjoy it.

"Yes, this time Sotomayor wrote her story so little ones can read it," she said. "Get it for Anna."

After this recommendation, I said goodbye to my friend and went back to the office, where the "story" of another judge was waiting for me. Only I won't be able to tell this one to Anna until she grows up a bit more and understands the world of earthly justice and its complexity. For a child, right and wrong are opposite and definite poles: throwing food on the floor is wrong, eating what your mom puts on your plate is right. For adults, right and wrong are painted with many complicated nuances, as would happen with the nomination and confirmation of this new justice.

After more than a year of delay with political games, the time had come to fill Anthony Kennedy's slot on the United States Supreme Court. Everything indicated it wasn't going to be easy. In large part because a great silence would have to be broken, with the help of a woman's voice.

It was September 2018, and in all my emails and on the news, Brett

Kavanaugh's face and name demanded attention. The controversy had been brewing since August but now it had entered the final stretch. In a few days the Senate would ratify President Donald J. Trump's nominee as the next lifetime member of the highest court in the land. It looked like a battle won, and an impending appointment, until a woman accused Kavanaugh of sexual assault while they were both in high school. The accusation was serious. It came from a professional woman with a good reputation and, after many deliberations, the Senate Judiciary Committee summoned her to appear and present her version of events.

We stood guard in front of the monitors the entire week watching the live broadcast of each word said in that committee room, where the investiture of a new justice would be decided, and where the entire country faced a political and public opinion challenge. Whether Kavanaugh's nomination would move to the Senate, where a Republican majority would undoubtedly approve it, now depended on what happened in the House of Representative's judiciary committee.

The explosion of the #MeToo movement had finally come to the highest reaches of power in this nation. And, again, conversations between friends in cafés, in stores, and on social media became real battles where you had to choose your jersey: team Dr. Ford or team Dr. Kavanaugh. The walls and profiles on Instagram and Facebook were filled with banners declaring "I believe her" or "I don't believe her."

Those of us who followed the hearings took note of every gesture and every phrase that came from the story's protagonists. From the trembling voice of the psychology professor who until recently had lived in total anonymity in California, to the furious expressions on the judge's face, unable to contain his frustration. At the end of that long morning, after both had concluded their statements, and after responding to questions from both sides, my colleagues and I were totally confused. Who to believe?

The committee's verdict came Friday: Brett Kavanaugh's nomination wouldn't be stopped, and in a matter of hours each senator would issue their vote. And so, shrouded by shadows of uncertainty,

Kavanaugh was ratified with a two-vote margin and became the newest justice of the Supreme Court of the United States of America. And doubt was sworn in with him: the doubt Dr. Ford planted in minds across the country, whether she was believed or not.

I had doubts too, even as I tried to understand the historic moment we'd just witnessed. On the one hand, there were the waves caused by #MeToo, #YoTambién, and Time's Up. On the other, Dr. Ford went home to a life that would never be the same, while many carried a sense that, from now on, young people would believe it wasn't worth reporting harassment because they wouldn't be believed.

The country had a new justice, rewarded and crowned, but the country also had a new hero, a woman who broke the silence and raised her voice although the price she would pay ended up being very high.

Kavanaugh appeared days after his appointment at the annual convention of the Federalist Society in Washington, DC, and got a standing ovation from the present lawyers. Meanwhile, Ford continued to receive death threats and very serious insults that forced her to go into hiding and radically alter her life.

Two weeks after the Kavanaugh-Ford crisis, while I focused on preparing for my trip to The Hague, where I'd been invited to moderate a panel on refugees for One Young World, my work would take me back to the Supreme Court issue. This time I'd sit face-to-face with one of its members. But it would be in a very different scenario and in a very special context.

"Ilia," said Claudia Rondón, on the phone, as I was packing my bags for my trip to Europe. "We got an interview with Sonia Sotomayor. Jorge Ramos wants you to interview her in Spanish and he'll do it in English."

I remained silent. I was already used to my colleague's generosity, but this time Jorge was giving me the opportunity to sit with the most influential Hispanic in the most powerful country on the planet. An amazing opportunity! A few days after the intense controversy of Kavanaugh's appointment, Justice Sotomayor was a much sought-after voice.

Like other members of the Supreme Court, she doesn't make many appearances in the media, despite the fact that her positions and concepts generate great expectation and countless opinions and interpretations.

I was told Sotomayor agreed to meet with us because of the publication of her new illustrated children's book, *Turning Pages*. "The book!" I remembered I still hadn't bought it for Anna.

"I'd love to interview her, but I have to go to The Hague on Friday, I don't know if I can reach . . ." I tried to explain to Jorge, thanking him first.

"Please, try to make it work before your trip. This interview is very important for you," Jorge said, encouraging me, like always.

Without thinking, I delayed my departure to Europe one day, packed my bags, and changed my route to The Hague so I'd have a stopover in New York, where Justice Sonia Sotomayor would welcome us. At the hotel suite they'd chosen for our meeting, Jorge surprised me again with another gesture.

"Ilia, you go first," he said, giving me the chair before the justice had arrived.

In the art of interviewing, whoever goes first can take more time, and the one who goes last runs the risk of falling short. But Jorge knows fully well that even five minutes would give him ample time to get the most out of any situation.

As I sat down, I adjusted my jacket, fixed my hair once more, and then suddenly she was there. A simple woman, short, with little makeup, and a huge smile. She wore a black dress with yellow flowers, a purse, everything was normal. Her voice was normal when she greeted us. Her way of shaking hands was normal. She could have been any of the thousands of ladies we meet every day at the store, at school, at the doctor's office, or in line at the bank. I stood up to welcome her and invited her to sit with me.

"Do you want your makeup retouched?" I offered before starting.

"No, just the hair, but don't straighten my curls, please." The justice was proud of her Caribbean heritage.

Suddenly, once this normal woman, wearing normal clothes, with a normal attitude sat down, I saw the most powerful change and transformation. This short and simple woman with a pleasant smile became the great justice from the Supreme Court: strong, bright, powerful. It was not her gaze, nor did she change her tone of voice or attitude toward me. It was something invisible. It was an energy that only people accustomed to managing power at very high levels know how to project. Sonia Sotomayor grew before my eyes and became enormous. I have to say, I was a little nervous, and I don't mind admitting it. Rather, I think of it as a sign of the immense respect I have for her. And she, as someone who has no doubt about her preparation or abilities, let me know with that same smile that everything was fine.

Other people with power, or those who think they have it, take advantage of moments like this. They exploit the strong impressions they make on others. For a few seconds I remembered Barker, how he received me at his home in North Carolina, and how he had used that controlling energy to try to intimidate me, to make me feel inferior because of the color of my skin. Harmful beings want to infuse inferiority. Positive beings instill confidence. And I can attest to it, Sonia Sotomayor puts her power and intelligence at the service and benefit of those around her. It's a strange art this Bronx-born and -raised woman handles perfectly.

"Well, how were the first days in court, with the arrival of the new member of the family, Judge Brett Kavanaugh?" I dared to ask point-blank.

"There's always a warm welcome for a new member of our court," she replied, making small pauses. "We have to work with him in a friendly way. We all welcomed him."

Her response was so political that she didn't convince me. I couldn't believe that when Kavanaugh arrived on his first day of work at 1 First Street Northeast in Washington, DC, where the other eight members of this select club were waiting for him, no one raised an eyebrow, coughed, or exchanged furtive glances.

So much to say, so few minutes, and so little freedom! Justice Sotomayor is expected to stick to the evidence and interpret her favorite text: the Constitution of the United States, which she carries with her as a little book wherever she goes. My role is to report, communicate, and question, and keep my opinions to myself. After all, I represent a whole team and a community that trusts us. Crossing those lines would be dangerous but Sonia Sotomayor, to my surprise, decided to be blunt when I asked my next question.

"After the scourge of Hurricane Maria, what do you think about the way Puerto Rico has been treated?"

"I'm not supposed to talk about politics, but I can answer that question: Puerto Rico still needs a lot of help. What makes me sad is that we have to rebuild our beautiful island. And to do that we need a lot of help and it hasn't been forthcoming. That pains me."

Sonia Sotomayor said what millions of Puerto Ricans on and off the island had been thinking: the current administration and the rest of the authorities weren't helping at the level that this U.S. territory, birthplace of their parents and grandparents, needed and deserved. The justice took off her robe for a few seconds to express her dismay, and I didn't blame her. I'd do the same if they asked me about El Chocó or Colombia. Titles and rules are meaningless when it's your people who suffer.

That tiny and kind woman quickly returned to her role as a jurist who measures what she says and I decided to ask her about just that: How does she deal with the difficult task of handling and weighing so much power on a daily basis? It is a huge responsibility!

"The difficult thing about being a justice is that, every time I make a decision, there's a party who won, but that means there's also a party who lost," she concluded, as she receded into another of her brief but profound silences.

She was thoughtful about everything she said but even more so when she kept silent. I asked her two more questions about her book and we parted warmly. Jorge was waiting to take my chair and start his interview.

After this meeting, I visited The Bronx and the apartment complex where Sonia Sotomayor spent her childhood. Walking through those streets where she grew up, her last words echoed in my head: "That means there's also a party who lost." In this world where we all want to be right, we don't realize that to win, others have to lose. Some are always affected, even if we do the right thing and fight for what's fair.

That night, sitting on the plane to The Hague just in time for my presentation at a conference with young people from different continents, I called Gene and shared my concerns with him.

"She didn't say much about Kavanaugh, she was too diplomatic, but that's what people want to know. I was left with so many questions I didn't get to ask . . ."

"Babe, c'mon, take it easy on yourself," said Gene, who's used to my harsh self-criticism. "Sometimes things go your way and sometimes they don't. That's life. Now focus on your trip and your presentation at The Hague. Anna and I will be waiting for you with open arms."

"Thank you, my love." Suddenly I remembered the book again. "Please be sure and buy Anna Sotomayor's book! Show her the justice's photo and tell her Mom interviewed her. I'll tell her more when I get home."

When I returned from my long trip, I'd tell my daughter more stories about judges, justice, the law, and how some lose so others can win. Perhaps that's why we shouldn't rejoice immediately after a victory without knowing the history of those defeated.

I just hope Justice Kavanaugh always keeps in mind that, in order for people to believe him, they had to stop believing her. That in order to achieve his much-desired appointment, Dr. Christine Blasey Ford had to experience cruelty and rejection, that her life and her family's lives will never be the same. He'll continue to speak and assert his voice and his opinions from that powerful chair, while she returns to the silence that has accompanied her for so many years. That suffocating silence.

23

The Last Word

I'm so proud of you,
my people always respond.

Johnny Pacheco, "Mi Gente"

"I'm drowning, I'm drowning!" I tried to scream, but nothing would come out of my mouth.

It was nighttime and the street noises were deafening. I didn't feel well. I didn't feel well at all. I was having a hard time breathing, my eyes burned. I couldn't breathe! I fell to my knees and looked around for something to hold on to. "What do I do, my God, what do I do?" That was my only concern. With my lips increasingly swollen, my throat irritated, it was difficult to breathe through my nose and, when I thought I couldn't take it any longer, I began to cough heavily and a little oxygen slipped into my lungs.

Evelyn and Juan Carlos couldn't stop coughing either, but we looked at each other and knew we'd get through this, even if, for a few minutes, we'd fallen prey to the impotence that comes from not being able to breathe. Like the helplessness experienced by those who can't speak, can't report abuse, injustice, and cruelty. Cries for help that die in the throat, suffocated. And Puerto Rico, torn by tear gas and demonstrations that could only compare to those that forced the U.S. Navy from Vieques Island, was about to cough and heave and be heard all over the planet.

"Here, wash off with this." One of the young people who lived in the apartment where we had set up to broadcast live from their balcony for *Noticiero*, Univision's nightly news, sprayed my face with a mixture of water, dish soap, and vegetable oil.

The young man and his girlfriend had equipped themselves every day since the protests began with this homemade recipe and masks, which they had managed to put on just as the tear gas exploded on the balcony.

I was still stunned, and unable to open my eyes completely, but Evelyn was able to reach her cell phone and dial the production control room in Miami. Seconds before starting my live report up on that old balcony on a street next to the square that flanks the Fortaleza, we'd been hit by tear gas bombs the police had thrown into the crowd. We can't confirm that the small device was directed toward us, but it fell at our feet, on a second floor, far above the demonstration. Our producer David, always stoic and very practical, reacted from Miami with speed and a composure that reassured and calmed us down. As soon as he'd seen me disappear from the frame, seconds before my on-air report, he'd ordered the control room to keep rolling from Juan Carlos's camera—now lying on the floor, but still on—and directed me to the telephone line: "Speak, Ilia, speak as best you can. We're listening; if you can't do it on-screen you can do it by phone."

And so, with a voice choked up by my nerves and a cough that wouldn't leave my throat alone, our viewers listened to me, from coast to coast and throughout the American union. Still on my knees inside the apartment where we went to take refuge from the tear gas, I didn't recognize my own voice. A hoarse, rough voice, as if I'd swallowed a huge pot of black pepper. I kept talking as best I could: "The Puerto Rican people are fed up. They won't give up. Nobody's leaving the streets until they get Governor Ricardo Rosselló's resignation. The police force is here with megaphones to disperse the crowds of people who are peacefully protesting in this unprecedented and historic movement..."

As soon as I finished broadcasting via telephone, I wiped off the water and soap that was still dripping down my neck and, looking around the apartment, I understood two things I already knew subconsciously: one, that my team—Juan Carlos Guzmán, an experienced camera operator, and Evelyn Baker, a dedicated and courageous producer, who both had red eyes and swollen lips like me—were my family, in that moment, not just my colleagues. There are experiences that bind you beyond work, and I had no doubt about that. Two, Puerto Rico was about to make history. The Puerto Rican people were on the streets and they were going to overthrow their governor.

Two years ago, right after Hurricane Maria, I'd seen that island mired in need, in institutional abandonment and corruption, but I left it singing a song of hope to the rhythm of the music I love so much. Today, Puerto Ricans, accompanied by that same rhythm, were going to reclaim everything they'd suffered. The music was not going to stop. Because, even though time had passed and all seemed lost, the last word was about to be delivered.

This odyssey began the same day we experienced the tear gas. It was Monday and we'd just arrived in San Juan to start our new assignment. "You're going to Puerto Rico and will be staying there until we see what happens," the bosses in Miami told me. The number of protesters in front of the legendary Fortaleza, the government house in Old San Juan, increased with each passing hour, and although we already had correspondents present from day one, the news and the popular movement rose like sea foam.

The origin of so much discontent had been leaked messages written by Governor Rosselló, which were being monitored by the Center for Investigative Journalism of Puerto Rico. In the leaked messages, Rosselló bluntly insulted his political adversary, Carmen Yulín Cruz, the same woman I'd met as the mayor of San Juan in my coverage of the destruction caused by Hurricane Maria. She'd just announced her candidacy for governor in the 2020 elections a few months earlier. Rosselló referred to this adversary as *"hijaeputa"* (bitch)! He also insulted the artist Ricky Martin as a patriarchal macho and lashed out at his sexual orientation. But what was most horrible and cruel was that he mocked those who'd died during the hurricane. The so-called Ricky-Leaks, or Telegramgate, revealed something much more serious: an entire network of corruption and embezzlement of funds for health and public education, to list some of the transgressions evidenced in that long text chain between him and his collaborators.

The leaks were the straw that broke the camel's back, the wick on the powder keg of corruption and impunity that had accumulated in government agencies since even before the hurricane. And they would be the spark that would blow up the island's general fatigue. This was not the result of a political cause of this or that side. This is how I perceived it as soon as we deplaned and got lost in the streets of San Juan in search of a balcony where we could put our camera and broadcast. A movement of hundreds of thousands of souls was protesting in front of us, along the sidewalks and avenues, singing, dancing, chanting, and pounding pots and drums, without any specific ideological seal. The crowds weren't organized by any union or public leader. I'd never witnessed such an event. Citizens left their homes and businesses organically and joined the tide of people, regardless of race, religion, or economic status. The pressing need to decry the abuse the island had suffered was much stronger than any social division. Then, celebrities such as Ricky Martin, Olga Tañón, Bad Bunny, Karla Monroig, among others, began to offer support, but the actual movement had begun with the people: first, the dozens who joined together to protest across the Fortaleza gates, and before they knew it, there were more than half a million compatriots behind them, pleading in chorus: "Ricky, resign!"

As soon as we reached the square, I surveyed the crowd: grandparents, children, teenagers . . . all ages. Logically, the largest numbers were the young, like the students who captained the Youth Uprising in Soweto. Young people are always responsible for raising their voices and fighting for change. Hundreds of thousands of young people in a perfect dance in which they weren't going to allow even Carmen Yulín, one of Rosselló's main targets, to benefit politically from the moment. This was not a partisan battle. It was an "enough is enough" from the heart of the island.

To the surprise of many who saw the images of thousands of people dancing, waving flags, and improvising festive atmospheres on every street corner, this was not a celebration, nor was it a group of opportunists at a party, because there were nights where even twerking was used as a form of protest.

What the world had trouble understanding was the language of protest by an entire island that lives, laughs, cries, and fights with the language they know best: music. I wasn't surprised, nor did I doubt the demonstration would have serious results. All I had to do was dig two years back in my memory to recall Hurricane Maria's veteran survivor singing in his practically destroyed house, or the music that accompanied us on our last night with a generator in that small restaurant. Now, the whole island was singing and dancing.

The sounds and rhythms immediately transported me to El Chocó. In my heart my country was bonded with this island. I remembered that on May 26, 1987, when I was a teenager, a similar popular revolt broke out in my region; a strike that lasted two days. I wasn't allowed to participate because I was very young, but thousands of Chocoanos took to the streets, tired of so much institutional abuse and abandonment. And they did it with cultural events, dances, hornpipes, poetry, and harangues. Like in Puerto Rico, the critics raged, and then the governor, Eva Álvarez de Collazos, described the protests as "a revolt by black people painted in a folkloric hue." These words further inflamed the mood, and the protests escalated into confrontations with the police that, unfortunately, ended in the death of a twenty-three-year-old.

My cousin Flor, older than me, joined these demonstrations and, despite the fact that nothing was accomplished as promised by the authorities, she felt victorious, because although nothing had changed (nor has it changed in the more than thirty years since), at least they tried with all their hearts, with all the vigor that drove thousands of young unaffiliated people to demand a change, crying out: "Not for more, not for less, there's no fucking way we're going back." How I would've liked for something like this, like what I was seeing now with my own eyes on the streets of Puerto Rico, to take place in my forgotten and needy El Chocó!

Back on the streets of Old San Juan with the Puerto Rican people, we had to hurry to continue with our work. Asking around, we found a young woman, Lisandra Montañez, who rented a small studio with her boyfriend on a street several yards from the main square. We asked them if we could set up on their balcony. From up there, away from the noisy sidewalks, we would be able to appreciate the magnitude of the protest. That balcony would be our center of operations during the following decisive forty-eight hours.

All of a sudden, that was when a helicopter flew by, sweeping the crowd on the street with a powerful reflector, while, on the ground, officers with a loudspeaker asked them to leave, to disperse, because congregating was illegal. With no time to react, and the countdown to go on air already started, I saw the tear gas canister fall right at Juan Carlos's feet. He was focused on the camera. It was no use running into the apartment and closing the windows and doors. The gas had already reached us and slipped through the slits in the natural ventilation system these eighteenth-century houses have above the doorframes. And the gas masks Univision had given us were in our car!

This wouldn't be the only time the gas would affect us. That same night, we counted more than ten grenades on that narrow street, and the tear gas reached our balcony every time. At around three in the morning, when the crowd of young people facing off with the police had slightly dispersed, we decided to leave the apartment and go back to our hotel, dragging several cases filled with light and cable equipment. And right there, in the middle of the street, we once again suffered gusts of tear gas carried in our direction by the wind.

The next day, when the antiriot squads had taken it down a notch when realizing the people weren't giving up, I was able to walk the entire square and reach the barricade next to the government house. On the way, I met a few unique characters, such as young Bryan Hernández, almost a teenager, who every morning arrived punctually, climbed up the barricade, and tirelessly waved an enormous Puerto Rican flag for hours on end. The people had been protesting for eleven days and Bryan had been waving the flag for eleven days. That was the role he decided to take on, with his parents' support, and he took it very seriously. "I'm doing it for my mom and my dad who are at home and can't be here. My dad is on dialysis, he's a patient with renal disorders who greatly suffered the corruption after Maria," he explained, emotionally. "And I'm not leaving this spot until Rosselló leaves."

In another square corner, a man in his eighties appeared on a balcony, impeccably dressed. From his second floor he raised a glass of wine and toasted with the people, encouraging them to continue protesting.

The more protagonists I met, the stronger my gut feeling: they were going to be successful. The governor would resign from his position, and, for the first time in Puerto Rican history, and possibly for many neighboring countries, the people's voice would be even more decisive and effective than an official election and the votes in the ballot box. I could see it in the thousands of smiles that greeted me with each step! I could hear it in each chorus and song coming from every corner. While most of the world thought this was just another pot-banging Caribbean-style protest, I had no doubts: that festive air was the prelude to victory. They were already unconsciously celebrating the success that was about to arrive! That was why they didn't tire. That's why I didn't see anyone sitting on the sidewalk taking a breather. Everyone was overflowing with the certainty that comes with knowing that you're on the winning team.

On the morning of Wednesday, July 24, Puerto Rico was beginning its thirteenth day of protests and confusing messages began to spread. A group of journalists had been allowed inside the Fortaleza for the imminent statement being prepared by Governor Rosselló. Then, they moved all of my colleagues from the press room, outside, with no statement or explanation, leaving them empty-handed. Outside, the crowd's intense demands were relentless.

For me, that was the day to leave the balcony behind and broadcast the news from the protest itself, amid the people. Suddenly, while I stood on top of one of our equipment cases to get a better view of the entire square, the Fortaleza flag was lowered and thousands of citizens stopped chanting and sat on the ground expectantly. It was all so surreal and new that no one could anticipate what would happen, or what each gesture or sign coming from the government's team meant. "That only happens when a governor is about to speak," explained a young couple next to me. The rumbling began to spread like wildfire, but the official balcony remained closed, and no one came forth to provide explanations to an entire people on pins and needles. Slowly, everyone began to stand up and resume their protests, with even more fervor. Each strange sign served as an incentive, a prelude showing that inside the blue building, where the history of Puerto Rico had been decided for centuries, they were lost, without knowing how to row nor in what direction. The people's voice had them cornered.

With nightfall, rumors that Rosselló had in fact prepared the statement everyone expected grew even stronger. We finished our last report for the West Coast and sat down to wait at the hotel's restaurant, which was already closing up shop. Suddenly, we saw the frozen image of the governor's face on all the TV screens, as a sign that it was a prerecorded video that they were about to transmit. Without saying a word, we ran out to the street. With impressive skills, Juan Carlos positioned his camera and a light while Evelyn called the control room to connect us with Miami. Since my cell was busy connecting to Univision, a kind woman lent me her phone to follow the governor's words, which were being transmitted through several Facebook accounts.

Suddenly, straight out of a Hollywood movie, before the key moment, or the end of the world, I don't know, everywhere around me, the sound dropped, disappeared. It was surreal. The people, the cars, the loudspeakers, the drums and thousands of voices, the tree leaves, and even the wind, everything stopped and went silent. "Today I announce that I will be resigning from my position as governor effective on August 2, 2019, at five in the afternoon." After these words resounded in thousands of televisions, phones, and radios, the movie-like silence lasted a few seconds longer and then exploded. What Puerto Rico expected, happened: Ricardo Rosselló was leaving, and the explosion of happiness that this triggered was as loud and powerful as Hurricane Maria itself. People were crying tears of joy and satisfaction, embracing amid a colossal uproar. Everything regained its sound: music, wind, applause, drums. Everything returned like an avalanche of unstoppable emotions.

When the dust settled slightly, Carolina Rosario, our correspondent, arrived and, while we shared anecdotes and experiences, the party was coming to an end, and the protesters were slowly heading back home. This would be the first night that they would get a sound night of sleep in almost two weeks, and with the satisfaction of having succeeded.

Carolina said, "Why don't we go to the beach to see the sunrise?" And we all agreed with the plan, because with the plethora of emotions our need for sleep had disappeared. Once we were sitting on the sand, accompanied by the sound of the waves, we reconsidered what we had just experienced.

Puerto Rico had spoken. Puerto Rico did not remain quiet. Puerto Rico broke the silence and had the last word in a story of corruption that made life on this small island unbearable since Hurricane Maria's destruction. The people's voice was their weapon, and silence stopped being the choice for a tired people. Puerto Rico, that island whose sovereignty is always up for debate, who some question or look down on with a measure of pity and condescension, had just imparted the biggest lesson of the last years to the powers and countries that have great democracies.

Puerto Rico, a territory that few bet on, was the teacher that taught the rest of the planet how to carry out a protest without causing anyone's death, and how to overthrow an elected leader without having to suffer long months of political games and referendums.

The so-called Island of Enchantment demonstrated with actions that, no matter how small or abandoned you may be, or how much corruption you have to face, when you raise your voice in unity, anything is possible.

This second work visit to the land of the music with which I was raised helped consolidate my lifelong theory, which I was slowly unraveling in my mind: silence has many colors, and many hues, but when it is over, life reemerges and once again flows. Who knows in what direction or for how long, but life reemerges, blooms, and is filled with that energy that is provided by the courage that comes with speaking up. Because the voice is the only tool needed to initiate change.

To the millions of Puerto Ricans who that night slept soundly, exhausted from so many emotions, this new dawn that I was witnessing with my colleagues would bring them fresh air, new challenges, and the consequences of this great change. Because it doesn't all end with those first rays of sunlight. On the contrary! It all began with the new day. Now everyone had heard their voice, that same voice they'd lost a while back, and they'd have to put it to good use. They'd already proven to the rest of the planet that leaders could also be toppled through song and dance. The next step would be to demonstrate that they were capable of continuing with this change, without losing their way in new networks and new roads of corruption.

On that note, another event was about to shake the world, and break the silence, but this time with the most heartbreaking cry. Because there are times when the sound of bullets and pain seems to be stronger than that of justice and truth. But that does not mean we should no longer have the last word.

24.

Returning to Kerosene

Where I come from
Things ain't easy but we always survive.
    ChocQuibTown, "De donde vengo yo"

"Did you hear what happened? Where are you? Are you available?" said one of the news department executive producers after calling me, with a more serious voice than usual.

"I don't know, I'm home alone with Anna . . ." I said, hesitantly, watching my daughter play with some boxes in the kitchen.

I'd recently gotten back from our coverage in Puerto Rico, and was trying to recover every minute of lost time with her, far from the TV and cell phones, focusing on being her mom.

"There was a shooting at a Walmart in El Paso, Texas. There may be more than twenty dead. It's terrible. Change of plans. Keep an eye on your emails for instructions."

El Paso? I quickly tried to find some logic to this barbaric act. More than 80 percent of El Paso's population is Hispanic.

As the hours rolled by, our biggest fear was confirmed: Hispanic last names flooded the lists of people who were dead, injured, or had disappeared. Soon enough, the possible manifesto of the alleged author of the massacre was dug up from the internet, and among other things, it said: "This attack is a response to the Hispanic invasion of Texas."

Like in *Chronicle of a Death Foretold*—title of the legendary novel by Gabriel García Márquez that we so often quote in different situations—this was a chronicle of a tragedy foretold, motivated by the hate speech that is articulated from the highest spheres of power.

Because words have real consequences, and they wait for no one. And the word "invasion," used time and again by President Donald J. Trump when referring to undocumented immigrants on the southern border during the last few months, was the same one used by the self-confessed attacker.

An armed white man shot at a mostly Hispanic crowd, in a place where he knew the bullets would precisely reach Mexicans, on a day when they were out buying their children's back-to-school supplies. With this act, immigrants, especially Hispanics, had officially become a target.

The saddest part of August 3, 2019, which has already left a mark in history, and in which twenty-two human beings were massacred in a matter of minutes, was that we received several red flags way before it happened. First, videos of people insulting Hispanics started to pop up much more frequently, demanding that they speak English in stores, and they always ended with them getting yelled at, "Go back to Mexico!" regardless of their actual nationality or immigration status. Then came the threats, the raids, the derogatory qualifiers in some media. Slowly, the tragedy was being foretold, it was taking shape, and we saw it coming and could do nothing to stop it. On August 3, 2019, Patrick Crusius was the one who confessed to pulling the trigger of the AK-47 he legally bought online. He surrendered himself and said, "I'm the shooter." But behind this young man was an entire part of the country that contributed with their silence. All of the United States saw it coming and no one was able to prevent it.

A silence that moves rampant within the same party in power to back its main leader, regardless of how offensive his statements or language may be. Silence from the legislators who received contributions from the National Rifle Association and don't promote or approve stricter measures for buying weapons.

What kind of country are we leaving the new generations? Or rather, what kind of society are we handing over to them? One where fundamental rights are violated and no one says anything?

It's impossible to forget the videos published by the desperate survivors, who tried to film their path while trying to escape the bullets, the stifled breathing, the screams of "Oh my God!" "Help!" I was overcome with a feeling of helplessness, of pain, of frustration when seeing our community, our viewers, attacked. We've been a part of their lives, we're in their homes every day, telling them what's going on in the world. We're part of that family that gathers around the table after work or school to watch Univision. How could it not pain us? We're present in their lives, and they're present in ours.

After a few hours, when we received details of the captured suspect and of that manifesto, also foretold, my outrage swelled: "The heavy Hispanic population will make us a Democrat stronghold . . . immigrants are taking jobs from natives . . ." The same phrases repeated by extremists and nationalists, the president's electoral base, who attend his public events.

On that August 3, it was El Paso's turn, tomorrow it could happen in any other community where we Hispanics live. We've advanced as a nation, but we've backtracked as a society.

Now I felt that differences were being condemned rather than celebrated and respected. Not being of the white race can turn you into the target of minds fed with hate speech and rhetoric, and there is increasingly more talk of rejection than welcoming. We no longer talk about the wealth of our differences but rather about inferiority and superiority. The country that once received immigrants arriving through Ellis Island, today rejects them at the Mexican border. Even the interim director of U.S. Citizenship and Immigration Services, Ken Cuccinelli, suggested changing the poem engraved at the Statue of Liberty's base, which reads, "Give me your tired, your poor . . ." by adding something worthy of the current government, ". . . who can stand on their own two feet, and who will not become a public charge."

Some days I feel breaking the silence is a double-edged sword. For several decades, immigrants in this country walked on tiptoes, trying to go unnoticed, to avoid calling attention to themselves, and barely complained or demanded the rights they deserved.

As I thought of this, I recalled the time Lori Montenegro took me Capitol Hill to meet Hispanic legislators. I had just launched my career in the United States, and was taken aback when I noticed that our Hispanic community had so little representation in Congress.

Eighteen years later, we still have few Hispanics in the legislative branch. However, now, our community's voice makes more noise in the media, at meetings, and even at electoral debates and the ballot boxes. Nevertheless, the harassment that comes from the highest level of power has also increased, because breaking the silence has inevitably made us more visible and, simultaneously, more vulnerable.

During the five or six days following the El Paso tragedy, the scenes of pain remained a priority in our newscasts. When I saw the El Paso residents' faces of distrust, I understood: This is how young people of color feel when they walk outside at night and see the police car lights. Singled out, marginalized, with a sign on their foreheads serving as the target for all attacks, discrimination, and hate.

I also felt vulnerable. Despite being in the middle of a newsroom, thousands of miles away from Texas, everything had changed for Hispanics; after that terrible event, we were left at the mercy of a fear created for us. We already had to deal with how the color of our skin makes some look at us a certain way when we walk into a store, what it means to be a woman walking around certain areas at certain times, but now we have to add our papers, last names, or nationality to the mix!

Now Hispanics are the center of all that hate, and it deeply affects me. We're as vulnerable to attacks as the other millions of citizens, human beings in this country, the country I chose to put down my roots. A country I admire and love profoundly, but where, at times, I see us floundering in helplessness and, on occasion, in silence.

The one person who doesn't remain silent, as I've said earlier, is President Donald Trump. He's probably aware that speaking the way he does is like lighting a match near gasoline-filled drums, tempting the fire. And even a child knows that playing with fire is dangerous. But the nation's top leader does not keep quiet or measure his words.

Gasoline-filled drums, inflammatory words, direct threats, silence imposed by fear, and that sense of vulnerability that overwhelmed me . . . with all this emotional baggage, I inevitably recalled my memories of Chris Barker, the leader of the Loyal White Knights of the current Ku Klux Klan; I recalled that hot and sticky night in the middle of a North Carolina forest. I remembered how Barker coldly observed me at the start of our interview, and how I debated whether to keep quiet in response to his threat or continue asking my questions, challenging him, contradicting him, and letting him know how wrong he was. To keep quiet or to speak up . . . ignore or protest.

"We're going to burn you out." His words once again resounded in my ears with the same hatred that we face today, all of us who now live under this created halo of fear.

With crosses and torches, it's time to share how I got out of that forest, and how I ended that interview where speaking up was a question of life . . . or maybe even death. Because it all begins with simple words, or threats, until someone takes them literally.

It is said that words mean nothing. Well, that's not always the case. Some words leave such a deep mark they end up becoming a tragic reality. And I had no way of knowing if Barker wanted to burn me alive just in his imagination to scare me or if his wish was real. In a moment like that, any insinuation can be taken literally.

I've already explained how I got to be sitting across from Barker, and now it is time to tell you how I left that strange and terrifying situation where I too was an easy target of hate.

"Thank you for having us." I remember that's how I decided to conclude our interview with the leader of the Ku Klux Klan.

I had already challenged him by asking how he was planning to burn me out, and how he was planning to get rid of millions of beings that he believed were undesirable, and I had argued that we were human and as worthy of respect as his people. But when I realized he was only willing to listen to his own words, I ended the interview. Expecting another type of conversation that night was a lost cause. At least I tried and I didn't remain silent, and I said what I had to say. Above all, I had gone there as a journalist to do my job, not as Ilia, the Afro-Latina.

When Chris Barker stood up, with his wife by his side, I reached out to shake his hand, and as reflex, he pulled away. Amanda looked at him disapprovingly and the man extended his hand somewhat begrudgingly, until it grazed the tips of my fingers. He didn't manage to join his palm with my own. "Lukewarm" was the word that came to mind. Barker's handshake was lukewarm.

In the following minutes, Martín and Scott filmed the sinister ceremony of the cross in flames, while Barker's words thundered in my mind, "We're going to burn you out." We still weren't out of there, safe and sound. I was still a black woman only a few feet away from six hooded Ku Klux Klan members.

Crosses, white hoods, torches, chants praising their nation, race, and the Klan. The ritual was wrapped in a surreal halo, in which I had to constantly remind myself that we were in the twenty-first century, in the United States, and that I was a journalist of color, surrounded by followers whose leader said he was going to burn me out. The entire scene seemed like it was from one of those movies that shows images of horror experienced by African-Americans. It was like a grotesque dream from which I wasn't sure I'd be able to wake up, but at some point in our past, it was real. When the last torches were extinguished, I breathed with somewhat of a sense of calm.

"Can we go inside the house to film some last images?" asked María, once they'd gathered the sticks and rope that remained after the ceremony.

She didn't want us to leave without all of the necessary elements to tell this story to the world, including some scenes of the Barkers in their family setting.

"Yes, come in," replied Barker, when we arrived at the tiny dwelling, after driving down the path flanked by trees to the property's entrance.

Our host's attitude had slightly shifted.

"But . . . can Ilia come in?" asked María.

"She shouldn't, but since she's here, let her in," said Barker, perhaps to make me feel even more uncomfortable, taking me inside his world, within the four walls of his lair.

When I walked into the living room, I noticed it was smaller than what it seemed from the outside. It was decorated with old furniture, endless framed photos of the Klan, and an old TV. Among a pile of magazines, papers, and empty bottles spread over the only table in the room, what most caught my attention was an ashtray shaped like a black slave's head with a rope around its neck. The grotesque object was overflowing with butts, and the entire room smelled of cigarettes.

From what I could see, the house had no more than two bedrooms, in which the two couples and the two youngsters slept, all piled up. Instead of doors, there hung curtains and once again I recalled El Chocó: dilapidated furniture, cheap fabric curtains . . . in the end, poverty is poverty, and it's the only thing that does not discriminate.

And amid that scarcity were the two teenagers, Amanda and Chris Barker's sons. During the interview, they'd remained quiet, watching everything. Then, they participated in the fire ceremony, repeating phrases and rituals like good students. Now, they listened attentively to the grown-ups talking. See, hear, stay quiet, repeat, that was their indoctrination, even though their mother insisted that they gave those kids the total freedom to believe what they want.

"We allowed our kids to be with black people . . . they had a black friend when they were in school," Amanda had said to us during the interview. Then, she went on to explain that they stopped hanging out with the children of color because one of them stole their skateboard. According to Amanda, they reached the same conclusions and beliefs shared by her and her husband on their own, without the need of any indoctrination.

But now, observing them in their living room filled with Klan photos, and with that abominable ashtray on the table, I wondered, how much freedom did these two teens really have to choose who to love and who to hate?

"Guess what, I have a friend from Argentina at work who also speaks Spanish," said Barker, in an effort to make small talk.

It surprised me to see him resorting to the old argument, "I'm not a racist, I have a black, Hispanic, or Asian friend." Some people think that if they work with someone from another race, and they talk to them, that means they're not racist. But they belittle other races and trample on their rights, and would never allow their children to marry a Latina or a black woman.

And so, among racist comments—because in the presence of a black woman, nothing else was coming out of their mouths—the Imperial Wizard of the KKK didn't seem in a rush to see us leave, but the clock was close to striking ten and we decided to cut out in time. We wanted to reach our hotel as soon as possible and avoid any regrettable endings.

Amanda and Wendy, the other Klan member's wife, were the only ones to walk us out. The night was dark and the two women were momentarily illuminated by our headlights, and ten seconds later, we were on the highway, outside of the property, and on our way back to the city. As soon as our phones had coverage again, I called Gene.

"We're all okay, the interview went well," I said, trying to calm my husband, who sounded worried after five hours of not hearing from me. "Tomorrow, when I get home, I'll tell you all about it."

Once at the hotel, I couldn't sleep a wink, and I cried my eyes out thinking about the country in which my daughter will live. A country that seemed to be increasingly closing itself off from diversity while other countries celebrated it. The images of the burning cross, the mosquitos, the kerosene, the whiskey they were drinking all came back to mind. I also couldn't forget that house, so poor and small, and the Barkers' two teenage sons standing there, listening to their parents' jokes and conversations with other Klan friends. I couldn't help but compare that scene with that of my grandfather, presiding over the huge kitchen table, on the second floor of the house of the enormous guaiacums perched on the river. I remembered all of us, surrounding Don Carlos Chamat, attentive, listening to every word of the long conversations with him, while the smell of coffee met that of the heater's kerosene. Outside, the heat and mosquitos were oppressive, like the poverty that reigned the streets of my beloved Istmina.

On those streets, at that table, next to the ravine, I discovered myself. I learned about loyalty and humility, about generosity and solidarity, about compassion and patience. Life lessons that I reaffirm every day. We are, undeniably, a product of what we learn from where we come from. Such is the case of the Barkers' children, receiving information in that living room teeming with hate and the smell of cigarettes, absorbing the speeches and phrases that are conceived in fear. Phrases of racial inequality, of rejecting those who aren't like them, of belittling those who come from somewhere else. Lessons that are completely contrary to what my mother and grandfather taught us. Understanding, equality, fairness, solidarity, generosity, those were the messages that were repeated at the Chamats' eat-in-kitchen table. And life itself added two basic ingredients to that list: education and opportunity. Two tools that can change and affect the course of humanity more so than wars, politics, diseases, or technology.

Education and opportunities, two elements that I had the great fortune of having in my life, and which I also sought out within my small world: my school, my grandfather, my mother, and that first job at Teleantioquia in Medellín. Without that initial education and those first opportunities, and the others that I had to seek out when they were denied to me, I would have never made it to Bogotá, or Miami, I wouldn't have sat with Justice Sonia Sotomayor in New York, or been invited to present an event at One Young World in The Hague, or been at the helm as a national news anchor.

By the same token, the education and opportunities that opened the journalism door for me had taken me inside the Barkers' house, into their world, to look hate straight in the eyes and understand that I would never remain silent again.

Because, when someone says to your face that they are going to burn you out, and you get out of there alive, remaining silent is no longer an option.

We've all had reason to remain quiet at some point, but silence doesn't work forever. Those of us who have turned to silence for one reason or another (all respectable) feel in some moment of our existence the need to break it, to speak.

When I look back at everything I have shared on these pages, and I look forward, toward our future, the only word I see is "voice."

The voice can provide us with convincing and transformative power. It can change a divided country and a broken society, and unite them. It can allow us to be a part of the global evolution, and come closer to becoming a fairer country where there's no space for fear or hate.

The voice is not only your first instrument when you are born and burst out crying, but also the most powerful throughout the rest of your life. Of course, as children, we are taught to speak, but we each must learn to use our own voice once we grow older. I'm talking about our real voice, the one that only comes with our experiences. A voice that, even if it was turned off or at a low volume, can emerge strong, sharp, clear, and precise among the constant noise that wants to keep us quiet.

This voice, which is not mine or ours, rises from our gut to become someone else's voice, that of many, even thousands, hopefully millions. That instrument that no longer belongs to me. The same voice that is your voice, and says goodbye to silence.

American Girl

I, who was born in America, don't see
Why I can't be American
     Los Tigres del Norte, "Somos más americanos"

"Gene, help me out. I need to work and make progress with the book. Since I've come back from my last trip, I haven't had much time," I pleaded on a Saturday morning to the best father in the world.

"Okay, don't worry. I'll take Anna for a drive. We'll see you later, at lunchtime." And just like that, as with all that he does, my husband left me alone for a few hours.

Lately, everything had revved up around me. A year after I was named primetime news anchor, political news was unfolding at dizzying speeds, and Anna was growing up even faster. My daughter, curious, restless, and rebellious, required permanent attention. If I was inquisitive, noncompliant, and curious as a child, Anna was making me pay for all the uncomfortable situations I put my mother through. That's life! You reap what you sow. What will be of me when this girl hits puberty! Her enormous heart is as sweet and generous as it is independent and challenging.

Hours later, Gene and Anna came back home with a huge paper bag.

"We went to the American Girl store," said Gene when Anna went to play in her room. "I told her she could choose her first doll from this brand, and we had a small crisis."

Gene explained that our daughter couldn't find a doll that looked like her. That's what this famous brand is all about; they have dolls of all colors and races so that girls can buy the one that looks most like them, and they even have the same dress and hairstyle, girl and doll, as if they were twin sisters.

Anna wandered around the store and couldn't pick one, so Gene suggested, "Check out the Hawaiian doll, what do you think?" Our daughter looked upset and replied, "No, I don't dress like that, and her eyes aren't like mine." Anna, with her clearly almond-shaped eyes, long and curly black hair, and her different skin tone, didn't fit any of the categories. Gene remained quiet and let her browse freely until she decided on her own what to do. Finally, our daughter grabbed one of the hundreds of perfectly aligned dolls from a shelf and said, "This one, Daddy."

"And?" I asked Gene, intrigued.

"Anna!" said my husband, calling our girl to come to the living room. "Show Mom your American Girl."

Anna walked in and showed off her new doll, which she'd already unboxed, proud and happy. She was black! Our daughter, on her own and unaware of what an important moment this represented, had chosen a doll with dark skin and curly hair, and I had to turn around for her not to see my eyes fill with tears. They were tears of pride: my daughter, heir of five different and beautiful ethnicities, had just identified with the one that most represented my mother, my grandmother, my sisters, and my El Chocó. Anna could have chosen to be whatever she wanted, and at six, she decided to be black, without this meaning that she was rejecting her other roots, which she will always carry proudly in her being. It also doesn't mean that, in the future, she can't identify with her Asian side, or with any of her other roots.

I felt so incredibly lucky and, I won't deny it, somewhat worried. With our black heritage, and as a woman, come wonderful experiences and others, whether you like it or not, that are somewhat painful. And a few days later, as if the universe were waiting for this moment of personal identity in Anna, one of those complicated situations was going to happen. It would be a first for her, and very similar to what her cousins experienced a few years earlier. Someone was going to burst her bubble of blond, brunette, bald, Hawaiian, or African dolls.

"Mami, some girls called me black face," said my daughter so candidly that it moved me.

"And how did they say this to you?" I asked, trying to buy myself some time to prepare my answers.

What we, as parents, respond in these first moments will be what will mark them forever. It will become the script with which they will act each time this scene is repeated in their lives. Being a parent is not easy!

"The girls were, like, mean, making fun of me," explained Anna, not hiding that those words had affected her.

"And what do you want to do?" I continued, cautiously, before starting the real heart-to-heart conversation.

"Nothing, I want to keep playing with them." There was no doubt in her eyes about this decision.

"You want to keep playing with them?" I asked.

"Yes, Mom, because I can change that and make it good."

Her answer impressed me and taught me a big life lesson. So, with all the care in the world, I sat next to her and, although I hadn't planned on doing this so early in her life, I was forced to have the conversation about races, colors, and physical differences.

"Anna, you love your mom. And what color is your mom? You love Abi, and what color is your grandmother Betty? You love your cousin Luciana, and what color is your cousin?"

Anna answered each of my questions with a yes, confirming that she loved us just as we were.

"And do you see a difference with your cousin in New York, your dad's nephew?" I asked, guiding her with my questions so that she came to her own conclusions.

"No, not at all, Mom; they're all the same."

"Then, don't let other people make you believe that we are different. We all laugh, cry, have good and bad moments. We're all exactly the same."

Like my mom taught me, I tried to explain that she should never feel like a victim. But now, as times have changed and I have also evolved with my odyssey through difficult roads of silence and its effects, I added another important part to this crucial piece of advice: She should not remain quiet when facing injustices and offenses. She can and should respond to them politely, if she decides to do so. She shouldn't be afraid to raise her voice. She should keep in mind that each time she speaks, she will be doing so for those who can't. That silence—although it is in many cases respectable and we should understand this—isn't always, and for everyone, the best option because sometimes you're left with a sense of frustration given what you didn't do in that moment.

In Anna's eyes, I could tell she understood; she clearly comprehended what I was telling her. But a few weeks later, the problem would come back with greater force. This time Anna confessed to me that she didn't want to be brown, the same thing my nephew said in New Zealand a while back. It's not always what is said, but how they make you feel. Now the explanation revolved around how "what is wrong" does not live within her, but in the perception of some people.

I talked with her, but she was still in dismay. We don't all react in the same way when faced with adversity. We can't judge a woman for her reaction to abuse or harassment, and we also can't judge someone for his or her way of responding to discrimination. For example, I was the girl who ignored that type of bullying, I minimized it and buried it deep in my heart. I always had a strong character. However, Anna is much more sensitive than me; she's very much like Gene. They are both incredibly empathetic but reserved, and sometimes they keep what they feel and what others make them feel to themselves. This can turn them into an easy target for those who cause pain in others for pure pleasure.

Since we've only started learning life lessons with Anna, this issue unsettles me. Gene and I want to be the parents she needs, respecting her sensitive personality. Since she was little, we've taught her to love herself just as she is, to appreciate her true beauty, and to grow up strong with tolerance and love.

Actually, the family of one of the girls who said those unfortunate words to Anna apologized to us. They're good people who were stunned and incredibly embarrassed about what happened. The little girl likely overheard it in some neighbor or relative's house, or at soccer, or on TV, internet, or from some of her classmates' mouths.

"Black drug addict." "Seedy Indian." "Smelly Hindu." "Mexican *mojado*." "It had to be a woman . . . they're such terrible drivers." "She probably brought it upon herself with that miniskirt." "She must've done something for him to beat her." Let's not turn a blind eye. We hear these and other phrases on a daily basis. What makes us think that our children, in the backseat of the car or at a family reunion, don't hear them too? Then, when they repeat them, let's not act surprised, because we all have an uncle, grandfather, neighbor, or friend who repeats and perpetuates what they in turn heard as children, and so the wheel of hate continues to turn, but now, it's in a world that is changing and is increasingly less likely to allow this intolerance.

That Mexico from the telenovelas where the main character was totally white is slowly becoming history due to the viewers' demand. That Colombia where the hunk's passion was only aroused by girls with distinguished last names and white skin tones is evolving. Now, Alfonso Cuarón comes and puts Yalitza Aparicio on the highest pedestal, with her Mixtec and Triqui features. Today, on Netflix, although I no longer spend as many hours watching as when I was single and didn't have Anna, I find Caribbean-Americans like Dascha Polanco and Selenis Leyva steal the show on *Orange Is the New Black*. Today, I look around the seats in Congress and see more women sitting there, representing their constituents. Some are white, others have darker skin, some are older, others younger, and some wear hijabs. And it's a positive thing to see, even if we are still far from equal representation.

The numbers do not lie, and colors don't either. The world is changing. The typical American profile is constantly evolving, as was the case with Romans in Rome, or Spaniards in the Iberian Peninsula. Exodus, migrations, mobilizations, colonizations. No country or empire has remained intact or isolated, genetically speaking. From Egypt to Mesopotamia, passing through the Incas and the Maya, all of these civilizations mixed with the new arrivals or even the "conquered," and their features and appearances began to change. The same thing is happening in this great country, and this great continent, even though Mr. Chris Barker and those who think like him aren't pleased by it. If you don't hop on the already unstoppable globalization bus, you will be left behind because, in this country, like in many others, the Annas are the new American Girls.

Tonight, my Anna, as she sleeps, is hugging her doll, which she still has yet to name. She doesn't seem to be in a rush to choose its name. It is simply her American Girl. And that's precisely how Anna is: free from all labels.

Tonight, my American Girl decided she is black. Black like her grandmother Doña Betty and her great-grandmother Ilia, and Afro-Colombian like the *mazamorreras* in our beloved Istmina. And hopefully she'll decide to raise her voice, breaking the silence like they did, fearlessly singing about their life stories in the hot afternoons of the tropics by the waters of the San Juan River.

Letter to Anna

Miami, 2019

My dearest Anna,

I know I've just devoted the last chapter in this book to you and have dedicated another one within these pages, as well as several mentions. But I can't send this manuscript to my editor without first speaking directly to you, in a letter that you will read and understand in a few years. So, here it goes.

Years ago, when I wrote the first letter to you and posted it on Twitter, encouraged by the echoes of discrimination that I had seen in the world, especially in your country, the United States, I sensed and anticipated that one day it would happen to you, as it had already happened to your cousins in Colombia and New Zealand. And I wasn't wrong. It's infuriating to know that I was right: that it was going to happen to you too.

Your mom's heart was shattered and I felt a huge desire to explode, cry, scream at the world about how unfair it was, when you told me about that episode where some little girls called you black face. And you were barely four years old!

The honesty and candor with which you told me you'd felt attacked gave me the strength to stay under control because I knew that the way I handled the situation would teach you how to respond to future attacks in your life.

I am so sorry I wasn't able to prevent you from experiencing such an upsetting moment, I'm so sorry I wasn't able to do anything to stop your ears from hearing those words and your eyes from seeing those eyes as they tried to offend you with the color of your skin. It hurts that you had to experience this moment right when your environment was beginning to open up to new social groups. It hurts that in that entrance to a new world, during your first days at school, away from home and your family, you had to face some hostility from someone as young as you.

In a matter of seconds, I relived, step by step, how difficult you've had it since forever, since being in my womb. The fight you waged to survive, to cling to life, to stick to my inner fibers so as to start growing even though we lost those who could've been your twin brother or sister. You were a warrior from the moment you became a life, and you continued to cling to me and I to you, and to the medicine that allowed for this to happen.

I had never experienced such anxiety as when you were about to be born. I felt my heart was about to explode into little pieces of paper of a thousand colors; I closed my eyes and imagined you, and imagined myself holding you, glued to my chest. Your daddy, by my side, never let go of my hand. We looked at each other, cried, laughed, all at the same time while he dried my tears and I dried his.

The thirty-eight weeks of waiting were about to end with the most beautiful event that would undoubtedly seal our love and our family forever. Holding you in my arms was ineffable; those first minutes hugging you, giving you my warmth, dreaming of the day you'd call me Mamá. Gene embraced us both, and Dr. Spiegelman, our ally in this struggle to become parents, contemplated the scene with a satisfied smile. It was a perfect moment.

Then came your baby years, followed by your first steps and, suddenly, your daddy and I began to discover that rebellious sheen in you. I want this, not that, and why should I tell you what to wear and what to eat. Ever since you started talking you've thought you are old enough to make your own decisions!

Ah, my Anna! I see so much of myself in you that I only hope that having gotten to know myself better in these last years of my life will help me understand you more.

You have so much of your dad! His eyes, which made me fall in love, and his sense of humor, "so silly," like you say. You are, like him, reserved, analytical, and observant. Sometimes you're so quiet I'd love to have a rod to fish out your thoughts . . . and feelings! But that's how you are: the perfect combination of two beings and many races. Of different cultures, and two very different yet so compatible personalities.

Now I understand why you still wanted to play with that girl who offended you "because I think I can make her good." You've always believed that things that aren't right can be changed and that fills me with immense satisfaction and hope. To know that at six you are capable of imagining everything in a better, or different, way confirms that inside that little person taking shape is a great human being, a great woman who is growing up and will always see difficulties from a different perspective.

At times you get frustrated with the world around you, and as parents we try to calm your eagerness to understand others, to understand yourself. With these lines I want to say to you: not so fast, my love, not so fast. Even so, with your uncontrollable impatience and momentum, I love your way of seeing the world, and your creative mind fills me with bliss. Watching you play and create stories is one of my small pleasures. I simply have fun and enjoy each time you dress up like a police officer or princess, a doctor or chef, because you're giving free rein to so many dreams you store in your little head.

To grow up in a multiracial and multicultural family is the best foundation to become a tolerant, caring, and generous person. Just like I was taught, you already learned that there are truly no physical differences that can separate us from another human being. And, when you face obstacles and are denied an opportunity that is offered to someone else, I'm sure that you will have the resources in your mind and heart to gracefully overcome the situation.

To see you dance in front of the mirror to the beat of ChocQuib Town's songs and the "bunde" of the choruses we sing in the El Chocó dances and festivities is priceless. To see you enjoy the Korean food prepared by your grandmother or repeat the numbers in Korean to the rhythm of a song with your aunt Sue is a privilege that few can enjoy, and we make sure that you understand this.

Your little cardboard box that we use to place clothes and toys to send to the children in El Chocó, whom you know don't have much, reminds me of the Ilia who grabbed food from the pantry to give it to those who came around asking for spare change, or to my friends in the San Agustín neighborhood on the other side of the ravine.

Almost at the end of this letter, my little flower, I'd like to ask you what you're going to be when you grow up, although I know you're going to give me several answers. You want to be so many things it's still hard to guess correctly. Whatever you choose, we want you to be happy, to do what you do with passion and responsibility, with commitment and rigor. Whatever you choose, you will make mistakes while you learn, and I know that worries you, but I want you to see each blunder as an opportunity to start over, fix the mistakes, and succeed. We don't want you to ever give up because perhaps the following attempt is the one that will work for you.

I want you to know that your dad and your mom are not perfect, we've made a lot of mistakes and blunders. No one taught us how to be parents. But we're learning day by day, constantly motivated by our profound love for you and by the desire to shape an exceptional human being. We don't want to be the perfect parents, just the parents that you need.

My sweet Anna, when someone asks you why you forgive so altruistically, why you tirelessly fight for change, and why you give people who haven't treated you well another chance, I just want you to answer the way you replied to me today, when I asked you about those girls who offended you, and say, "Because I can change that and make it good."

The world is yours, my love, it's of the people who look and feel like you: genuine, unique, different. Don't be afraid. Remember that you can change it all . . . for the better. That's your superpower!

Acknowledgments

Thank you, Betty (Mamá). Our lives would have been nothing without your resilience, discipline, guidance, and endless love.

Liz and Titi, my sisters, we are one.

Abuelito Carlos . . . this book would've made you so happy! You will continue to be everything in my life.